Le Sacre du printemps

Seven Productions from Nijinsky to Martha Graham

Theater and Dramatic Studies, No. 48

Oscar G. Brockett, Series Editor

Leslie Waggener Professor of Fine Arts
and Professor of Drama
The University of Texas at Austin

Other Titles in This Series

No. 42 *"Only a Paper Moon":*
The Theatre of Billy Rose   Stephen Nelson

No. 43 *Mikhail Chekhov as Actor,*
Director, and Teacher   Lendley C. Black

No. 44 *Dancing in the Sun: Hollywood*
Choreographers, 1915–1937   Naima Prevots

No. 45 *Silence in Shakespeare:*
Drama, Power, and Gender   Harvey Rovine

No. 46 *Historical Consciousness in Nineteenth-*
Century Shakespearean Staging   Nancy J. Doran Hazelton

No. 47 *O'Neill's* The Iceman Cometh:
Reconstructing the Premiere   Gary Vena

No. 50 *The Autobiography of*
Bolossy Kiralfy, Creator of
Great Musical Spectacles   Barbara M. Barker, ed.

Le Sacre du printemps
Seven Productions from Nijinsky to Martha Graham

by
Shelley C. Berg

Le Sacre du printemps
Seventy-fifth Anniversary of the Premiere
1913–1988

U·M·I Research Press
Ann Arbor / London

Produced and distributed by
UMI Research Press
an imprint of
University Microfilms Inc.
Ann Arbor, Michigan 48106

16900838

Library of Congress Cataloging in Publication Data

Berg, Shelley, C., 1952-
Le sacre du printemps : seven productions from Nijinsky
to Martha Graham / by Shelley C. Berg.
p. cm.—(Theater and dramatic studies ; no. 48)
Bibliography: p.
Includes index.
ISBN 0-8357-1842-5 (alk. paper)
1. Rite of spring (Ballet)   2. Dance production—History.
I. Title.   II. Series.
GV1790.R5&B47   1988
792.8'42—dc19   87-29421
                                                  CIP

British Library CIP data is available.

To Lola R. Berg, 1917–1987

Although she never saw this book in print, my mother shared its creation with me. That mystical bond between mother and daughter—as primal as any in nature—was never stronger than when we talked, argued and watched dance. She had a dancer's eye, if not the feet. She knew my dancer's heart and helped it grow into a woman's as well. We went through life as true partners and formed a bond that can never be broken.

Contents

Acknowledgments   *ix*

Introduction   *1*

1   A New Temple to Terpsichore   *5*

2   The Prelude   *19*

3   A Song of the Earth   *33*

4   *Reigen*   *43*

5   Counterpoint   *63*

6   Epithalamion   *89*

7   Movieola   *107*

8   Pictures of Pagan Russia   *125*

Epilogue: The Monster Serpent and the Maiden Sacrifice   *141*

Appendix 1   Chronology   *153*

Appendix 2   Léonide Massine's Work Film of
   Le Sacre du printemps   *157*

Notes   *161*

Bibliography   *191*

Index   *201*

Acknowledgments

Katherine Mansfield once said that she could not burn the candle at one end and write a book with the other. Perhaps she never had the sort of support and help I did. The staff of the Dance Collection of the New York Public Library provided research material and photographs and patiently answered queries. John Shepherd, of the Library's Music Collection, was especially helpful in making available letters, programs and other documents from the Stravinsky Archives before they were transferred to the Paul Sacher Collection in Basel. The staff of the Theatre Museum, London, were generous with their time and resources, as was Parmenia Migel Ekstrom of the Stravinsky-Diaghilev Foundation in New York. Tatiana Massine graciously granted permission to view a film clip of her father's 1948 production of *Le Sacre du printemps* for La Scala.

Both Maurice Béjart and Richard Alston took valuable time to discuss their versions of *Le Sacre* with me, and Mr. Alston also provided numerous reviews and articles from his private collection. Jane Pritchard, the archivist for Ballet Rambert, was unfailingly helpful in locating sources and providing photographs. Henry Lisle, general manager of the Paul Taylor Dance Company, and Eugene Lowry of the Martha Graham Dance Company kindly searched out and sent photographs.

Friend and colleagues, including Joan Ross Acocella, Martha Swope, Jack Vartoogian, William Dupont and David Buckland generously allowed their photographs to be reproduced for this book. Barbara Naomi Cohen, Lynn Garafola, Steve Nelson and Sally R. Sommer, offered valuable advice and suggestions. Suzanne Levy shared not only her time and knowledge but also innumerable evenings of tea and sympathy. Mary Smith typed the manuscript from handwritten drafts and was always patient, good-humored, accurate and prompt. Steve Vallillo cheerfully took the photographs for the first five chapters on a wet and chilly morning.

Dancers who had performed in the productions discussed in this study were invariably generous in sharing their experiences. The late Errol

Addison, Bessie Schönberg and Lily Mehlman gave telephone interviews, while five "Chosen Virgins," the late Lydia Sokolova, Bella Lewitzky, Monica Mason, Ruth Andrien and Sally Owen graciously spoke with me about their roles. My deepest appreciation goes to the late Dame Marie Rambert, who spent several afternoons sharing her memories of Nijinsky and the original 1913 production of *Le Sacre*. Finally, my special thanks to Naima Prevots, who was the first to encourage my work on this project, to Brooks McNamara, my endlessly patient adviser, and to my parents and my brother, Gordon, whose love and support make all things possible.

Introduction

I sat in the darkened auditorium of the Slovene National Opera and listened, it seemed for the first time, to Stravinsky's vociferous hurricane of sound. Temporarily incapacitated by an injury, I was able to watch, rather than perform, Czech choreographer Karol Toth's ballet, *Le Sacre du printemps*. Although I had seen other productions of the work, I was now struck, forcibly, unexpectedly, by a powerful visceral reaction to music with which I had been familiar since childhood. *Le Sacre* seemed to me, in the words of its first choreographer, ''all different, new and beautiful.'' Unable to account for my sudden fascination, I stored my reaction safely away for later analysis and consideration.

When I stopped dancing and began teaching, *Le Sacre* proved fertile material for various academic projects. As I progressed in my research, *the* ballet, the Nijinsky–Stravinsky–Roerich creation for the Ballets Russes in 1913, became the matrix for a canon of *Sacres*, the legendary ancestral motherlode for generations of choreographers. *Le Sacre* became, for me, a family of ballets, each sibling unique and individual, but all related to their common parentage by Stravinsky's commanding score.

What made the original *Le Sacre du printemps* so compelling, so fascinating; the object of obsessive discussion, speculation and critical inquiry for three-quarters of a century? Although the first production of the work received only nine performances in all, the ballet has had an unprecedented afterlife.[1] The spirit, the inspiration, the urgency of *Le Sacre*'s theme of life, death and rebirth, has had an impact far beyond its fabled tumultuous premiere.

The first performance of *Le Sacre du printemps* provoked greater storms of controversy than any other ballet in history. The action of the ballet was intended to evoke a primitive Slavonic ritual glorifying the rites of spring. The Russian impresario Serge Diaghilev commissioned Igor Stravinsky to compose the score, which remains a touchstone of innovation in the chronicles of music.

The ballet's first performance at the Théâtre des Champs-Elysées on 29 May 1913, by Diaghilev's Ballets Russes, is a legend in the annals of theater, music and dance. It caused the most provocative theatrical scandal since "the battle of *Hernani*" in 1830, an event which symbolically proclaimed the beginning of the Romantic era. Just as *Hernani* presaged the tidal wave of Romanticism in the nineteenth century, the premiere of *Le Sacre* in 1913 was the most significant declaration of Modernism to appear up to that time in twentieth-century music and dance.

The scenario for the ballet was conceived by Stravinsky and planned in collaboration with the Russian painter, designer and ethnologist Nicholas Roerich. Diaghilev chose the great dancer Vaslav Nijinsky to choreograph *Le Sacre,* and the results were as controversial as Stravinsky's score. In his two previous ballets, *L'Après-midi d'un faune* (1912) and *Jeux* (1913), Nijinsky had begun to experiment with *plastique*—the form and line the body makes in space—with gravity as alimentary energy, with the proportion of human limbs as abstract shape. Accused of choreographic heterodoxy, of crimes against beauty and grace, Nijinsky defended the integrity of his work, believing that his ballet was "really the soul of nature expressed by movement to music."[2]

It is impossible to fully judge the validity of Nijinsky's convictions as the original choreography has long been considered "lost" and no complete dance notation score for this ballet has been discovered.[3] Despite this fact, *Le Sacre du printemps* is viewed by dance historians as a seminal work. Choreographers have been seduced by both the ballet's score and its larger-than-life mythology. There have been more than thirty major productions of the ballet in the last seventy years, all using an orchestral or four-hand piano arrangement of the score.

In this book, I will discuss seven versions of *Le Sacre du printemps,* their impact and significance in the extensive genealogy of productions of the ballet. The first four chapters are devoted to the conception and realization of the original ballet of 1913. Later chapters examine two versions by Léonide Massine, created in 1920 and 1930 respectively, and productions by Maurice Béjart, Paul Taylor, Richard Alston and Martha Graham. These particular works were chosen because they demonstrate a broad range of choreographic sensibilities and varied approaches to the score. Each version is a landmark revival, a breakthrough in style or an innovation on the part of the choreographer.

The one constant in any discussion of *Le Sacre* is, of course, the music. Choreographers have challenged Stravinsky's vision by discarding his scenario of ancient Slavic rites, but none has dared alter his syntax. Many have, in fact, demonstrated the validity and universality of the score by presenting their own interpretations of *Le Sacre.*

From the moment of its premiere, the score for the ballet has been termed "revolutionary," a description the composer has frequently repudiated. Stravinsky believed that Maurice Ravel, "practically alone," was able to see that the novelty of *Le Sacre* was "not in the 'writing,' not in the orchestration, not in the technical apparatus of the work, but in the musical entity."[4] Despite its aura of "newness," *Le Sacre* was more of a return than a departure; the homage of an artist to his history, his heritage and his culture. Indeed, revolution, too, can imply a return to the point of origin, the completion of a cycle. In that sense, perhaps, the score must be considered "revolutionary." The agent of change, the catalyst of disruption, *Le Sacre du printemps* remains subject to interpretation and argument by choreographers, historians, musicians, dancers and critics. It also remains uniquely, impossibly, undefinably itself.

1

A New Temple to Terpsichore

In late spring of 1909, Serge Diaghilev's Ballets Russes made its debut at the Théâtre du Châtelet in Paris.[1] During the course of the next two decades this remarkable Russian impresario and his corps of choreographers, dancers, composers and designers collaborated to create one of the most exciting artistic adventures of the twentieth century. The era of the Ballets Russes became "un style d'époche." When Diaghilev and his associates presented their reformed vision of ballet to the West over seventy years ago, the waning specter of Noverre's *ballet d'action* drew new life from this concept of a "synthesis of the arts." The foundation for "a new temple to Terpsichore" had been laid and the renaissance of ballet in the present century had begun.[2]

Since the close of the Romantic period in 1847, ballet had gradually undergone a decline in the European capitals it once had captivated. Where ballet and opera had shared the stage as equals, the former now became a handmaiden to the extravagant spectacles of grand opera. While the ballet school of the Paris Opéra remained intact, the female *danseuse* was its exclusive product. Male roles were performed by women *en travesti*. In Milan, the name of La Scala Ballet became synonymous with mere virtuosity. Technical brillance was the central focus of the dancer's art. The expressive and dramatic qualities and the artistic integrity so important to the Romantic ballet had been supplanted by unending displays of *tours de force.* Thus, ballet, in the form in which the Diaghilev company presented it, "was a striking novelty to Western Europe, a strange resurrection of something long since defunct and forgotten."[3] The Ballets Russes was, in fact, "the culmination of a long-developing vogue for Russian dancers in the West—a trend that can be traced back before the turn of the century."[4]

Russian prima ballerina Olga Preobrazhenska had created a sensation in Monte Carlo in 1895. In 1909 she appeared at the Paris Opéra, nearly simultaneously with the Diaghilev company, where Mathilda Kschessinska had performed the year before. Anna Pavlova and Nicholas Legat had a tremendous success in Berlin prior to Pavlova's appearance in the first Paris season of the Ballets Russes. Historian Debra Goldman states that when, in 1910, the Russian press mentioned ''our ballet abroad,'' they were referring not only to Diaghilev's ballet but also to the ''various concert tours and ad hoc ballet companies that were consolidating around a couple of dance stars and a theatrical contract.''[5] The ballets performed by these free-lancers were, for the most part, truncated versions of works from the standard repertoire and short pieces in the classical style of the *danse d'école.*

Although ballet had all but vanished from the artistic mainstream of Western Europe, it still flourished in Russia under the patronage of the tsars. Since the eighteenth century, Western performers had been drawn to Russia. The salaries and working conditions were attractive to many who came to perform and often remained to teach. These artists established a performance tradition and built an audience, not only in the royal court, but at productions in noblemen's homes and in privately run companies where serfs from the estates could view the entertainments. By 1800, it was impossible to discern that almost a century before, Western theater was all but unknown in Russia.

This emphasis on the theatrical traditions of Western Europe disenfranchised much of Russia's own cultural heritage. Because Russia had no theater professionals of its own, it imported the best from abroad. Great artists of the Romantic ballet appeared successfully in Russia, among them Marie Taglioni, Fanny Elssler and Jules Perrot. Indeed, Perrot remained in St. Petersburg to teach and choreograph from 1848 to 1859. ''The Russians are great connoisseurs of ballets,'' wrote Théophile Gautier, the French poet and critic, who traveled in Russia in the late 1850s, ''and the dancer who has withstood the marksmanship of their opera-glasses must be very confident of herself.'' He praised the Conservatory of Dance, stating that it supplied excellent soloists and a *corps de ballet* ''knowing no equal for perfection and the speed of their evolutions.''[6] The art of ballet, he admitted, was more developed in Russia than in France. Russian ballet, Gautier felt, had been protected from the corruption which ballet had suffered in Western Europe.

Goldman notes, however, that the twenty-year dominance of ballet romanticism in St. Petersburg and at the Bolshoi was ''already an anomaly on a larger stage of Russian cultural life.''[7] While sylphs and forest nymphs danced on the stages of the Imperial theaters, Russian literary journals published stories in imitation of Gogol. Although Taglioni's and Perrot's effects on the development of Russian ballet were significant, it is notable that in discussing them, we must remain within the ballet world itself. Dancers and technique became the focus of ballet history, while ballet itself was severed from the mainstream of creativity in Russian culture. The continual importation of foreign talent had eroded much of the

Russian content in the Imperial ballet and contributed to its increasing artificiality. This situation would continue until the advent of the Ballets Russes. Meanwhile, the chief architect of the evolving formalism in late nineteenth-century Russian ballet was a Frenchman, Marius Petipa. Like his compatriots and predecessors, Charles Didelot and Perrot, Petipa came to Russia as a dancer and remained to become a ballet master to the Imperial theaters. Unlike them, he did not come with maturely formed artistic policies or with a portfolio of accomplishments to his credit. Petipa's brand of Russian classicism was to be created "from the blood and bone of the Imperial ballet—from its dancers [and] its school."[8]

The training of a dancer for the Imperial theaters began at the ballet school on Rossi, popularly known as Theatre, Street. The aim of every student was to become an artist of the Imperial Ballet. At the turn of the century, the Maryinsky Company was comprised of nearly 180 people, mostly women. Salaries were decided according to rank, and promotions were announced in the official weekly gazette, the *Journal of Orders*.[9] This hierarchy, and its codified standards, together with the tradition and continuity inherent in the dancers' training, all consolidated by the organization of the Imperial Ballet, was mirrored in the highly structured ballets of Marius Petipa.

The "Age of Petipa" in Russian ballet began with the *maître*'s first important work, *La Fille du pharon*, in 1862. He created over forty ballets, including the famous Tchaikovsky trilogy, *Swan Lake*, *The Nutcracker* and *The Sleeping Beauty*. Taking the art of ballet back to its pedagogical roots, he used the classroom as a choreographic laboratory. He would try out new choreography in his classes and would subtly alter *enchaînements* from the classes of the great Swedish teacher, Christian Johansson. As his repertoire evolved, the Petipa "recipe" emerged as a clearly recognizable formula.

Ballets of the period were divided into acts, each containing at least one major *pas d'action*, or dramatic scene. The basic themes of the ballets were developed in these sections. The forms of the *pas de deux*, classical solo and ensemble dances, also became canonized. The *pas de deux* was divided into an adagio movement, two solos and a coda. Solos were usually arranged in an ABA form—carefully constructed movement mini-sonatas. Both *pas de deux* and solos could be used as components of the ensemble, which in turn could be combined to form huge *divertissements*.

Within the strictures imposed by these forms, Petipa used the academic vocabulary of ballet as a "paradigm of potential."[10] Although his choreography was endlessly inventive, the "sense of luxury in the choreography itself provided the soul of the art of spectacle that Petipa practiced, with his bejeweled ballerinas, vast corps and elaborate stage business."[11] The complex scenarios were designed to present the maximum opportunities for dancing rather than dramatic congruity. His ballets were triumphs of technique over content and existed almost totally apart from the Russian culture that surrounded them. Petipa's work had little or no *âme russe.* Indeed, Petipa's answer to those who insisted on "nationalism" in art was to give them superb dancing. For him, the true Russian content of his ballets was their Russian dancers.

Russian art by and for Russian artists became the byword in *fin-de-siècle* art and literature—often referred to as the Russian Silver Age. A generation of young artists and intellectuals, the emerging Russian avant-garde, began to realize that their own cultural heritage had much to offer. They understood that "a renewal of artistic content could come about through a revival of national traditions."[12] This idea was the crux of a Neonationalist or Neo-Russian movement in painting and the applied arts, and became identified with a concurrent revival of interest in Russian folk art and culture. This increased awareness of a renewed national consciousness became evident in music, with the works of Nicolai Rimsky-Korsakov and Modest Mussorgsky; in theater, especially in the establishment of Konstantin Stanislavsky's Moscow Art Theater; and, finally, in ballet, with the advent of the Ballets Russes.

Two influences are important to this preamble to *Le Sacre du printemps.* The first is the establishment of two artists' colonies in the late 1870s and 1880s. In 1877, the wealthy industrialist Savva Mamontov opened Abramtsevo, his country estate near Moscow, to young artists, promising "no confines . . . no demands . . . no code of conduct."[13] A St. Petersburg noblewoman, Princess Maria Tenisheva, followed Mamontov's example and, in 1893, formed her artists' colony on her country estate, Talashkino, near Smolensk. Many artists frequented both retreats, inspired by the beautiful surroundings and the new interest in propagating traditional Russian culture.

In November of 1898, the second influence appeared in the form of a luxuriously produced new art journal called *Mir iskusstva* or *The World of Art,* the first issues of which were subsidized by Mamontov and Princess Tenisheva. *Mir iskusstva* was the vehicle for the artistic and literary ideas of its editor, Serge Diaghilev, and his cabinet of *miriskustniki,* and would provide "the real foundation of the Ballets Russes established by Diaghilev in 1909."[14] The magazine served as a propagator of both Russian and Western European art, familiarizing Russians with their own culture and history, as well as with that of the West. The participants in these three ventures—Abramtsevo, Talashkino and *Mir iskusstva*—formed connections that contributed to the work of each of the others and to the burgeoning "russification" of Russian art.

In an effort to "rescue" Russian folk art, Mamontov, a railroad millionaire, designed a series of projects to highlight interest in national traditions of art and architecture. The artists who came to Abramtsevo, including Victor Vasnetsov, Mikhail Vrubel, Elena Polenova, Alexander Golovin and Nicholas Roerich, shared his enthusiasm.[15]

Roerich was also a member of the Talashkino colony, where the artistic community pooled its creative talents in a variety of joint projects, including theatrical spectacles, workshops and the building of a church. One of Princess Tenisheva's most important contributions to the appreciation of Russian arts and crafts was the foundation of a museum of rare antique artifacts, including embroideries, woodcarvings and metalworks. By 1905, she had accumulated ten thousand pieces, and in 1907, she organized an exhibition entitled "Objets d'art russes anciens faisant partie des collections de la princesse Marie Tenichev" at the Musée des Arts Décoratifs in Paris.[16]

By the 1890s, art exhibitions had become popular as a way of guiding and developing the intellectual vanguard. A young artist named Alexandre Benois was appointed curator of Princess Tenisheva's art collection in 1895.[17] Benois was part of a select company of young men, "artists, literati, musicians and esthetes" who had banded together under the rubric of the "Society for Self-Education."[18] The core of the group had attended the same *gymnasium* and remained in close contact.

The society's activities consisted of "discussions of literature, musical performances, and reading of art periodicals, which the Benois household received in great number."[19] Later referring to themselves as the "Nevskii Pickwickians" (New Pickwickians), the members included Benois, the artists Léon (Lev) Bakst, Konstantin Somov, Eugene Lanceray and Walter Nouvel, Dimitre Filosofov and his cousin Serge Diaghilev. The society's interests were eclectic, embracing Ancient Greece and Egypt, the Italian Primitives, Far Eastern art, and the French eighteenth and nineteenth centuries, as well as Russian art and artists.[20] The young men attended exhibitions, concerts and the theater. Benois, especially, was passionately devoted to the ballet. Members of the group frequently traveled elsewhere in Europe, and the effect of this cross-fertilization helped develop and mature their artistic sensibilities.

The idea of an art journal that would propagate the ideals of this group of St. Petersburg aesthetes had been proposed by Diaghilev as early as 1893. The project gradually crystallized and the first issue of *Mir iskusstva* was published in November of 1898. The magazine's aim was "to encourage the development of modern Russian art in its purely aesthetic manifestations as well as in its application to applied art."[21] A primary concern of the *miriskustniki* was the reevaluation of the history of Russian art, and Diaghilev, as the journal's editor, maintained a broad interest in everything pertaining to Russian culture. This latter penchant carried through to the seasons of symphonic music and opera which he brought to Paris. The Ballets Russes, of course, was to premiere many works based on themes from Russian folklore, among them *L'Oiseau de feu, Petrouchka, Le Sacre du printemps, Contes russes* and *Les Noces.*

The objective of *Mir iskusstva* was outlined by Diaghilev in a quartet of articles in the first two issues of the journal. Although designed by Diaghilev, they expressed the outlook of the entire group—they were the *Mir iskusstva* aesthetic manifesto. In the course of these articles, the editor maintained that "the great strength of art is that it is independent, disinterested and—the main thing—free."[22] For Diaghilev, beauty in art was "the personality expressed in images."[23]

It was the work of artists who exemplified the Diaghilev cabinet's precepts that appeared in the pages of *Mir iskusstva.* The staff's bias toward Symbolist and Russian Neonationalist styles is evident, especially in early issues.[24] The Neonationalist painters who appeared in the journal adopted certain stylistic traits of folk art, particularly simplified form and vivid color. The scenes they portrayed were "generally far removed from everyday life: myth, history and lyrical landscapes." Roerich's work in *Mir iskusstva* reflected these concerns. He produced scenes of ancient Russia that evoked the remoteness of the past, "infinite spaces, elementary forces, pagan spiritual mysteries."[25] Russia's rich and venerable folk art heritage was a significant ingredient in the composition of *Mir iskusstva's* aesthetic canon.

The wide-ranging interests of the *miriskustniki* were reflected in the scope of the journal. Art, writ large, was represented by a variety of articles on music, theater and literature, as well as the visual arts. Essays on ballet, however, began only in 1902.

Critiques of ballet were written by both Diaghilev and Benois. Both expressed dissatisfaction with the productions mounted by the Imperial Theaters, then headed by V. A. Teliakovsky. Diaghilev, in particular, had ample reason to feel bitter toward the Imperial Directorate.

Prince Serge Volkonsky was appointed Director of the Imperial Theaters in 1899. Well acquainted with the activities—and the philosophy—of the *Mir isskustva* group, Volkonsky brought Diaghilev into the sphere of the Imperial Theaters, making him a special assistant on his staff. As his first assignment, Diaghilev was made editor of the traditionally conservative *Annual of the Imperial Theaters* for 1899–1900. Diaghilev and the *World of Art* cabinet transformed the uninspiring journal into "a bibliophilic rarité."[26] His handling of the project was termed a "triumph" and he won Volkonsky's approval to supervise a production of the ballet *Sylvia,* in collaboration with Benois, Bakst, Serov, Korovin and Lanceray.[27] The complication of "unofficial people, working independently in an institution so bounded by red tape" caused a confrontation between Diaghilev and Volkonsky. A subtly orchestrated *coup d'état* finally resulted in Diaghilev's dismissal from service to the Imperial Theaters.[28] With this rupture, "the possibility of creative theatrical work in Russia on the scale he wanted" was denied Diaghilev forever.[29]

The immediate consequences of this rift were twofold. Diaghilev channeled his energies in new directions, especially in organizing and presenting art exhibitions under the aegis of *Mir iskusstva*. Although the magazine ceased publication in December of 1904, Diaghilev's *World of Art* efforts were to culminate in the extraordinary historic portraits exhibition of 1905.

Benois records that the idea for such an undertaking was originally his, but that it was Diaghilev who did the legwork. He traveled extensively in Russia and Western Europe, searching out "portraits in forgotten palaces and estates," and borrowing works from museum collections.[30] The "Exhibition of Historic Russian Portraits," generously subsidized by the Tsar, opened at the Palais Tauride in St. Petersburg in February 1905. This grand visual record of Russia's Imperial history had a profound social and cultural effect. It was, in Diaghilev's estimation, the culmination of a search for "the brilliant images of our forefathers"—both a tribute and a summing up. The exhibition, which was open during the October Revolution of 1905, in fact presaged the end of an era. The pictures bore witness to a "great historical moment of reckoning . . . ending in the name of a new, unknown culture."[31]

Harbingers of a new culture were evident to the emerging Russian avant-garde. Not the least of these messengers was the young American dancer, Isadora Duncan. Her first performances in St. Petersburg in December of 1904 proved an enlightening experience for the Russian intelligentsia. Isadora's charismatic personality and impassioned dancing made a powerful impression on "those dilettantes of the gorgeous ballet," as she labeled her St. Petersburg audience.[32] Her philosophy that "the dance of the future will be one whose body and soul have grown harmoniously together," had no less impressive impact.[33]

Mikhail Fokine, a young dancer and aspiring choreographer at the Maryinsky, also saw Duncan and found in her dancing an example of the new ideals of expression he envisioned. Unhappy with the "iron rules of tradition," he felt ballet must be freed from the conventional strictures that were *de rigeur* in the Imperial Ballet.[34]

In 1904, Fokine read Longus's story of "Daphnis and Chloë," and submitted a two-act scenario to the director of the Imperial Theaters. In order to elucidate his concept for the ballet's production, he submitted explanatory notes with his proposal. In brief, he wrote that the whole meaning of a story could be expressed in movement; that dancing should be interpretive. He felt that ballet "must have complete unity of expression . . . a harmonious blending of three elements—music, painting and plastic art.''[35] In the dancing of Isadora Duncan, Fokine saw the realization of some of his precepts.

For Fokine, technique was a means to an end, and in this regard he was more a renegade than a radical. His aim was not to discard the principles of classical ballet, but to breathe new life into its choreographic idiom. A. V. Coton noted that Fokine lived in an age when ''man was discovering again the splendor and beauties of past cultures and civilisations, and with the rest of the forward-thinking artists he realized that *all* living, *all* knowledge, *all* imagination were to be drawn upon by any artist using any form.''[36]

It was inevitable that Fokine should be attracted to other ''forward-thinking artists''—the *Mir iskusstva* circle. Benois saw Russian ballet entering ''a new era of rebirth; the academic hothouse suddenly burst its frame and passed into the fresh air,'' a sentiment with which the choreographer agreed.[37]

Between 1905 and 1907, Fokine continued his choreographic experiments, creating ballets for charity performances and the Imperial School's graduation exercises. One such work was *Le Pavillon d'Armide*, created in collaboration with Benois and the composer Nicholas Tcherepnine for the Maryinsky Theater. Benois devised a three-act libretto, creating a fantastical tale of enchantment based on Théophile Gautier's *Omphale*.[38]

While the root of Fokine's choreography for *Le Pavillon d'Armide* remained the classical *danse d'école*, his ideas of expressivity and coherent dramatic action were at odds with the autotelic formulas of Petipa's era. The facade of abstract beauty exemplified by the Imperial Ballet was no longer sufficient; dance must express both character and emotion. The successful premiere of *Le Pavillon d'Armide* in November 1907 was Fokine's first major statement of his ideas of choreographic reform. The ballet also became the impetus for the World of Art group to take this new vision of Russian ballet to the West. Diaghilev and Benois saw the opportunity to transform ballet from ''an entertainment for children, hussars and ranking dignitaries'' into ''something young, full of enthusiasm, passion, strength, full of genuine life and color.''[39] In Fokine, they had found an intelligent, talented and sympathetic collaborator. According to Benois, Diaghilev appeared backstage after the opening of *Le Pavillon*, shouting, ''We must take this abroad.''[40]

Diaghilev's mission to produce Russian art in the West had begun the year before. His 1906 ''Exhibition of Russian Art'' at the Grand Palais had given Paris a glimpse of Russian tradition ''as seen through modern eyes.''[41] Following the success of the exhibition, Diaghilev became acquainted with *le gratin*, the cream of Parisian society. He met entrepreneurs such as Gabriel Astruc, the founder and first director of the Théâtre des Champs-Elysées, as well as artists, critics, composers and influential *literati*.[42] He next planned to present a series of concerts of Russian music in Paris in 1907.

Five programs of orchestral music and opera, entitled "Russian Music through the Ages," were presented at the Paris Opéra in May of 1907. Along with works such as Rimsky-Korsakov's *Mount Triglav* and Rachmaninoff's Second Piano Concerto (played by the composer), Diaghilev shrewdly included excerpts from colorful, dramatic Russian operas. Parisian audiences first heard Feodor Chaliapin in scenes from Borodin's *Prince Igor*, and Mussorgsky's *Boris Godunov* and *Khovanshchina*. The concerts, which French critic Robert Brussel declared surpassed all his expectations, encouraged Diaghilev to lay the groundwork for an opera season in 1908.[43]

The centerpiece of the opera venture was to be a complete production of *Boris Godunov*, with Chaliapin in the title role. The basso scored a personal triumph, while the critic of *Le Gaulois* acclaimed the entire production. "The admirable thing," he wrote, "was the color and pungency derived from a base of folk song: every country should insist on popular folklore being taught in musical conservatories."[44] Diaghilev, having masterminded a *campagne russe* of art, music and opera in Paris, decided upon the next logical step. He would bring ballet to Paris; he would present a traditional art form to the West which had been "miraculously preserved" in Russia, and there "transfigured and revived."[45]

In St. Petersburg, Diaghilev gathered his artistic committee to plan a *saison russe* of opera and ballet for presentation in Paris in the spring of 1909.[46] The ballet repertoire was to consist entirely of works by Fokine: *Le Pavillon d'Armide*, *Les Sylphides*, *Le Festin*, *Cléopâtre* and the "Polovtsian Dances" from *Prince Igor*.[47] The dancers included some of the finest young artists of the Maryinsky Ballet. Tamara Karsavina, Anna Pavlova, Adolph Bolm and, especially, Vaslav Nijinsky, were overnight sensations. The beauty, glamour, mystery and enchantment exerted by the Russian Ballet fostered the cult of *les fervents des russes*. This was a "group of painters, intellectuals, poets and poetasters, with Misia Sert at its head, that haunted the rehearsals and dined with Diaghilev and Nijinsky . . . after the show."[48] The Parisian public was dazzled, titillated and awed. Anna de Noailles wrote, "There was something new under the sun in the world of art, not conceived of until it appeared, in sudden splendor, the phenomenon of the Ballets Russes. . . . It seemed as though the creation of the world had something added to its seventh day."[49]

The ballets of the first Paris season foreshadowed the development of the pre-World War I repertoire of the Diaghilev company. Each of these works formed a link with the classical ballet heritage of Imperial Russia, and at the same time presaged the avant-garde works for which the Ballets Russes would become renowned. The tradition of *Le Pavillon* and *Les Sylphides* was continued in such ballets as *Le Carnaval* (1910), *Le Spectre de la rose* (1911), and *Daphnis and Chloë* (1913). *Cléopâtre* proved the forerunner of the "Oriental ballets"—*Schéhérazade* (1910), *Thamar* (1912) and *Le Dieu bleu* (1912). The singularly Russian thematic material first developed in the "Polovtsian Dances" found fuller realization in many of the landmark ballets of the Diaghilev company—*L'Oiseau de feu* (1910), *Petrouchka* (1911), and *Le Sacre du printemps* (1913). Prior to 1919, Diaghilev presented at least one "russkii" ballet per season and each was "a rousing display of Russian temperament."[50] Diaghilev, shrewdly, was feeding the public exactly what it wanted.

In Europe, and especially in France, there was, by the late 1880s and 1890s, a passion for things "russkii." The Russian Pavilion at the Exposition Universelle, for example, had a sensational impact. French translations of Dostoevski novels were in vogue, and even the writer Péladan declared in his *A coeur perdu* in 1888 that Europe would be saved by an infusion of "vigorous, instinctive Russian culture."[51]

The "Russian ballets" of the prewar Ballets Russes supplied an image of what "Europeans felt they had lost: innocence, passion, folk 'roots,' and unself-conscious responsiveness to spiritual mysteries."[52] Three elements contributed to the atmosphere of "primitivism" in the Ballets Russes evocations of *l'âme slave*. The first was the decorative exoticism of the sets and costumes. These designs, with their strange barbaric images, were provided by Neonationalist artists like Golovin and Roerich. The use of stylized folk dance also contributed to the aura of Primitivism, as did the music of composers such as Borodin, Rimsky-Korsakov, Balakirev and Stravinsky, who often used folk tunes for inspiration, orchestrating their compositions with exotic and colorful harmonies.

The third element was Fokine's development of the *corps de ballet* as an emotionally expressive ensemble. Although to today's ballet audiences Fokine's choreographic conception of wild abandon appears rather tame, it was a long way from the conventional, static groupings of the Paris Opéra *corps de ballet* of the period. Cyril Beaumont felt that Fokine "had no equal in the arrangement of dances that required to be imbued with a mad frenzy."[53] Critic and historian Joan Acocella views this "pure energy, both terrifying and liberating" as a "kinetic metaphor for primitive 'wholeness.' "[54] The Parisians were intoxicated by such ballets as the "Polovtsian Dances" from *Prince Igor*, with its depiction of savage warriors and captive women swept up in a "seething tumult of brutal rage."[55]

The ballets choreographed by Fokine and designed by the *Mir iskusstva* and Abramtsevo artists were consciously sophisticated productions that "assailed the [ballet] audience like an involuntary memory."[56] Some were fantastical fairy tales for grownups, like *L'Oiseau de feu* and *Schéhérazade*. *Les Sylphides*, *Le Carnaval* and *Le Spectre de la rose* evoked long-forgotten poetic images of the Romantic ballet. The Russian Butterweek fair, with its *balagani,* or Harlequinade puppet shows, was lovingly recreated in *Petrouchka.* The creators of the ballet made it a magical recollection, crammed with bittersweet nostalgia for the Russian fairs of their youth.[57] "It was as if Benois, Fokine and Stravinsky boxed the whole experience of the *balagan,*" writes Debra Goldman, so that the audience might remember "its own lost, simple savage self."[58]

This sort of theatrical historicism was an important element in the prewar Ballets Russes repertoire. The free and eclectic treatment of history, fantasy and mythic subject matter allied Fokine's ballets to the *Mir iskusstva* group's interest in Symbolist aesthetics. Fokine's works showed an unmistakable tension between the evolving realism in dance and the purity of the academic *danse d'école;* in other words, "the pull between description and abstraction."[59] Fokine never completely discarded the classical ballet base; rather, he attempted to translate iconography borrowed from artifacts, paintings and sculpture into exotic, mythic or Romantic movement analogues.

Fokine's choreography was more inventive than innovative and, by today's standards, rather conservative. But he—and the Ballets Russes— were able to give Europe something it had not seen in a long time: ballet as a "synthesis of the arts," the form of the French *danse d'école* enhanced by visual presentations with mysterious, hot-blooded and emotional overtones. Writing in the Russian magazine *Rech'* in 1909, Benois explained the Russian Ballet's success. "The barbarians once again conquered Rome," he declared, "and it is curious that contemporary Romans welcome this, their captivity, for they feel they will benefit from it, that the newcomers with their fresh blood and clear art will infuse new blood into their exhausted bodies." It was not Borodin, or Chaliapin or Diaghilev who was victor in Paris, "but rather all Russian culture, all the particularity of Russian art, its conviction, freshness and spontaneity, its savage power."[60]

Benois pointed out that the "wild primitiveness" and "simplicity" was more refined, more advanced and subtle than anything comparable in ballet or opera then being produced in Paris.[61] With Loïe Fuller's debut at the Folies-Bergère in 1892, the Symbolist artists and writers of the time saw their aesthetic exemplified in her work. Fuller, however, was outside the tradition of academic ballet and it remained for Diaghilev's Ballets Russes to offer Paris a glimpse of the apotheosis of Symbolism in the art of classical ballet.

Unlike Romanticism, "literary and pictorial Symbolism had no contemporary counterpart in ballet."[62] As noted earlier, European ballet, like its Russian counterpart, had been cut off from the prominent artistic and intellectual movements of the late nineteenth century. By the first decade of the twentieth century, the vogue for Symbolism had receded in Europe without affecting either the form or the conceptual development of

Western ballet. The Symbolist aesthetic reached Russia after its European heyday, where it was embraced by the *Mir iskusstva* group. Diaghilev and the *miriskustniki* artists, therefore, "were left with an aesthetic that was *démodé* but which they were in no way tired of. The solution was to transfer that aesthetic to a new medium, ballet, and a new theater of operations, Europe."[63] Petipa had worked within the parameters of the classical ballet tradition, canonizing the structure of his ballets and extending the dancers' technical range and proficiency. In contrast, Fokine drew his inspiration from outside the circumscribed world of the Imperial Ballet. The theories and precepts of Symbolist art, the resurgence of interest in Russian folk culture and the "new" school of dancing introduced by artists such as Isadora Duncan all contributed to the iconography of his ballets and defined their style. It was, therefore, Fokine's ballets for the Diaghilev Ballets Russes that presented Paris "a resurrection of Symbolism."[64]

The portents of Modernism, however, especially in the visual arts, were already sweeping through Europe. In the years between 1907 and 1913, Cubism, Futurism, Vorticism and other *isms* became full-fledged art movements. Giacomo Marinetti, the Italian Futurist painter, published his manifesto in 1909 and the following year Roger Fry organized the first Post-Impressionist exhibition at the Grafton Galleries in London. In 1911, the editors of the German *Blaue Reiter* art movement, presented their first exhibition in Munich, setting the tone for Vasily Kandinsky's tract *Uber das Geistige in der Kunst,* while Fry's second Post-Impressionist exhibition in October of 1912 contained a section devoted to Russian art.[65]

Clearly, a change was at hand. The tempo in the art world accelerated, racing to keep pace with innovations in science and technology. Rhythm "denoted modernity" and, not coincidentally, John Middleton Murray chose *Rhythm* as the title for his avant-garde literary journal.[66] While the Ballets Russes was giving Paris and (from 1911) London an effusion of *âme slave* in ballet form, Diaghilev was keenly aware of the new aesthetic on the horizon. According to Robert Brussel, nothing irritated Diaghilev more than to see Russia treated "like an exotic country that is curiously regarded by the West as a picturesque bazaar."[67] Diaghilev, however, needed his public, and "barbarism" was good box office. So was anything ancient, exotic, mythic and colorful when presented under the aegis of the Russian Ballet.

Late in 1910, following the success of *L'Oiseau de feu,* Igor Stravinsky told Diaghilev about a "musical-choreographic" work he had begun to compose, conceiving the libretto in collaboration with Nicholas Roerich. It was to represent "pagan Russia . . . the mystery and surge of the creative power of Spring."[68] The climax of the ballet was to be a solemn ritual in which a maiden danced herself to death to propitiate the god of Spring. For Stravinsky, the work was a paean to his homeland, to what he loved most in Russia: "the violent Russian spring that seemed to begin in an hour and was like the whole earth cracking."[69] For Diaghilev, it was the consummate synthesis, an extraordinary opportunity to bring together the ancient world of Slavic myth and ritual and the modern sensibility and power represented by Stravinsky's music. If it was primitive barbarism Europe really wanted, they would have it with *Le Sacre du printemps.*

2

The Prelude

I think the whole thing has been done by four idiots. First M. Stravinsky who wrote the music. Second M. Roerich who designed the scenery and costumes. Third M. Nijinsky who composed the dances. Fourth M. Diaghilev who wasted money on it.

Enrico Cecchetti

Thus did the great Italian ballet master Enrico Cecchetti dismiss *Le Sacre du printemps,* one of the seminal works in twentieth-century dance and music history. He was understandably shocked and disturbed by the primeval creation of his gifted protégé Vaslav Nijinsky, and he would not be alone. Vivid descriptions of the battles that ensued at the ballet's premiere—onstage, backstage and in the front of the house—are legion. Yet the shockingly brutal evocation of a primitive Slavonic ritual, glorifying a rite of spring, catapulted ballet into the twentieth century. Diaghilev saw the ballet as "a magnificent opportunity for shattering the Parisian audience. . . . [T]he new ballet was to contain nothing of European or any known civilization. If such barbarian rites had been practiced in Western Europe, thousands of years of culture had eradicated all trace of them."[1] *Le Sacre du printemps* was to be the prewar Ballets Russes' most extraordinary tribute to Russia and its most primitivist work.

The details concerning the conception of the ballet and the formative stages of its development are nearly as controversial as the work itself. A. E. Johnson, in his history, *The Russian Ballet,* published the same year as *Le Sacre*'s premiere, provided an imaginative account of the ballet's inception. He fantasized the three collaborators, "one had almost said conspirators," assembling in council and hatching a plot to be "primitive." Stravinsky would invent music which would "defy all accepted canons, and thus presumably be eloquent of a time when 'music' in any conventional sense, was not," while Roerich would devise a *mise-en-scène* so crude "that it must represent the furthest degree of unsophistication." Finally, Johnson imagines Nijinsky, "fresh from his meditation on a primitive phase of art," enthusiastically embracing a new opportunity to "apply the principles of gesture and movement which he believes himself to have divined."[2]

Johnson's idea of a premeditated plot by the ballet's creators to shock the audience seems somewhat extreme. The Diaghilev Ballets Russes had become famous for the synthesism of its ballets—the fusion of different artistic media into a single vision. The contributions of individual artists were subsumed in the process of creating an organic whole. There were three authors' names on the poster for *Le Sacre du printemps:* Roerich, Nijinsky and Igor Stravinsky. The writings of and about Stravinsky, however, seem to establish *Le Sacre* as his brain child. While the idea of creating a ballet based on primitive rites may have occurred to Stravinsky, Diaghilev, Roerich and Nijinsky at various times and in different ways, it was Stravinsky's score that provided these artists with a theme and focus for the creation of the ballet.

There are two somewhat contradictory accounts of Stravinsky's inspiration for *Le Sacre.* The first description comes from an interview with the composer when the ballet was revived in 1920, with new choreography by Léonide Massine. Stravinsky compared Massine's "architectonic" treatment of the original libretto, noting that the idea for the ballet "came from the music and not the music from the idea."[3]

The composer's *Autobiography,* published in 1936, presents a different story of the original inspiration for *Le Sacre,* and it is this version that generally has been adhered to by both Stravinsky and his biographers. After completing *L'Oiseau de feu,* the composer writes of seeing a fleeting vision; "a solemn pagan rite: sage elders, seated in a circle, watched a young girl dance herself to death." Stravinsky states he immediately told Roerich of the idea and ensured the painter's collaboration. Diaghilev, too, was told of the "vision," and was "at once carried away by the idea."[4]

Stravinsky's friend and associate, Robert Craft, believes that the composer's "dream" occurred in March 1910. Stravinsky probably discussed the ballet, then tentatively titled "The Great Sacrifice," with Nicholas Roerich that spring.[5] In a letter to Roerich dated 2 July 1910, Stravinsky writes that Diaghilev is encouraged by the success of *L'Oiseau de feu* and will have to be told about "The Great Sacrifice" "sooner or later."[6] By 9 August Stravinsky had begun to create musical sketches for the ballet and inquired whether Roerich had "done anything for it yet?"[7] Stravinsky was anxious to contact Roerich, as he had "much to say about our future child."[8]

The composer, meanwhile, had interrupted work on *Le Sacre* to begin composing a *Konzertstück* for piano and orchestra, a piece which eventually became crystallized as the ballet *Petrouchka.* "I had already told Diaghilev about *Le Sacre* when he came to see me in Lausanne at the end of

September 1910,'' wrote Stravinsky, ''but he did not know about *Petrouchka*. . . . Though Diaghilev may have been disappointed not to hear the music for 'pagan rites,' in his delight with *Petrouchka*, which he encouraged me to develop into a ballet before undertaking *Le Sacre du printemps*, he did not show it.''⁹ Nijinsky accompanied Diaghilev on this visit, and both were expecting to hear the music for ''The Great Sacrifice.'' It was to be included, along with Nijinsky's first choreographic effort, *L'Après-midi d'un faune*, in Diaghilev's 1911 season. Both ballets, however, were postponed.

Diaghilev decided to go ahead with *Petrouchka*, with Fokine as choreographer and Benois as co-librettist with Stravinsky. *Faune* was also put off, partly, according to Richard Buckle, because the Greek ballet *Narcisse* would have a starring role for Nijinsky and partly ''because Diaghilev was afraid Fokine would walk out if Nijinsky was brought forward as a choreographer even more radical than himself.''¹⁰ No doubt the impresario's concern was well founded.

A rift was undoubtedly brewing between Diaghilev and Fokine. Stravinsky considered offering ''The Great Sacrifice'' elsewhere, and, writing from Clarens in November of 1910, told Benois he would postpone ''The Great Victim'' until *Petrouchka* was completed. ''Also,'' he declared, ''I could never finish [it] by April, the time limit Diaghilev has imposed on me.''¹¹

Although Fokine, Benois and Stravinsky were absorbed in preparations for *Petrouchka* in the winter of 1911, Diaghilev kept an eye on his new protégé. Nijinsky had become a member, albeit a silent one, of Diaghilev's ''cabinet'' of artists as early as 1908. According to Bronislava Nijinska, before Diaghilev left for Paris to complete negotiations for the first Ballets Russes season, he made her brother Vaslav a gift of a complete set of *Mir iskusstva* and the catalogues of all his exhibitions of Russian art.¹² By 1910, Nijinsky regularly attended the meetings of ''the elite of St. Petersburg intelligentsia,'' and although he preferred to remain apart from the group, ''he listened avidly and absorbed everything that could perfect his art.''¹³ As one of the ''innovators,'' as members of the Diaghilev circle termed themselves, Nijinsky had begun to develop his own ideas about choreography. In the fall of 1910, he told his sister that he was going to invent a ballet for Diaghilev: *L'Après-midi d'un faune*, to Debussy's tone poem. He wanted to portray ''the archaic Greece'' that was less well known as opposed to the ''classical'' Greece Fokine liked to interpret. ''However, this is only to be the source of my inspiration. I want to render it in my own way,'' Nijinsky asserted.¹⁴

Nijinsky's advent as choreographer coincided with Diaghilev's need to present the new, the innovative and the controversial, as well as with his growing disenchantment with Fokine. ''Not long ago,'' Nijinska wrote in her journal during the winter of 1911, "Fokine freed himself from the old classical school and the captivity of Petipa's choreography, and now Vaslav is freeing himself from the captivity of Fokine's choreography so that, again, we enter a new phase in our Art."[15]

The "new phase" was postponed until 1912. Nijinsky showed Diaghilev and Bakst, who was to design *Faune*, the preliminary sequences of the ballet in St. Petersburg during the winter of 1911. While Bakst saw a number of unusual details in the work, Diaghilev "was made uneasy by the unexpected and unusual severity of the composition and the lack of dance movement."[16] Whatever his reaction, Diaghilev decided to postpone the premiere of *L'Après-midi d'un faune* until 1912, and Fokine remained the sole "Choreographic Director" for the Ballets Russes in 1911. By this time, Diaghilev wanted his own ballet company, for which he planned to create a new repertoire and which would perform year round.

In preparation for the 1911 season, Nijinsky and Diaghilev met with Stravinsky at Beaulieu in March. It is possible that they discussed not only *Petrouchka*, which was planned for the 1911 season, but also the embryonic "Great Sacrifice." In any case, after the successful premiere of *Petrouchka* in June of that year, Stravinsky met Roerich in July at Talashkino, the country estate of Princess Tenisheva. Roerich was eager for the composer to see the Princess's collections of Russian ethnic art.

Stravinsky began work with Roerich, deciding on the sequence of the action and the titles of the dances. Roerich also sketched his "famous Polovtsian-type backdrops" and designed costumes after original models in the Princess's collection.[17] The composer also notes that at this time their title for the ballet was *Vesna Sciaschennaia*, "Sacred" or "Holy" Spring. "*Le Sacre du printemps*, Bakst's title, was good only in French. In English, 'The Coronation of Spring' is closer to my original meaning than 'The Rite of Spring,'" wrote Stravinsky.[18]

It was Stravinsky's idea to divide the ballet into two sections representing day and night. Roerich suggested the specific ceremonies and rituals and the titles of the separate movements.[19] Robert Craft calls Roerich the "catalyst" of the ballet and both Benois and Grigoriev agree that the painter was both an equal and valued collaborator from the outset.[20] Indeed, the score of *Le Sacre* had as great an impact on Roerich as the designer's visions had on Stravinsky.

Roerich's thoughts on the ballet are detailed in a letter to Diaghilev, written at the beginning of 1913. "I wanted," he wrote, "to portray scenes of the joy of the creation of the Earth and the Heavens in a Slavic conception." A mystic, as well as a noted ethnologist, Roerich describes scenes of "blazing, earthy joy" and "celestial mystery," noting that he loved antiquity, "so high in its joy and so deep in its thought."[21]

The ballet was divided into two parts: "The Kiss of the Earth" and "The Sacrifice."[22] A definite program of dances was set down. The first part included: "Introduction" (The Prelude); "Auguries of Spring" (Dance of the Young Girls); "Ritual of Abduction"; "Spring Khorovod" (Round Dance); "Ritual of the Two Rival Tribes"; "Procession of the Oldest and Wisest One"; "The Kiss of the Earth" (The Oldest and Wisest One); and "The Dance Overcoming the Earth." The second part, which was called "The Exalted Sacrifice," contained "Introduction" (Pagan Night); "Mystic Circle of Virgins"; "The Naming and Honoring of the Chosen One"; "The Evocation of the Ancestors"; "Ritual of the Ancestors"; and "Sacrificial Dance" (The Chosen One). With this scheme in mind, Stravinsky began composing the score. The first section to be completed was the "Auguries of Spring." Stravinsky then wrote the entire first section before returning to "The Prelude," in which he wanted to evoke "the awakening of nature, the scratching, gnawing, wiggling of birds and beasts." The second part emerged in a "more helter-skelter fashion": the "Sacrifical Dance" was already in germination during the composition of the "Introduction." The dances for this section were composed very quickly, until Stravinsky reached the "Danse sacrale" (Sacrificial Dance), which, he recalled, "I could play, but did not, at first, know how to write."[23]

When Diaghilev commissioned the score in July of 1911, the agreed date of the premiere was June of 1912. In January, however, Diaghilev decided to postpone *Le Sacre* until 1913, meanwhile encouraging Stravinsky to score the ballet for a huge orchestra.[24] As a result, Stravinsky's work on the ballet slowed down and the instrumentation of the work was not written until late spring. The final pages of the "Danse sacrale" were not completed until 17 November 1912.[25]

In March of 1912, the Ballets Russes went to Monte Carlo to rehearse three new ballets, Fokine's *Thamar* and *Daphnis and Chloë*, and Nijinsky's *L'Après-midi d'un faune*. The spring season was to prove a turning point in the history of the Ballets Russes. By now, everyone knew that Nijinsky was to make his choreographic debut, and the relationship between Diaghilev and Fokine had deteriorated. The company's *régisseur*, Serge Grigoriev, records that the impresario was no longer attracted by the work of his principal choreographer. "Diaghilev," wrote Grigoriev, ". . . thought he [Fokine] had no more to say and was in search of someone to take his place. Moreover, it was clear that his choice had fallen on Nijinsky."[26]

At the beginning of 1912, however, Stravinsky still thought Fokine might be entrusted with the choreography for *Le Sacre*. He was dismayed at the prospect and wrote to his mother that he considered Fokine "an exhausted artist,'' incapable of creating the ''new forms'' of which the composer dreamed.[27] Diaghilev, however, could see the emergence of ''new forms'' in Nijinsky's *Faune*, which was unlike any ballet yet produced by the Russian Ballet.

L'Après-midi d'un faune was to prove a strange and challenging experience even for the choreographer's sister, Bronislava. She was to be one of the nymphs in her brother's first ballet. During early rehearsals of the ballet in 1912, Nijinska recalled a particularly difficult jump, noting that she had to ''preserve in the air the same pose as when running across the stage—a bas-relief form, with the knees slightly bent.'' The jump had to be performed with no perceptible preparation, with the landing and an ''abrupt half-turn'' and run into the wings executed in the same two-dimensional bas-relief form.[28]

Clearly this type of movement, so intractable in its sheer simplicity and unremittingly demanding call for *plastique*, was very different from Fokine's ''curly classicism.''[29] The six women who were to portray the nymphs were confused by this new style of choreography and did not seem to know what was expected of them. Nijinsky demonstrated the required movements with apparent ease and was unable to understand why the dancers looked so awkward. The ''nymphs'' remained exasperated, but applied themselves nonetheless. Nijinska asserts they were ''very effective'' when standing still, but were unable to preserve the flat, ''bas-relief'' form when moving.[30]

By the time the Ballets Russes opened its Monte Carlo season in the spring of 1912, *L'Après-midi d'un faune*, and its choreographer, were the focus of publicity. Fokine, who was working on *Daphnis and Chloë* at the same time, was depressed and disturbed by the attention to what he perceived as an ''amoral work.'' After seeing a rehearsal of *Faune*, he claimed that Nijinsky had copied the style of dancing from his *Daphnis*, and before the Paris season he angrily tendered his resignation.[31] Diaghilev received his decision ''almost with indifference,'' as he had begun to expect great things of Nijinsky.[32]

The premiere of *L'Après-midi d'un faune* was a ''*succès de scandale.*'' Critics and audiences professed shock at its ''erotic bestiality and heavy shamelessness.''[33] The originality of the choreography was nearly eclipsed by the moral outcry against the ''lasciviousness'' of Nijinsky's final pose in the ballet, which suggested to some critics an indecent sexual act. While some protests centered on the sexually suggestive nature of the ballet's theme, others argued that Debussy's music had been ''misused'' and that the synchrony of music, choreography and design had been ignored. In any event, the audience at the dress rehearsal received the work in silence; whether stunned or awed it is impossible to determine. Fokine reported that ''after a few strained minutes,'' Astruc appeared in front of the curtain. He explained that "such a new exhibition" could not be understood in a single viewing, and the ballet was repeated.[34]

The action of *L'Après-midi d'un faune* is based, as is the Debussy score, on the poem of the same name by Stéphane Mallarmé. An idle Faun "observes seven Nymphs, and his desire is aroused by one who undresses to bathe in the stream; but when he confronts her, she flees, and he has to console himself with the scarf she has left behind."[35] Bakst's backcloth, with white rocks, trees and a waterfall in russet, green and gray, was hung far forward, on a line with the second set of wings. The Nymphs' pleated tunics, stenciled with bold geometric designs, matched the angular movements Nijinsky had created. Cyril Beaumont described the look of the ballet as "a frieze of living figures."[36] Certainly the tension inherent in the two-dimensional movement style devised by Nijinsky added to the atmosphere of suppressed eroticism in the ballet.[37]

Critic Eugène Belville noted, Nijinsky's "claim to link his inspiration (for *Faune*) to archaic monuments, angular attitudes and broken gestures of Greek art, has been strongly disputed."[38] The choreographer remarked that he spent a good deal of time at the British Museum, finding inspiration in the ancient marbles, bas-reliefs and vases for "dances, gestures, physical balances and purity of movement." The ballet, stated Nijinsky, was "simply a fragment drawn from a classic bas-relief."[39] Perhaps Nijinsky most fully revealed his intentions when he told a reporter before the premiere of *Faune*, "Je ferai de l'art cubiste."[40]

Although the ballet had its detractors, many members of the Parisian artistic community recognized and applauded Nijinsky's achievement, including the sculptor Auguste Rodin and the artist Odilon Redon. Delighted with the publicity engendered by the ballet, Diaghilev asserted that *Faune* "represents the furthest step we have yet taken in the development of ballet."[41] Having decided to champion the ballet as both beautiful and original, the *deus ex machina* of the Russian Ballet was determined that Nijinsky would be the choreographer for *Le Sacre du printemps*.

It was during the Ballets Russes' 1912 season that Parisians first heard of *Le Sacre*. When Stravinsky joined the company in Monte Carlo, prior to its Paris performances, he had completed the bulk of the score. He performed the piano version in unfinished form for Diaghilev and conductor Pierre Monteux in Monte Carlo and for Debussy and Louis Laloy in Paris.[42] Monteux recalled that before the composer "had got very far, I was convinced he was raving mad." Noting that, heard without the "color" of the orchestration, "its stark primitiveness was emphasized," and the conductor concluded that "such music would surely cause a scandal."[43] Years later, Monteux remembered that Diaghilev had told him, prophetically, "This is a masterpiece . . . which will completely revolutionize music and make you famous, because you are going to conduct it."[44]

Even the conductor of *Le Sacre du printemps* was bemused by the complex nature of the score's rhythmic structure. Realizing that the music would present hitherto unprecedented problems for both the choreographer and the dancers (to say nothing of the musicians), Diaghilev and Nijinsky decided to employ someone from Emile Jaques-Dalcroze's school in Hellerau, near Dresden, to help both the dancers and the choreographer cope with the difficulties of Stravinsky's score. Dalcroze had created a system of analyzing music by bodily movement, a method that became known as Eurythmics. There were two sides to the concept of Eurythmics: the immediate response to music and the "more intellectual, analytic response of the will to the music."[45] One aspect of the work concentrated on the memorization and analysis of rhythmic patterns and phrases, which seemed to make this area of training advantageous for the study of a score such as *Le Sacre*.

Dalcroze and his work were well known in Russia. He and his pupils had visited St. Petersburg in January of 1911, where they gave a demonstration of Eurythmics.[46] Diaghilev, intrigued by the method, visited the school in Hellerau in December of 1912, accompanied by Nijinska, Baron de Gunsburg and dancer Adolph Bolm. Nijinska was unimpressed by what she termed the students' "pseudomusicality." Diaghilev, however, was concerned that his dancers would not be able to cope with the intricate rhythms of Stravinsky's score. Accordingly, he hired Miriam Ramberg, who became known as Marie Rambert, to teach the company Eurythmics. Nijinska, "burning with indignation," protested, but to no avail, while Nijinsky "made no comment one way or the other."[47]

Much has been written about Nijinsky's—and the dancers'—difficulties with the score of *Le Sacre*. In his *Autobiography*, Stravinsky wrote that Nijinsky's "ignorance of the most elementary notions of music was flagrant. The poor boy knew nothing of music."[48] Nijinska asserts that her brother could play a number of musical instruments, including the piano, balalaika and clarinet, although she acknowledges that he often had no patience for reading conventional piano scores.[49] It is therefore unlikely that he "never understood musical metres" and had "no very certain sense of tempo," as Stravinsky later claimed.[50] By all accounts, Nijinsky was acutely musical, with the dancer's sensitivity to and awareness of the shape of a musical phrase.

Nijinsky's method of working with the score of *Le Sacre* was established before Rambert joined the Ballets Russes. He had begun choreographing the "Danse sacrale" in the early weeks of November 1912, working with Nijinska who was to dance the role of the Chosen Maiden.[51] Nijinsky would have the rehearsal pianist, Maurice Steiman, play the section in its entirety, then play each musical phrase separately, until he thoroughly comprehended and assimilated the rhythms.[52]

Nijinska felt that the rhythm of the movements created by her brother "had never been used before by a choreographer" and that he was following the "breath" of the music to create his choreography.[53] The composer, however, had his own very definite ideas about the kind of movement that should accompany his music.[54]

Stravinsky plotted an extraordinarily detailed plan of choreographic movement for Nijinsky.[55] Eventually both parties became exasperated with each other. Stravinsky felt the choreographer made no attempt to understand his ideas for *Le Sacre*, while Nijinsky complained that the composer treated him as though he had never studied music at all.[56] As Stravinsky conceived the synchronization of music and choreography, the dance would almost always be in counterpoint to the score. Nijinsky, for his part, although content to work within the composer's thematic framework, was determined to realize his own choreographic vision.

The "Danse sacrale," which was to be the climax of the ballet, was created in two rehearsals.[57] In this solo, Nijinsky established the style and developed the movement material he would later use in the ensemble sections of the ballet.[58] He did not explain the story of *Le Sacre* to his sister before working with her on the solo, saying only that it was a "ritualistic sacrificial dance." While working on the "Danse sacrale," Nijinska recalled the intense, stormy atmosphere of Roerich's painting "The Call of the Sun."[59] "As I envisaged the primitiveness of the tribal rites," she wrote, "where the Chosen Maiden must die to save the earth, I felt that my body must draw into itself, must absorb the fury of a hurricane. Strong, brusque, spontaneous movements seemed to fight the elements as the Chosen Maiden protected the earth against the menacing heavens."[60]

Nijinsky was now ready to begin work on *Le Sacre* in earnest. Rambert joined the Ballets Russes in Budapest at the close of 1912. Meanwhile, the company had begun rehearsals of the ballet, but with few results. The choreography that Nijinsky was creating demanded an almost unprecedented precision of execution. For the dancers, brought up in the tradition of the Imperial Russian Ballet, Nijinsky's demands for exactness in every detail seemed unreasonable. Nijinsky, who could demonstrate the most difficult movements with ease, believed that the inability (or unwillingness) of a dancer to repeat his movements precisely "was a deliberate act of obstruction, and he accused the artists of wanting to sabotage his ballet."[61] By the time Rambert arrived, Nijinsky's difficulties with the dancers, the dancers' dislike of the score, the choreographer's extraordinary demands, and Stravinsky's misgivings about both the choreography and its creator, produced an atmosphere fraught with tension and frustration. Rambert proved to be a blessing for all concerned. She befriended the usually shy and withdrawn Nijinsky, placated the confused and exasperated dancers, and attacked the score of *Le Sacre* with relish.

Due to the demands of the ballet's music and choreography, an unusual number of rehearsals were required. Rambert recalled the problems which the work engendered in creation:

> We arranged that I would give a class—in Eurythmics—at half past five when rehearsals were over. Well, that was just not on . . . people were dead tired. We very soon gave up *that* and started straight away on the score. I took the piano score and started counting out the bars. We had "Kolossal"—Diaghilev named our pianist "Kolossal"—and he would play a few bars and I would analyze it and teach it to Nijinsky. Then he would say that would be for say, a group of six. . . . And so we went on. (Lydia) Sokolova describes it very well when she says that everyone had little booklets, writing down their bars! Nijinsky wanted every note of the music interpreted. He would study the score. . . . He was terribly keen on the score.[62]

Work progressed tediously. Painstakingly, Nijinsky taught the movements, and the dancers recorded in their notebooks how to start, the number of bars needed for phrases of movement, and how to count them. The *dénouement* took place when Stravinsky arrived to view rehearsals. He observed for a few moments and then stormed, "that's a funeral march, what you are playing. It's terribly slow." According to Rambert, Nijinsky told the composer it was impossible to do the movements more quickly. "Finally," she recalled, "Stravinsky jumped up and banged his feet and banged the top of the piano, trying to 'orchestrate,' to give Nijinsky the idea. Of course we understood we had to do it quicker . . . because we were doing it at *very* comfortable tempi."[63]

The choreographer's demand that the dancers perform movements to which they were unaccustomed, coupled with the difficulties inherent in remembering the counts of the score, were undoubtedly the cause of much of the dancers' exasperation. Rambert insisted that Nijinsky knew precisely what he wanted and gave exact and painstaking instructions. "He was indefatigable the way he showed movements again and again." She recalled that Nijinsky insisted that a choreographer should oversee even the most minute details of his work.[64]

Many members of the Diaghilev entourage who saw *Le Sacre* in rehearsal were dismayed, and did not attempt to conceal their disapproval.[65] Only Roerich, Nijinska asserts, supported Nijinsky. The painter often came to rehearsals, encouraging the choreographer, recounting the pagan rites and prehistory of ancient Slavic tribes.

Roerich's influence on Nijinsky is readily apparent in the choreographer's comments in an interview printed in the *Pall Mall Gazette* on 15 February 1913. *Le Sacre*, said Nijinsky, was to be danced only by the *corps de ballet*, as the choreographer saw the ballet as a work of "concrete masses, not individual effects."[66] Earlier in January, Nijinsky had written to Stravinsky, assuring the composer that the ballet would be "something great." "I know what *Le Sacre du printemps* will be when everything is as we both want it," he wrote, "new, and, for the ordinary viewer, a jolting experience. For some it will open new horizons flooded with different rays of sun. People will see new and different colors and different lines. All different, new and beautiful."[67]

Nijinsky's search for "resolutely modern movement" was leading him to pursue thematic material that would reflect his concern with the plasticity of movement for its own sake. The choreographer had declared that "the human being that before all else I would see on stage is modern man. I dream of . . . attitudes and movements that are characteristic of our time."[68]

Simultaneously with *Le Sacre*, Nijinsky began work on *Jeux*, a ballet which used the contemporary and *au courant* theme of a tennis game as a "metaphor for psychological patterns in modern manners."[69] Tennis was very much in vogue in 1912, making its sports motif an ideal vehicle for a "modern" ballet.

There are, of course, several versions of the genesis of the ballet. Although it was undoubtedly another collaborative effort, involving contributions from Nijinsky, Diaghilev, Bakst, Debussy and writer Jacques-Emile Blanche, it was Blanche who received program credit for the scenario.[70] According to Blanche, Nijinsky wanted to choreograph a "Cubist" ballet, with no *corps de ballet*, no ensembles, no variations, no *pas de deux*, "only boys and girls in flannel and rhythmic movements."[71]

Jeux was an attempt to fuse the aesthetics of the current avant-garde movements in the visual arts—especially Cubism and Futurism—with Nijinsky's evolving *plastique* style of movement. Indeed, an interview with Nijinsky in *Comoedia*, published the morning after the ballet's premiere, has the echo of a Futurist manifesto on the modernization of ballet.[72] After proclaiming that dance must do away with "puerile choreographic storytelling," the choreographer makes an impassioned plea for progress through "the interpretation of harmonious and resolutely modern movement . . . the plasticity of movement for its own sake."[73] In its spare action and use of strong, athletic and uncompromisingly simple movement, *Jeux* was, as Nijinska described it, "the forerunner of Neoclassical ballet."[74]

The scenario of *Jeux* was slight. Set in a moonlit garden designed by Bakst, the ballet began with a tennis ball bouncing across the stage. Three dancers, two girls and a youth, followed it, carrying tennis racquets. The boy flirted first with one girl, then the other, then both at once. Another ball bounced onto the stage, all three ran after it and the ballet was over.[75] The dancers were to be Tamara Karsavina and Nijinska as the girls and

Nijinsky as the youth.[76] As with *Faune* and *Le Sacre,* Nijinsky did not explain the ''libretto'' in rehearsals. The dancers often attended tennis
games, however, where the choreographer studied the players' body
movements, ''the technique of striking the ball [and] the position of the
arm and the grip of holding the tennis racquet.''[77]

From his observations, Nijinsky developed a highly stylized basic
body position for *Jeux.* The dancer stood on demi-pointe in a turned in or
''natural'' second position, with the body flat to the stage proscenium. The
arms were held out from the sides of the body at shoulder height, bent at
the elbows and wrists. The hands were held in half-clenched fists and the
head inclined to one shoulder. The choreographer was attempting to
devise ''stylized gesture'' with an ''angular as opposed to [a] curved
beauty.''[78]

To a number of observers, the geometric configurations and fragmentation of movement in *Jeux* had much in common with Cubist
aesthetics. The quick, attenuated shards of motion gave the effect of a
rapidly changing stereopticon. Accordingly, *Jeux* was labeled a ''ballet
cinématographique.''[79] The ballet also included sculptural posings and
groupings, effectively extending the angularity of *Faune* from a two-
dimensional frieze into three-dimensional space.[80]

The critical reaction to *Jeux,* which premiered on 15 May 1913, was, for
the most part, negative. It was termed a ''succès de ridicule,'' a novelty,
and an example of Diaghilev's need to astonish. Louis Laloy declared that
it ''would be impossible to conceive a more grossly pedestrian interpretation, one more contrary to all the laws of harmony, of body as well as of
sounds.''[81] Pierre Lalo railed against the ''rigid posturings'' and
''sharpened silhouettes.'' ''Willfully [Nijinsky] chooses ugliness and
freakishness instead of the demanded desired beauty.''[82] Lalo's despair
was echoed by other critics, but Nijinsky would not, could not, conform
to the conventional, traditional modes of expression canonized by classical ballet.

Nijinsky's use of Debussy's music also aroused controversy. One critic
felt that the composer and choreographer took absolutely no notice of one
another, while Debussy himself accused the choreographer of being
''Dalcrozian.''[83]

The criticisms leveled at *Jeux* represented an important precedent for
the premiere of *Le Sacre du printemps* a fortnight later. The audience at the
opening night of *Jeux* greeted the ballet with laughter and hissing, thus setting the tone of the season for the audience which would shortly see the
new Stravinsky–Nijinsky work.[84] *Jeux* also raised serious concerns in the
critical community regarding Nijinsky's competence as a choreographer.
At issue were his capacity to create choreography in the traditional balletic
mode and his mistreatment of French music. Nijinsky critics came to the

Ludmilla Schollar, Vaslav Nijinsky and Tamara Karsavina, in *Jeux*
(Photo courtesy of the Dance Collection, The New York Public Library at Lincoln Center, Astor, Lenox and Tilden Foundations)

defense of Debussy and opposition to the ballet became an "occasion for patriotic posturing and for decrying the violation of French artistic life by Russian influence."[85]

Diaghilev had planned to present *Le Sacre du printemps* in 1912, but neither the score nor the choreography had been completed in time. Now, in 1913, he judged, and rightly, that the time was ripe for a massive dose of *âme slave*. The success of Stravinsky's two previous "Russian" ballets, *L'Oiseau de feu* (1910) and *Petrouchka* (1911), coupled with Nijinsky's growing notoriety as a choreographer made *Le Sacre*'s triumph seem predestined. Here was a thoroughly Russian ballet—primitive, raw, arcane and ritualistic—to revitalize the fading "russkii" image of the Ballets Russes. *Le Sacre du printemps* was a work which had its roots in ancient Russian culture and reflected the artistic synthesism for which Diaghilev's company was renowned. *Jeux* may have failed to make a deep or memorable impression, but, in the words of Victor Debay, "*Jeux* prépara la révolte."[86]

3

A Song of the Earth

In the spring of 1912, Louis Laloy, the editor of *La Grande Revue* and a friend of French composer Claude Debussy, first made the acquaintance of Igor Stravinsky. The Russian musician had brought Laloy an arrangement for four hands of his new work, *Le Sacre du printemps*. Debussy, Laloy recalled, agreed to play the bass part, and Stravinsky immediately asked if he could remove his collar. "His sight was not improved by his glasses," wrote Laloy, "and, pointing his nose to the keyboard, and sometimes humming a part that had been omitted from the arrangement, he led into a welter of sound the supple, agile hands of his friend." Debussy followed the score without a hitch and seemed to make light of the difficulty. When they had finished, recalled Laloy, "there was no question of embracing, nor even of compliments. We were dumbfounded, overwhelmed by this hurricane which had come from the depths of the ages, and which had taken life by the roots."[1] Debussy later wrote to Stravinsky that their reading at the piano of *Le Sacre du printemps* was always in his mind. "It haunts me like a beautiful dream, and I try in vain to reinvoke the terrific impression."[2] Laloy, too, knew he had heard one of the most extraordinary musical scores of the twentieth century.

When *Le Sacre du printemps* had its premiere in Paris in May 1913, Igor Stravinsky had been intimately associated with the Ballets Russes for four years. He had had his first success in Paris in 1910 with the presentation of *L'Oiseau de feu*, the only ballet to new music performed by the Russian Ballet that year. In 1911, *Petrouchka*, the Russian *commedia* ballet celebrating the St. Petersburg Butterweek fairs, established Stravinsky as the Russian Ballet's most distinguished living composer. Both ballets were nationalistic in subject matter and were the first major musical scores composed specifically for the Ballets Russes. All the other ballets from 1909 to 1911 made use of various musical formulas. Some used shortened musical scores, such as *Schéhérazade*, or excerpts from other pieces, such as the "Polovtsian Dances" from *Prince Igor*. There were also arrangements of a single composer's work (e.g., Chopin's *Les Sylphides*) and amalgams of the works of several composers (e.g., *Cléopâtre*). With the scores for *L'Oiseau de feu* and *Petrouchka*, it was the coherence of the musical work which became an important concern of the Ballets Russes. A "new unity between the narrative aspect of the choreography" and the descriptive elements of the musical score was also established.[3] Both *L'Oiseau de feu* and *Petrouchka* were collaborative efforts, conceived in the spirit of the "synthesis of the arts" advocated by *Mir iskusstva,* for which the Russian Ballet became famous.

Stravinsky acknowledged that the philosophy of the *Mirisskustva* group was the single greatest aesthetic influence of his youth. Especially important to the nascent composer was the *miriskustniki*'s recognition of folk art and tradition for their "inherent aesthetic and stylistic values."[4] Stravinsky's use of Russian folk music as thematic material is easily discernible in his first three Ballets Russes commissions, *L'Oiseau de feu* (1910), *Petrouchka* (1911) and *Le Sacre du printemps* (1913). Indeed, Richard Taruskin, the noted historian of Russian music, states that "no Russian composer before or since surpassed the early Stravinsky's creative utilization of 'native folklore,' and no Russian composer was ever more profoundly inspired and influenced by it in forming his own personal style."[5] *L'Oiseau de feu* and *Petrouchka* represented Stravinsky's first attempts at composing for the ballet and adapting Russian folk music for theatrical scores. For this reason, it is important to examine these two works as stylistic antecedents to *Le Sacre du printemps.*

When Diaghilev wanted a new ballet, and "a *Russian* one," for his 1910 Paris and London seasons, he first approached the composer Anatol Liadov to prepare a score for the fairy-tale story of the Firebird.[6] The scenario was a patchwork of several Russian folk tales and fairy stories, and although Fokine is generally credited with the libretto, the ballet was, in the fashion of some early Ballets Russes creations, a collaborative effort.[7] In any case, Liadov proved a slow worker and Diaghilev finally offered the commission of *L'Oiseau de feu* to Stravinsky, who accepted it with some reluctance. The composer later stated that *The Firebird* did not attract him as a subject. It was a "story ballet," needing descriptive music which he emphatically disliked.[8]

The libretto concerns the young Prince Ivan, who captures a magical Firebird in an enchanted forest. In exchange for her freedom, the Firebird offers the Prince a golden feather. He assents and allows her to go free. As he is about to leave, twelve maidens enter the glade, led by a beautiful Tsarevna. Ivan watches them dance and falls in love with the Tsarevna. She warns him to go, as he is in the domain of the evil enchanter, Kostchei the Immortal. Suddenly Ivan and the maidens are surrounded by a motley horde of demons and goblins. Kostchei enters and is about to place Ivan under a spell when the Prince waves the Firebird's magic feather. She appears and compels the demons to dance until they fall into an exhausted sleep. Ivan discovers an enormous egg, which contains Kostchei's soul, and dashes it to the ground. The evil magician and his court are destroyed, and in their place a group of young noblemen is seen. In a final solemn procession, Ivan is invested with a crown, scepter and ermine robe, and "the assembly acclaim him as their deliverer and sovereign lord."[9]

Stravinsky and Fokine worked together on the synthesis of movement and music. The composer, noting that he liked "exact requirements," played melodies on the piano while Fokine interpreted various roles.[10] When Stravinsky had finished each section of the score, the choreography would be set on the dancers.

Ultimately, however, Stravinsky thought the results were less than perfect, feeling the words "For Russian Export" were "stamped everywhere, both on the stage and the music."[11] Benois concurred, noting that the realization of *Firebird* was less than ideal. The designer felt Stravinsky's score, however, which he termed "poetical, expressive and beautiful," was one of the composer's finest creations.[12]

L'Oiseau de feu, with its story drawn from *skazki*, or Russian folk myths and legends, was the Ballets Russes' dance equivalent of the highly successful Russian operas which Diaghilev presented in his early Russian seasons. Musically, the ballet was essentially unrelated to the tradition of Petipa–Tchaikovsky classicism. Its heritage was rather "folkloric 'magic' operas," beginning with Glinka's *Ruslan and Ludmila* and continuing through Rimsky–Korsakov's *The Snow Maiden* and *Le Coq d'or*.[13] It was a deliberately "Russian" sensibility, then, on which Stravinsky drew for inspiration for *Firebird* and, later, for *Petrouchka*.

In *L'Oiseau de feu*, Stravinsky effectively differentiated the natural elements of the ballet—represented by Prince Ivan and the princesses—and the supernatural world of the mythical Firebird, Kostchei and his demonic court. In musical terms, he used a convention that extends back to the work of Glinka. For his human characters, the composer used music adapted from the Russian folk song idiom, a device which made for a colorful contrast to the "fantastic harmonies" which he devised for Kostchei.[14] The sequences of mimed and danced episodes, like recitative and aria in opera, are especially effective in *L'Oiseau de feu*. This is a technique which the composer may have borrowed from the operas of the "Mighty Five" as well as from the great ballet scores of Tchaikovsky, whose work Stravinsky greatly admired.[15]

The two songs that Stravinsky used in *L'Oiseau de feu* are to be found in Rimsky–Korsakov's collection, *One Hundred Russian Folk Songs* (1877). The *khorovod*, or round dance, called "In the Garden," was adapted for the "Ronde des princesses." For it, Fokine devised a lyrical, feminine dance reminiscent of Russian women's folk dances. The other tune, also a *khorovod,* became the Coronation processional in the ballet's finale.[16] Another distinctive aspect of the score concerned the syncopation of the bass rhythms in the "Firebird's Dance" and the dynamic surge of the "Infernal Dance," "with its insistence on a constantly sustained, undeviating beat."[17] The *ostinato*—the persistent, repeated, fragmentary pattern played without any change in pitch of the repetitions—became an important feature in Stravinsky's style between 1910 and 1920. The chief advantage of this device is that "it supplies a rhythmic consistency for the dance."[18]

In the score of *Petrouchka* (1911), Stravinsky developed a more sophisticated and unconventional style in both his treatment of folk music and in his manipulation of rhythmic structures. After the success of *L'Oiseau de feu,* the composer wanted to "refresh" himself and began work on a sort of *Konzertstück,* an orchestral piece with a prominent role for the piano. "In composing the music," wrote Stravinsky, "I had in my mind the distinct picture of a puppet, suddenly endowed with life, exasperating the patience of the orchestra with diabolical cascades of arpeggi." Searching for a suitable title for the piece, Stravinsky finally decided on *Petrouchka,* "the immortal and unhappy hero of every fair in all countries."[19]

Diaghilev visited Stravinsky in Lausanne in the summer of 1910, and, hearing the music which would eventually become the second scene of *Petrouchka,* persuaded the composer to develop the theme into a new ballet. The two men settled on the general action of the plot and on the ballet's setting, the St. Petersburg Shrovetide Fair—the Butterweek pre-Lenten carnival festival which Stravinsky and Diaghilev remembered from their youth. Benois, a devotee of the *balagani,* was to design the decor and costumes.[20] Although he is credited as "half-author" of the libretto, Benois noted that his participation was primarily that of helping Stravinsky coordinate the action with the music.[21] As with *L'Oiseau de feu,* the choreography was to be done by Fokine.

The action of the ballet begins at the Shrovetide Fair in St. Petersburg's Admiralty Square in the 1830s. Crowds stroll among the swings, roundabouts, food-stalls and the Charlatan's little theater. A street musician with a hurdy-gurdy accompanies one dancer, while her rival performs to music-box tunes. Suddenly the Charlatan appears before the theater curtains and reveals three puppets on their stands—Petrouchka, the Blackamoor and the Ballerina. Each performs a dance to the melodies of the Charlatan's flute.

In the second scene in Petrouchka's cell, the puppet rails against the cruelty of both his master and his fate. When the Ballerina visits him, he tries to win her love, but she is frightened by his antics and flees, leaving Petrouchka in despair. The third scene takes place in the Blackamoor's exotic room. He is playing with a coconut when the Ballerina arrives and they dance a flirtatious duet. Presently, they are interrupted by a furiously jealous Petrouchka, who is thrown out by the Blackamoor.

The final scene again takes place at the fairground. It is evening and the festivities have reached their height. There is a performing bear and gypsies, and a group of wetnurses and coachmen perform a dance. Finally, some masqueraders—including a devil, a goat and a pig—dash onto the scene. But at this moment, the crowd hears a commotion in the Charlatan's theater. Petrouchka rushes out from behind the curtain, followed by the Blackamoor, whom the Ballerina attempts to restrain. The Blackamoor strikes Petrouchka with his scimitar and, to the astonishment of the crowd, the puppet dies. The Charlatan is summoned and he reassures the bystanders that Petrouchka is nothing more than a sawdust doll. The crowd disperses as night falls, and the Charlatan is left alone. As he begins to drag the puppet away, he is shocked to see Petrouchka's ghost appear above the roof of the theater, jeering and mocking in his final salute.[22] The crowds in *Petrouchka* are festive and boisterous, both unaware and, until the end, untouched by the realities of life. In contrast, the puppets are seemingly endowed with human emotions, fears and frailties. Stravinsky exploited this dichotomy in his handling of the ballet's music.

In *Petrouchka*, Stravinsky makes imaginative use of vernacular folk music. The scenes at the Butterweek Fair use not only Russian folk songs, including tunes played on a *sharmanka*, or barrel organ, but a popular melody which Stravinsky heard played on that instrument outside the window in Beaulieu.[23] It is the composer's orchestration, however, which gives the fair scenes the effect of *faux semblant*. The musical features of these sections—the use of popular tunes, the insistent *ostinato* and "flat" dynamics—sound convincingly "folklike" to the ear. Yet, as Taruskin points out, "applied in such a heavy dose, they are unnatural, inexpressive, mechanistic and toylike, and so they characterize the human crowd."[24]

Stravinsky was never completely satisfied with Fokine's choreography for *Petrouchka*. Specifically, he considered that the movements of the "crowd" in the Fair scenes had been neglected, having been left to the 'arbitrary improvisation of the performers instead of being choreographically regulated in accordance with the clearly defined exigencies of the music." Prince Peter Lieven, however, felt a large part of the ballet's success was due to "the convincing and authentic nature of the 'folk' scenes."[25] What seemed colorful, remote and picturesque to the Parisians, appeared to Stravinsky simply familiar, nostalgic and, in Fokine's rendering, even chaotic. With his next "Russian" ballet, the composer was to reach back beyond nineteenth-century St. Petersburg, away from magical fairy tales and into the realm of the myths and rituals of ancient Russia. *Le Sacre du printemps* was a significant departure from "story" ballets such as *L'Oiseau de feu* and *Petrouchka*. Instead of beautiful firebirds or tragi-comic puppets, the audiences of the Ballets Russes were to be subjected to a world still plunged in barbarity.

Le Sacre du printemps has long been seen as a turning point, not only in the composer's career, but in the history of twentieth-century music. Stravinsky's ingenious handling of rhythm and tonality, together with an unusual use of instruments of the orchestra, combine to give *Le Sacre* its explosive impact. But the music of *Le Sacre*, like that of the two ballets which preceded it, owes a considerable debt to Russian folk melodies and their traditions.[26]

Although Stravinsky asserted that "the opening bassoon melody in *Le Sacre du printemps* is the only folk melody in that work," research by musicologists has shown that the composer appropriated significantly more material from folk sources. Indeed, Taruskin states that there are at least as many Russian folk melodies in *Le Sacre* as there are in *Petrouchka*.[27] Lawrence Morton, an old friend of Stravinsky's, checked the score of the ballet against an anthology of over one thousand Lithuanian folk songs compiled by a Polish priest named Anton Juszkiewicz. Morton was able to demonstrate that Stravinsky used ideas from it for "The Auguries of Spring," "The Ritual of Abduction," and the "Spring Khorovod," in addition to the Introduction to Part One. Subsequently, Taruskin added four more folk-song identifications after studying Stravinsky's sketchbook for *Le Sacre*.[28]

In the "Spring Khorovod" section of the sketchbook, Taruskin discovered the tune of a round dance associated with a folk holiday known as *semik*. This is an observance of the appearance of the first green vegetation, known as Green Week, and is celebrated on the Thursday of the seventh week after the first full moon in spring.[29] According to musicologist Tatiana Popova, "the customs and ceremonies of Green Week are bound up . . . with the cult of ancestors."[30] The melody, which Popova connects to the practice of divination and dancing spring rounds, appears in Rimsky-Korsakov's 1877 folk tune anthology, from which Stravinsky also culled two other motives for the ballet. Stravinsky does not quote the tune directly, but manipulates the material for his own uses. It is this process of "abstraction of stylistic elements from folk music that marked a turning point in Stravinsky's development as a composer."[31]

A number of interesting and significant folk music sources are identifiable in the score of *Le Sacre*. The "Mystic Circle of Virgins" uses a source melody that is allied with wedding *khorovods*—appropriate for this elegiac maidens' dance. A melody for three muted trumpets in the "Ritual of the Ancestors" has a similar harmonic structure to a group of *vesnyaki*, or Western Russian "invocations to the spring."[32] In a study of Russian "season songs," Soviet folklorist Izalii Zemtsovsky notes the term *vesnyaki* is used not only to refer to "invocation" to spring, but also to cover a whole range of springtime songs, games and *khorovods*. According to Zemtsovsky, various accounts attest to the "magic function of the songs whose purpose was to facilitate the quick awakening of nature."[33] Further, these songs were never performed without some sort of accompanying movement or action. There are, indeed, traditional dances for the *vesnyaki*, especially in the Ukraine.[34]

The function of the *vesnyaki* was purportedly that of "collective conjuration." They were performed chorally, usually in short phrases repeated several times.[35] These songs emerged primarily in the regions of Western and Central Russia, including the area called Volkynia. Stravinsky had a summer home in Ustilug, located in that region, until 1914. It is likely that the composer heard these tunes there or at Princess Tenisheva's Talashkino near Smolensk, as well as traditional Jewish folk songs that accompanied weddings, bar mitzvahs and other celebrations to which the Ustilug community invited him.[36]

Finally, Stravinsky's sketchbook makes note of a tune under the heading of *Vyplyasyvanie zemli*—the "dancing out" or "wearing out" of the earth. Taruskin notes that the melody is recognizable "as belonging to the genre of dance-until-you-drop vocal and ostinato dance tunes."[37] Stravinsky's teacher, Rimsky-Korsakov, pointed out that "the whole cycle of ceremonial songs and games . . . rests on ancient pagan sun-worship which lives unconsciously in the people. The people, as a nation, sing their ceremonial songs by force of habit and custom, neither understanding nor suspecting what really underlies these ceremonies and games."[38]

It is clear that such ceremonial songs and melodies became part of the fabric of Stravinsky's evocation of primeval Russia. In *Le Sacre*, the composer was able to assimilate Russian folk art "not as a nimble stylist who was able to hide his quotations, nor as a populist ethnographer, unable to absorb his material and elevate it to an artistic plane, but as a master of his native speech."[39] Stravinsky's new language was based on the abstraction, objectivity and analysis that were allied to the emerging aesthetic of modernism. This is especially vivid when he uses polytonality to separate discrete musical ideas. In "The Auguries of Spring," for example, the ear can distinguish a number of individual melodic fragments. Each line is introduced, continues its phrase, and drops out when its statement is completed. Often, these melodic "voices" are broken up and segmented, fragments of each phrase appearing at unexpected intervals. This contrapuntal treatment in a polytonal idiom emphasizes two or three distinct voices, giving the effect of a collage. Often, too, the use of different musical keys helps to further color the differentiation between the voices.

The almost visceral impact of *Le Sacre* is heightened by the work's astonishing rhythmic structure. Stravinsky wrote the score in constantly changing rhythmic meters, frequently against an insistent *basso ostinato*. Either the composer selects a regular metrical pattern and appears to upset it by violently syncopated accents, as in "the Dance Overcoming the Earth," or he allows his meter to follow the fragmentation of the melody. In the second event, as in the "Danse sacrale," the rhythms form irregular patterns calling for numerous changes of time signature.[40]

Musicologist Eric Walter White states that a "tremendous internal tension is set up in the score by the simplicity of the thematic material and the discordant complexity of the harmonic texture."[41] This sensation was further increased by the music's orchestration. The highly sophisticated instrumentation of *Le Sacre* was the composer's means of achieving a deliberately primitive effect. The technique of one instrument is applied to another; in some sections the violins are used as percussion instruments, the strings being struck by a bow to produce a highly distinctive sound. Here, too, Stravinsky adapted the folk traditions of Russian music, incorporating *dudki,* or peasant reed pipes, to add authentic "color" to the score.[42] But it is significant that although the composer was inspired by folk music, it was Stravinsky's manipulation and integration of his source material that gives *Le Sacre* its originality and musical integrity.

Over the years, Stravinsky first praised and then dismissed Nijinsky's choreography for *Le Sacre*. In the famous and much disputed *Montjoie!* article, "What I Wish to Express in *Le Sacre du printemps,*" the composer was reported to have said that he was happy to have found "for this work of faith M. Nijinsky, the ideal choreographic collaborator."[43] In an article in *Gil Blas* shortly after the ballet's premiere, Stravinsky declared that Nijinsky was an admirable artist who was capable of revolutionizing the ballet.[44] When *Le Sacre* was revived by the Ballets Russes in 1920, with new choreography by Léonide Massine, the ballet had long been acclaimed as a concert work. Stravinsky told the *Observer* in July 1921, that Nijinsky's work was of great plastic beauty, but "subject to the tyranny of the bar," while Massine's was based on phrases composed of several bars. "This last is [in] the sense in which [*Le Sacre*] is conceived [as] the free connection of the choreographic construction with the musical construction. . . . [*Le Sacre*] exists as a piece of music, first and last."[45] Robert Craft believes that Stravinsky had come to prefer *Le Sacre* in concert form rather than as a staged performance. The composer had forgotten that Nijinsky's original choreography, too, was based on phrases of several musical bars, and that it was Stravinsky's own "choreographic visions" that partly determined the ballet's musical form.[46]

In 1967, Stravinsky recovered the four-hand piano score he had marked for Nijinsky and used in rehearsals with the choreographer, which, since Diaghilev's death, had been in the possession of the dancer Sir Anton Dolin.[47] With this as an *aide-mémoire*, he reaffirmed his approval of Nijinsky's realization of the ballet. That same year, during the Bolshoi Ballet's visit to New York, Stravinsky told Russian choreographer Yuri Grigorovich that of all the interpretations of *Le Sacre* he had seen, the composer considered Nijinsky's the best.[48] Finally, in 1968 or 1969, Stravinsky read Irina Vershinina's monograph on his early ballets and made a notation in the margin that his criticism of Nijinsky's choreography had always been ''unjust.''[49]

Indeed, with Nijinsky, Stravinsky had found an ideal collaborator. The choreographer said it was the music that suggested a ballet to him, and he then put all his energy into making the dance accord with the spirit of the music. ''Modern music,'' Nijinsky declared, ''is 'my music.' . . . [It] is closer to me, it corresponds to my aspirations.''[50]

Le Sacre du printemps proved the ideal vehicle for both composer and choreographer to reveal their ambitions. It was a manifesto of the new that grew out of both men's veneration of tradition, a tribute by two artists to their cultural heritage, reflecting their nostalgia for a homeland lost to them forever. For Stravinsky, the creation of *Le Sacre* and, a decade later, *Les Noces*, a ritualistic celebration of a Russian peasant wedding, effectively ended his ''Russian'' period. Although the composer's later works were more closely allied to the Neoclassic aesthetic, the influences, if not the melodies, of Russian folk music and its ethnographic roots, were ever-present. *Le Sacre* remained the tangible proof of Stravinsky's own *âme russe*, his very personal song of the earth. The austere, mystic rituals of *Le Sacre du printemps* were the adaptations in art of the Russian folklore which had been cherished and kept alive for centuries. Over seventy years after its creation, the music of *Le Sacre du printemps* continues to fulfill Claude Debussy's prophesy that it would continue to be played throughout the world, ''for the piece tells of freedom, newness and the richness of life.''[51]

4

Reigen

The Ballets Russes began its eighth season in Paris in May of 1913. The adulation the company had inspired in its first seasons had begun to wane and there was a growing sense of disillusionment with the "phalanx of Russian geniuses" who invaded Paris every summer.[1] Jacques-Emile Blanche noted that the Théâtre des Champs-Elysées had opened its box office to a seemingly blasé public who had no patience and were already complaining.[2] The season's programs announced only three or four new ballets, among them *Jeux* and *Le Sacre du printemps,* both with choreography by Nijinsky.

The opening night of the 1913 season included the premiere of *Jeux,* which, as previously noted, was not well received. Although *Jeux* proved unsuccessful, Diaghilev had great expectations for his pagan Russian ballet, *Le Sacre du printemps.* Indeed, the success of the work was so important to him that the completion and polishing for *Jeux* had been neglected in deference to *Le Sacre.*[3]

The final rehearsals for *Le Sacre* took place in essentially three stages: rehearsals for the dancers with piano accompaniment, rehearsals for the orchestra and five full rehearsals. The last included the *répétition générale,* or invitation-only dress rehearsal, on 28 May, the eve of the official premiere. The final stages of the choreography had been completed in Monte Carlo, during the Russian Ballet's annual spring season.

Most of the more than one hundred rehearsals for the dancers in *Le Sacre* took place with only piano accompaniment. Stravinsky appeared sporadically at these run-throughs, keeping an anxious vigil over both Nijinsky and pianist Maurice Steiman.[4]

Monteux, however, conducted the initial full orchestra rehearsals of *Le Sacre* in late March of 1913, without the composer's supervision. At that time he wrote to Stravinsky that *Le Sacre* sounded at least as good as *The Firebird* and *Petrouchka.* "What a pity you could not be here," wrote Monteux, "above all that you could not be present for the explosion of *Le Sacre.*"[5]

The composer appeared, however, for the final seventeen orchestra rehearsals in what became known as the "Comédie des Champs-Elysées."[6] Many of the players were overwhelmed by Stravinsky's orchestration and the music's strange sonorities. "When we saw the parts for the first time we couldn't believe they could be played," wrote oboist Louis Speyer.[7] Some of the musicians even stopped Monteux to ask if their parts were correctly printed. The chaos among the ninety-seven orchestra members increased. Monteux realized that they thought the music was crazy, not to say unplayable, but he perservered. "We rehearsed over and over the small difficult parts," recalled the conductor, "and at last we were ready for the ballet."[8]

Whether the dancers were ready for the sonic hurricane of *Le Sacre* is a different matter. As previously noted, the ballet company had been rehearsing solely to a piano reduction of the score, which gives little indication of the unprecedented sonorities, harmonies and the formidable polyrhythms of the music when it is played by an entire orchestra. The five full rehearsals were held on the stage of the Théâtre des Champs-Elysées, the first on 18 May, and the last, the *répétition générale*, on 28 May. The dress rehearsal, according to Nijinska, went smoothly and irreproachably, an ideal execution, with perfect harmony between stage and orchestra. "All of us and particularly Vaslav were confident about the performance."[9] Double bassist Henri Girard, reflecting the view of the musicians, was less sanguine. "Despite work, care, and good will from everyone, nobody was sure of the outcome on the day of the first performance," said Girard.[10] Speyer noted that when the musicians saw the savage dancing and the strange scenery and costumes, they were at a loss. "Already *Le Sacre* was the talk of the town," he recalled, "so many telling stories making it even bigger and more impossible."[11]

Diaghilev had made certain that *Le Sacre du printemps* was the focus of the advance publicity for the 1913 Ballets Russes season. Always superstitious, he had reserved the first anniversary of the premiere of *L'Après-midi d'un faune*, 29 May, for *Le Sacre*. A promotional article in *Comoedia* on 16 May prominently featured an announcement of the ballet. Stravinsky, it declared, would complete his balletic trilogy with the most striking work of all, *Le Sacre du printemps*, and promised a visual presentation of "interest and astonishment."[12]

The spring performances of the Ballets Russes were part of the *Grande Saison de Paris*, along with other concert and art festivals. For Gabriel Astruc, a shrewd businessman as well as an impresario, the importation of the Diaghilev companies was part of his campaign to attract a subscription audience to the Théâtre des Champs-Elysées.[13] In devising these seasons, Astruc aimed for the tourists who descended on Paris in the late spring and summer and the aristocratic *clientèle mondaine*, who determined to do and see whatever was in vogue. In addition, the audience at the Théâtre included the requisite artists, aesthetes, intellectuals, students (particularly Russian ones) and critics, all of whom were part of the hard-core theater habitués in Paris.[14]

Both Diaghilev and Astruc were famous for their ability to "orchestrate" audiences. They were careful to invite a number of influential critics, as well as artists, writers and "the most cultured representatives of society" to the *répétition générale* in order to gauge their reaction. The run-through, according to Stravinsky, "went off peacefully."[15]

On 29 May, a number of influential newspapers featured a lengthy announcement, laced with superlatives, about *Le Sacre*. Termed "the most amazing creation" ever attempted by the Ballets Russes, it promised "the most startling polyrhythms ever produced by the brain of a musician," but warned that this "new sensation" would provoke "heated discussions."[16]

For many who attended the first night of *Le Sacre du printemps*, the event itself was to prove more memorable than the actual ballet. Jean Cocteau observed that the theater on the Avenue Montaigne was crammed on that hot, humid night; "all the elements of scandal were present. . . . The audience played the role that was written for it."[17]

Diaghilev planned the evening's program carefully, interspersing ballets that were romantic and introspective with works that were quint-essentially "russki." *Les Sylphides*, Fokine's elegiac homage to Romanti-cism, opened the performance. *Le Sacre* was next on the bill, followed by *Le Spectre de la rose*, another of Fokine's excursions "into the world of spiritual ecstasy."[18] The "Polovtsian Dances" from *Prince Igor*, the most popular ballet in the company's repertoire, concluded the evening.

By framing *Le Sacre* with two traditional ballets in the style of the classi-cal *danse d'école*, Diaghilev heightened the contrast between Nijinsky's raw, uncompromising movement style and Fokine's more conventional—and more familiar—choreography. By following *Le Sacre* with *Le Spectre de la rose*, Diaghilev also allowed the audience an emotional respite before the onslaught of the "Polovtsian Dances." Here, too, the audience could com-pare Nijinsky's vision of Slavic pagan rituals with Fokine's Symbolist primitivism. The arrangement of the program was brilliantly conceived.

In the thirty-four minutes following the rise of the curtain on *Le Sacre du printemps*, a work was revealed for judgment which had taken three artists to create, forty-six dancers and over one hundred rehearsals to realize, and two impresarios to produce. The riot that the ballet provoked has been documented exhaustively.[19] The artist Valentine Gross looked back "in delight" on the uproar of that evening. "The theatre seemed to be shaken by an earthquake," she recalled. "It seemed to shudder. People shouted insults, howled and whistled, drowning the music. . . . I thought there was something wonderful about the titanic struggle which must have been going on in order to keep these inaudible musicians and these deafened dancers together, in obedience to the laws of their invisible choreographer.''[20]

After the opening bars of the Prelude, the curtain rose on Roerich's first scene, ''an expanse of wild hilly countryside intersected by innumerable streams.''[21] The initial measures of the score were listened to in silence by the audience, and then the tempest broke. Monteux had specific instructions from Diaghilev not to stop on any account. Stravinsky's most vivid memory was of Monteux's back. ''He stood there apparently impervious and nerveless as a crocodile,'' observed the conductor.[22] Monteux, however, was fully aware of the battles raging both on and offstage. He recalled that the audience remained quiet for the first two minutes, but that boos and catcalls soon erupted from the gallery and the stalls. ''The anger was concentrated against the dancers, and then, more particularly, against the orchestra as the direct perpetrators of the musical crime. Everything available was tossed in our direction, but we continued to play on. The end of the performance was greeted by the arrival of the gendarmes.''[23]

The pandemonium increased as the performance continued. Astruc recalled that, at one point, he stood and shouted with all the strength in his lungs, ''Listen first! You can hiss afterwards!'' Carl Van Vechten, then the Paris music critic for the *New York Times,* became aware that the young man standing behind him was drumming with his fists on the top of Van Vechten's head.[24] Rambert, dancing with the group of small girls on stage, heard Diaghilev's voice calling, ''I beg you. Let the performance finish.''[25] In an attempt to alleviate the chaos, either Astruc or Diaghilev ordered the house lights turned on, probably between the first and second scenes. According to Girard, Astruc came before the curtain and requested that the audience restrain themselves during the playing of the second act.[26] ''Many in the auditorium are not antagonistic,'' declared Astruc, ''and would like to see and hear the performance without interruption, in order to be able to form an opinion on the value of this new departure in dance, pantomime and music.''[27] Astruc further offered to refund the price of a ticket to anyone willing to leave at that instant. No one made a move.[28]

On the other side of the footlights, the scene was at least as chaotic. Diaghilev had rushed backstage, where Nijinsky stood with his sister Bronislava. She recalled that Nijinsky appeared to be on the verge of rushing onstage to restore some kind of order in case the dancers went to pieces. ''I wanted to grab Vaslav to prevent him from rushing out, but fortunately this was not necessary.''[29] Stravinsky apparently thought otherwise. He had been sitting near the orchestra, but after the protests in the auditorium he left the hall ''in a rage'' and arrived ''in a fury'' backstage. ''For the rest of the performance,'' he wrote, ''I stood in the wings behind

Nijinsky holding the tails of his *frac,* while he stood on a chair shouting numbers to the dancers.''[30] Lydia Sokolova vividly described the commotion on the stage itself. ''We were all terrified that we were doing the fourth or fifth or sixth steps, while somebody else was doing the second; Nijinsky was in the wings stamping and trying to count for different groups all at once. . . . We must have been a lovely picture for the audience, racing round, jumping, turning, and wondering when the whole thing was going to collapse.''[31]

By the end of the ballet, the violence that had erupted in the audience very nearly exceeded the frenzy of the spectacle enacted on the stage. Everyone present bore witness to the birth of a legend. There were four or five curtain calls for Nijinsky, Stravinsky and the dancers, all the artists receiving ''vigorous applause from one side and . . . protests from the other.''[32] Diaghilev's only comment is said to have been: ''Exactly what I wanted.''[33] He was quick to realize the publicity value of the scandal, and *Le Sacre* was presented four more times in the course of ten days. The second performance was received more calmly, and Diaghilev seized the chance to put the ballet before the public at every available opportunity.[34] To the end of his life, *Le Sacre du printemps* remained one of Diaghilev's favorite works. When, in 1929, the Ballets Russes ended their Covent Garden season with a performance of Léonide Massine's version of *Le Sacre,* an ailing Diaghilev applauded its success. It was one of the last ballets he ever saw.

The Nijinsky production of *Le Sacre du printemps* received only nine performances, six including répétion générale, in Paris and three during the Russian Ballet's London season in July 1913. Extant records consist of contemporary reviews, a few rehearsal photographs, a series of sketches by Valentine Gross, Dame Marie Rambert's rehearsal score and the memoirs of those who saw or performed the ballet. The actual movement that Nijinsky devised to correspond with the libretto has been lost.[35] Nijinsky studied Stepanov dance notation at the Imperial Ballet School in St. Petersburg and a partial score of his notations for *L'Après-midi d'un faune* still survives.[36] There is also reputed to be a choreographic notation score for Nijinsky's *Le Sacre,* but if so it remains undiscovered.[37] Today's almost routine method of preserving dance works on videotape or film was not, of course, possible in 1913.[38] As with dance forms of preceding centuries, the ballets of the Diaghilev era were handed down from choreographer to company, from ballet master to dancer. The immense complexity of *Le Sacre* made it a difficult work to rehearse and, therefore, to revive. Because Nijinsky's *Le Sacre du printemps* was a seminal work, a harbinger of modern dance, indeed the ballet ''that broke the ground of twentieth century choreography,'' it has attained the status of legend.[39] Over the years, a mythology has evolved regarding the creation and performance of *Le Sacre,* sometimes shrouding the importance of the work itself. Choreographers, critics and historians, fascinated by its mystery, regard the few remaining artifacts connected with the ballet as relics of a lost masterpiece. But while there is no definitive documentation of *Le Sacre,* it is possible to have some idea of what the ballet looked like by piecing together descriptions from various sources.

With the aid of Dame Marie Rambert, Igor Stravinsky, Mme. Romola Nijinsky and other members of the Diaghilev company of the time, dance critic and historian Richard Buckle has developed one of the most complete descriptions of the ballet's dance sections, as they correspond with the score. There have been numerous "libretti" for *Le Sacre,* with Stravinsky himself having written at least three, which differ to some degree in minor details.[40] Buckle's account, according to Rambert, is the most complete and intelligible account of the original Nijinsky ballet. Robert Craft has provided commentary, based on Stravinsky's musical sketches and choreographic notes for Nijinsky, in his description of the stage action in *"The Rite of Spring:* Genesis of a Masterpiece."[41] In her efforts to reconstruct Nijinsky's choreography for *Le Sacre,* dance historian Millicent Hodson has uncovered material that adds additional details to the description cited above. The following account of *Le Sacre* is a composite, drawn from the sources cited above.

Following the "Introduction" in the score, the first violin pizzicato sets the pace for the opening dance, which leads into the "Auguries of Spring." The boys are taught certain spells and divinations to be performed every spring.[a]* A witch manipulates the forces of the earth, teaches fortune-telling and how to make spells.[c] Groups of boys dance and sit in turn. A Greek-like dance tune on the alto flute is followed by a Russian chorale melody on four trumpets. Gradually the whole orchestra joins in, the music building to a Bacchanalian frenzy, as the dancers fall to the floor. A presto in the orchestra signals the beginning of the "Ritual of Abduction." Two groups of red-clad girls enter and the sight of the boys induces sexual panic. The groups of challenging men and jumping women confront each other from opposite sides of the stage. As the orchestra emits staccato clashes of brass and drums, the men grasp the women in

---

*The material used in this description will be drawn from three sources: (1) Richard Buckle, *Nijinsky* (New York: Atheneum, 1979), pp. 293–99; (2) Robert Craft, "Genesis of a Masterpiece," in I. Stravinsky and R. Craft, *The Rite of Spring Sketches 1911–1913* (London: Boosey & Hawkes, 1969), pp. xx–xxiii; (3) "Restoring a Lost Work: Nijinsky's *Sacre* and Nijinska's *Noces,*" transcript of a symposium at the Dance Critics Association Conference, "Reconstruction and Revival: Which Dance Is This Anyway?" New York, 18 June 1982. Chaired by Anna Kisselgoff, with Millicent Hodson and Irina Nijinska. For the purposes of identification the above sources will be marked by the following superscription: (a) Buckle; (b) Craft; (c) Hodson.

a gesture of stylized rape; the section is briefly elaborated on by two pair of dancers.[a] There are groups of three women who stand shivering and trembling beside the couples.[c] There is a tremendous sense of adolescent fear radiating between the men and women in this act.[c]

The "Spring Rounds" or "Khorovod" describes a form of singing and dancing in a circle, "Khor" meaning "chorus" and "vod," leading.[b] This section is introduced by flutes and alto flutes, against a primeval melodic sequence played by the clarinets. The Russian chorale tune reappears in slightly different form. As the entire orchestra takes up this melody, men and women come together and revolve in circles.[a]42 As Stravinsky envisioned the first part of this section, five small circles of dancers slowly gyrate, then, in the orchestral tutti, coalesce into a single large circle. During what the composer calls the "Khorovod Chant," the women stand apart from the men, extending their arms in gestures of exorcism. The women then leave the stage and the men dance to the orchestral coda alone. The men then divide, thus establishing two tribes for the ritual games.[a]

The "Ritual of the Two Rival Tribes" begins with short bursts of warfare between the men. They perform a rituallike game in which a contest of strength is determined by, for example, a tug-of-war. These rites alternate with pleading gestures from the groups of swaying, clapping women, who have reentered the ceremony. A sequence of competitive dances concludes the section. A barbaric melody on the tubas weaves into the "Procession of the Oldest and Wisest One—the Sage." A clearing is prepared at the center of the stage.[b] The Elders lead on the Sage[a] with the women of the tribe following in his train.[b] An orchestral tutti signals the gathering of all the people.[b] The Sage lays himself spread-eagled face-down on the ground[a] and bestows his sacramental kiss on the earth in time with the chord of string harmonics.[b]43 The tribe senses the presence of a god, and runs to form a square to represent a tribal compound.[a]

After the Sage completes the ritual, "Kiss of the Earth," the dancers begin the "Dance Overcoming the Earth," which concludes the first scene of the ballet. This section is a frenzied celebration by the tribes in anticipation of the coming spring.[a] Stravinsky has said that he imagined the dancers "rolling like bundles of leaves in the wind" and "stomping like Indians trying to put out a prairie fire."[b] As the movement ends, to syncopated shrieks on the brass and woodwinds, the dancers, arranged in asymmetrical clumps, leap and fall convulsively to the ground,[a] with each cluster of dancers jumping repeatedly to a different set of musical counts.[c]44 The curtain is lowered on the first scene.

Part Two was begun in darkness.[b] The introduction to the second scene concludes with a gentle Russian folk tune on alto flute and solo violin. The curtain rises on the "Mystic Circle of Virgins."[45] All the maidens are standing, trembling, as if welded together in a circle, facing outward, knees bent, toes pointed inward. Each has her right elbow resting on her left fist, while her right fist supports her chin. This is a characteristic posture in the women's folk dances of Byelorussia and the Ukraine. Their dance once again is khorovod-like in character.

One of the girls will be chosen for the traditional sacrifice to Yarilo, the god of spring. The men and the Elders watch.[(a)46] The ring of girls slowly moves round, and on specific counts, they rise on tiptoe, dropping their right hands to their sides and jerking their heads to the left.[(a)] The dancers describe the perimeter of a circle (drawn on the ground) which represents the cycle of nature and in which the Chosen One is to die.[(b)] As a circuit of the ring is completed, every other girl leaps out of the circle and back again. To a melodic Russian tune, the girls begin to walk with a bell-like swinging gesture—starting and stopping.[(a)] "One of the maidens is chosen by lot to fulfill the sacrifice; from this point to the 'Sacrificial Dance' the Chosen One stands motionless."[47]

The next section is the tribe's "Naming and Honoring of the Chosen One." During the ensuing orchestral crescendo, the men appear at the sides of the stage, as though poised for an ambush.[48] Stravinsky imagined this dance as a choreographic ricochet of movement from stage left to stage right. The tribe divides into five groups, male and female, leaping and stamping convulsively. They approach and surround the Chosen Virgin.

The "Evocation of the Ancestors" is a male dance, a celebration of the ancient ritual of the consecration of the Chosen One. As the young women leave, the Elders appear, dressed in bearskins, and squat before the sacred circle like a court of judges.[(b)] The tribe recalls their forefathers in a slow reflective dance. To staccato shrieks and percussive chords the final ritual begins as the tribe stamps around the Chosen Virgin. She first assists and then leads her fellows in the celebration of her own sacrifice. The members of the tribe repeat a motif of jumps over and over, turning to the left and to the right—an emotional ritualistic counterpoint to the Virgin's movements. Her leaps become increasingly frenzied, until she falls exhausted. She tries to rise but falls again and, to a final chord, she dies and is raised at arm's length by six men and borne away.[(a)49]

The choreography that Nijinsky devised for Le Sacre du printemps may be viewed as an anthology of innovation, breaking completely with conventional precepts of classical ballet. Inspired both by Roerich's paintings portraying "the awakening of the spirit of primeval man," and by the rhythmic complexities of Stravinsky's score, Nijinsky created a ballet of unexpected beauty.[50] Indeed, the radical choreographic style of his Le Sacre anticipated many of the reforms in technique and theory associated with the development of modern dance.

In an interview in the *London Daily Mail*, Nijinsky stated that he detested what he termed "conventional 'nightingale-and-rose poetry'" and declared his own inclination to be "primitive."[51] In painting and sculpture, he noted, when suavity led to "banality" a revolt was always the result. "Perhaps something like this has happened in dancing," Nijinsky declared.[52]

Nijinsky was to apply to dance the dictums of the "revolt" that already had stirred the visual arts in Paris. Cubism developed with extraordinary rapidity between 1907 and 1914. With Pablo Picasso and Georges Braque as its leading exponents, the aesthetic of Cubism was viewed as "the conscious determination to establish in painting the knowledge of mass, volume and weight," as well as line and void, color and value.[53] Among these artists' resources for experiment was the art of other cultures, particularly the forms and motifs of African art. As art historian Robert Hughes notes, this interest on the part of Picasso and Braque brought to a climax "a long interest which nineteenth-century France had shown in the exotic, the distant, and the primitive."[54] Diaghilev's Ballets Russes had been exploiting this very fascination since 1909 by presenting Fokine's "oriental" and "russkii" ballets. But these works had their roots in *fin-de-siècle* Russian Symbolism, rather than in any modernist aesthetic. It was Nijinsky, with his avowed preference for the "primitive" and his assertion that he himself would make Cubist art, who was to apply the precepts of Cubism to the medium of dance.

It may seem paradoxical that a breakthrough in modernism, both in dance and in music, should come in the form of a ballet which portrayed the arcane rituals of a prehistoric Slavic tribe. But it is likely that Stravinsky and Nijinsky took note of the primitive source of much of the Cubist painters' early inspiration. Picasso had looked to African art as an untapped wellspring, to renew his vision of the vitality of form and perspective in art. He saw the masks and figures as "emblems of savagery [and] violence," prototypes to be reinvented from the Cubist perspective.[55] Similarly, the creators of *Le Sacre du printemps* wanted to produce something "new, beautiful and utterly different" through their evocation of primitive Slavonic rituals.[56] But while the ballet's theme was rooted in ancient folklore, this musical and choreographic "language" of its realization was emphatically modern.

At the time of *Le Sacre*'s composition, Stravinsky was concerned with "ethnological authenticity as the first step toward 'creating reality.'"[57] (The development of a new perspective about realism was also a crucial subtheme in Cubist artistic theory.)[58] Stravinsky "drew from life" in collecting folk melodies for *Le Sacre*, and Nijinsky used his knowledge of Russian folk dance as raw material for the choreography. His parents were superb character dancers, his father especially accomplished in the *lez-*

ghinka.[59] The traditional forms and steps of dances such as the Polish *mazurka* and *cracoviennes,* the Ukranian *hopak,* and the Russian *prissyatka* and *kazatchok* were ideal for stylization and adaptation to Nijinsky's needs in *Le Sacre.* The positions he devised for the women's hands and arms are especially evocative of their folk dance counterparts; in some instances, for example, the women rest their cheeks against the open palms of their hands, or lay their chins on their lightly clenched fists.[60] At one moment, the women clasp their hands behind their necks with the elbows pulled sharply forward. Valentine Gross described this gesture in her notes and sketched it in her quick hieroglyphiclike drawings of the ballet's performances.[61] It is a powerful image that has worked its way into the very bloodstream of twentieth-century dance.[62] This movement is characteristic of Russian folk dances, especially of the Ukraine. It is a gesture employed when a woman wants to "show off" her *kokoshnik,* or headdress, and display the ribbons that hang down her back. Performed by an individual woman, it is a sign of feminine coquetry and pride; done *en masse,* as Nijinsky used it in *Le Sacre,* it becomes a poignant image of vulnerability.

Many of the steps and postures that Nijinsky devised for both the men and women have reverberations in the vernacular of Russian folk dance. The "harvesting" movement for the women is especially typical. The legs and feet are held parallel, with the knees slightly bent and the body folded forward at the waist. The accompanying movement usually is a gentle, pulsing, sidestepping motion, found in many folk dance styles.[63] The dancer reaches down with her arms, gently "turning the earth," the hands first twisting in toward the body and then opening forward, with the palm flat and open.[64] A shuntlike skip, moving either forward or back, is another distinctive folk dance movement. The dancer holds the body erect, while one leg is drawn up in parallel alignment in front of the body, like a hook, with the knee and foot flexed. Nijinsky invented a number of variations on this spare motif for both the men's and women's dances.[65]

The Gross drawings and a number of written descriptions of *Le Sacre* emphasize the blocky, angular impression created by the choreography. The dancers were compared to "puppets on wires," "strange troglodytes," and "cells under a microscope."[66] The critics saw neither "light movements of the body nor graceful use of the limbs" in the heavy, awkward movements and austere gestures of *Le Sacre.*[67] Nijinsky had deliberately reordered and objectified the perception of the human figure in dance, as Picasso, in *Les Demoiselles d'Avignon,* had radically altered the conventional depiction of human anatomy in painting. For Picasso, the primitive sculptures of African art exemplified the "freedom to distort anatomy" for the sake of developing a rhythmic structure capable of creating new shapes. At the same time, its suggestion of a "supernatural presence" seems to have been equally stimulating.[68] Nijinsky found a

Valentine Gross, Scenes from Nijinsky's *Le Sacre du printemps*
The top sketches show Maria Piltz in her final solo. The bottom shows a group of men, probably from the first scene.
(*Courtesy of the Theatre Museum, London. Copyright ARS NY/SPADEM 1987*)

similar inspiration in the ethnography of the ritual ceremonies of ancient Russian tribes. In *Le Sacre,* by applying the precepts of Cubism to the dynamic image of the dancer, Nijinsky was able to reveal this new aesthetic as the visual artists never could—in movement through time and space.[69]

Like the Cubist painters, Nijinsky achieved the effects of distortion and fragmentation in a variety of ways. Critics had referred to the choreographer's "stylization of gesture" in *Jeux,* and this phrase reappeared in a number of reviews of *Le Sacre.*[70] A key element in Nijinsky's choreographic method was to establish a distinctive body posture for each ballet. In *Le Sacre,* he derived the grounded stance and "stylized" look of the movement by adapting the characteristic motifs and postures of Russian folk dance to the hieratic, two-dimensional body alignment he had first essayed in *Faune.* Folk dance forms provided the stylistic baseline in *Le Sacre* in the same manner as the action of a tennis game served as the foundation for the movement in *Jeux.*

The audiences that saw *Le Sacre du printemps* were treated to "profiles of faces posed on full-front shoulders . . . elbows glued to the body . . . horizontal forearms, rigid and open hands."[71] Gestures were fragmented and economical, facial expression was blotted out. The dancers' movements were heavy and awkward, their anatomies seemingly reduced to geometric lozenges of grotesque proportions. The arrangement of their limbs was designed to look foreshortened rather than extended. Poses looked fixed and deformed rather than symmetrical and designed. The fluidity associated with classical ballet had been replaced by splintered, percussive movements, the familiar vocabulary of the *danse d'école* was rejected in favor of agitated trembling, frozen stillness and spasmodic jumps. The dancers did not simply attack a movement; they wreaked violence upon it. Rivière felt that in *Le Sacre,* "the body is the real speaker. It moves only as a whole, it forms a totality and its manner of speaking is to leap suddenly with arms and legs outspread, or to move to the side with knees bent and the head on the shoulder."[72] Nijinsky saw his dancers as abstractions, vessels for the enactment of a ritual, "the incarnation of Nature—not human nature."[73] "One would think," wrote Rivière, that "he is witnessing a drama beneath a microscope . . . large turning masses of protoplasm, germinative slabs; zones, circles, placentae."[74]

The tribal ceremonies portrayed in *Le Sacre* were intended to mirror the violent beginnings of the Russian springs which Stravinsky remembered from childhood and wanted to express in the score. Nijinsky concentrated on the "driving power of the group," exploring the properties of mass and weight as elements in dance.[75] The movement vocabulary of the ballet was composed of technically simple steps—walking, running, skipping, jumping, stamping, together with a few more complex sequences.[76] Nijinsky achieved the sense of volume and density that is one of the principal characteristics of the ballet's choreography by having large groups of dancers clustered together repeatedly perform their *pas mouvements* in unison, canon and counterpoint. The lack of symmetry in these formations increased the sensations of tumult and chaos. As if hypnotized by some hidden force, the dancers executed the same steps over and over, "rough-hewn, stumbling, sinister. . . . Bereft of all personality and individual desire, these groups of liturgic dancers, pressing close upon each other, changed places, turning and winding, dominated by an overwhelming compulsion that seemed almost to disjoint their limbs and weigh heavily upon their bent necks."[77]

In order to achieve a starkly primitive quality in his choreography for *Le Sacre*, Nijinsky had to convert a company of highly trained ballet technicians into a "tribe of dancers." Stravinsky and Roerich had designed the ballet's libretto with particular attention to the ethnography of ancient Russian cultures. Nijinska has stated that her brother frequently discussed the pagan rites depicted in *Le Sacre* with Roerich, who was a recognized scholar and authority on the rituals of prehistoric Slavic cults. Roerich was Nijinsky's most important source of information on these matters and it is likely that some of the painter's ideas regarding ritual dance became integrated into the patterns, gestures and even steps of *Le Sacre*'s choreography.[78]

The very elements inherent in ritual dance—the sense of detachment, the repetition of movements, the pared-down gestures—forced Nijinsky to use the body in a nonliteral, nonrepresentational manner. The massed energy of the group became a metaphor for the "terror and 'panic' that accompanies the rising of the sap."[79] The dancers were compelled to reestablish contact with the earth, with gravity, to sense and exploit the weight of their bodies; a concept that was anathema in classical ballet. The angularity of Nijinsky's dance gesture directed the observer's eye toward the body's center, rather than outward to the limbs. Tension was cultivated rather than released. By using repeated percussive movements and avoiding graceful transitions between phrases, Nijinsky made the choreography appear unremittingly stark and austere. "In breaking down movement," wrote Rivière, "in bringing it back to simple gestures, Nijinsky has brought expression back to the dance."[80]

The influence of ritual dance forms is especially marked in the spatial designs of the ballet. The sense of being surrounded and encircled is a central theme in *Le Sacre*. The geometry of the first act is based essentially on circles, files and lines, with the exception of the formation of the tribal square at the conclusion of "The Kiss of the Earth." The first scene of *Le Sacre* was strategically conceived as a ceremonial preamble to the ballet's climax, the sacrifice of the Chosen Virgin to the god of spring. "The Mystic

Four Studies of Dancers from the Ballets Russes in Vaslav Nijinsky's 1913 Production of *Le Sacre du printemps*
(Photo courtesy of the Dance Collection, The New York Public Library at Lincoln Center, Astor, Lenox and Tilden Foundations)

Circle of Virgins," which opened the second scene, was described by André Levinson as "blooming with the sense of lyricism: young girls lead a 'branle,' shoulder to shoulder, with all the angelic affection of Byzantine saints. They designate and greet the Chosen Virgin, the victim of the sacrifice. In the magic circle, the victim is almost immobile; pale beneath her white headband, she executes her macabre dance."[81]

From the ancient circle, the ring, the maiden was chosen to perform a dance which celebrates both her death and her apotheosis.[82] Nijinsky used circular floor patterns throughout Le Sacre, but never with greater impact than in "The Mystic Circle of Virgins" and the "Danse sacrale." The use of form as metaphor—the circle representing the cycles of life and their constant renewal—is part of the ethnography of many ritual dance forms. Philosopher Susanne Langer has observed that the circle dance, or Reigen, symbolizes an important reality in the life of primitive man—the sacred realm, the magic circle. "The Reigen as a dance form . . . fulfills a holy office, perhaps the first holy office of the dance—it divides the sphere of holiness from that of profane existence. In this way it creates the stage of the dance."[83]

Together, Nijinsky and Stravinsky had set the stage for the only solo dance in Le Sacre du printemps—and one of the most extraordinary solos in the ballet repertoire. Its lineage can be traced to ceremonial ecstatic dances of ancient peoples. In the "Danse sacrale," Nijinsky attempted a feat of choreographic stamina and complexity which staggered the dance world. Marie Rambert described the solo as the greatest tragic dance she had ever seen. The role of the Chosen Virgin was originally intended for Nijinsky's sister, Bronislava, who would have been ideal in realizing both the dramatic and dance potential of the solo. But by the time Le Sacre was in rehearsal, Bronislava was pregnant, and Maria Piltz, a young soloist, was selected to dance the role. Rambert, who was sometimes present when Nijinsky rehearsed Piltz for the part, was dismayed at the choice. "She didn't in any way suggest a Russian peasant," said Rambert, who noted Piltz was unable to absorb Nijinsky's style. "More weight was needed for the role; it was [implicit] in the music. When Nijinsky showed a jump, it was as though he had fire under his feet [and] he tried to jump away from it. Of course, she couldn't do anything like that."[84]

Nijinsky was insistent about emphasizing the dancer's experience of weight as a positive use of gravity. The attempt to escape the ground was equaled by the emphatic implosion of physical force into the earth. He demanded that the dancers strive for an uncontrolled, heavy descent from jumps, as though they were being pulled to the ground by unseen hands. This was an audacious and unprecedented command from a choreographer who himself had seemingly conquered the physical laws of gravity. Nijinsky's use of movement was the very antithesis of that seen in classical ballet—the conquest of the air. For the "Danse sacrale," he insisted on the "obvious desperation of physical energy to proclaim the gross cost of psychic exhaustion. A girl's body was to dance itself out of humanity, transmitting its virtue into the soil, in order to renew fields, grain, the year."[85] Rambert recalled the dance as being "terrifying, very frenzied, incredible." Certainly the dance made brutal demands on the dancer's physical resources. The final jump sequence, with the knees tucked up and the upper body twisting on the spine, straining away from the legs, was executed at least five times in succession.[86]

Nijinsky composed the "Danse sacrale" first and its choreography became the conceptual matrix of the whole ballet. The strongly two-dimensional appearance of the movement and the emphasis on the angularity of knees, elbows and hands are clearly illustrated in the Valentine Gross sketches of the solo. The Gross drawings of the "Danse sacrale" emphasize the exaggerated inclination of the dancer's head, giving the images an eerily mechanical, disjointed appearance.[87] The suggestion that the Chosen Maiden is "possessed," that her movements were being manipulated by a supernatural power, occurred to more than one observer. To André Levinson, she seemed to dream, "her knees turn inward, the heels pointing out—inert. A sudden spasm shook her body out of its corpse-like rigor. . . . She trembled in ecstatic, irregular jerks."[88] Rivière was moved by the aura of devotion and self-sacrifice evoked by the dance. "She accomplishes a rite, she is absorbed into a function of the society," he wrote, "and, without giving one sign of comprehension or interpretation, she reacts to the powers and the shaking of a being more vast than she, of a monster full of ignorance and cravings, of cruelty and darkness."[89] Calling the "Danse sacrale" "the most overwhelming theatrical spectacle I have ever seen," Jean Cocteau saw in this "dance of an insect, of a doe fascinated by a boa, of a factory blowing up"—indeed, in the whole theme of Le Sacre du printemps—the prodromes of war.[90]

Le Sacre du printemps was both symptom and manifestation of the progressive, restless spirit that pervaded the arts in the year preceding the outbreak of the Great War. "Looking back upon it now," wrote Mabel Dodge Luhan in 1936, "it seems as though everywhere, in that year of 1913, barriers went down and people reached each other who had never been in touch before."[91] It was an eventful year: Marcel Proust and D. H. Lawrence each published important works, Du côté de chez Swann and Sons and Lovers, respectively; Edmund Husserl's treatise Phenomenology first appeared in print, as did Sigmund Freud's Totem and Taboo. The Armory Show aroused scandal in New York, and Vorticism, the English version of Cubism, appeared in London. The tumultuous premiere of Le Sacre du printemps marked a watershed in twentieth-century music and dance, and the critical reaction to the ballet reflected both admiration and dismay in terms of public response.

136

Valentine Gross, Sketch of Nijinsky's *Le Sacre du printemps,* Scene 2,
"The Mystic Circle of Virgins"
The two drawings at the bottom of the page are of Maria Piltz as she waited
to begin the "Danse sacrale."
(*Courtesy of the Theatre Museum, London. Copyright ARS NY/SPADEM 1987*)

For some of the French critics, neither the music nor the dance elements of *Le Sacre* was successful, for others one succeeded while the other failed and for a few critics both aspects were praiseworthy.[92] The reviews ranged from earnest and painstaking evaluations to contemptuous or skeptical dismissals. Several critics viewed *Le Sacre* as a daring experiment rather than a polished production; some even questioned the artists' sincerity in presenting this "almost bestial ballet."[93] Gustave de Pawlowski dubbed the work the "Massacre du printemps," declaring the collaborators had brought off an improbable *tour de force,* a display of "the unconscious, childish frenzy of primitive tribes, awakening to the mysteries of life."[94]

Leon Vallas wondered whether the music of *Le Sacre* was an example of "music of the future," a sentiment echoed by not a few of his colleagues.[95] The critic of *Le Figaro* compared watching and listening to the ballet to "torture," the Russian Ballet season to "occupation" by hostile armies and found Nijinsky "a kind of Attila of the dance."[96]

For many observers, Roerich's costumes and *mise-en-scène* represented the most obviously "russki" element in the ballet. The women's silk dresses and the men's white robes were painted with dozens of vivid colors—scarlet, orange, turquoise, magenta, golds and greens.[97] The weight and design of the costumes contributed to the sense of mass and volume which Nijinsky was trying to achieve in the choreography. Roerich's contribution to *Le Sacre* reinforced the ballet's link with the traditions of Russian folk art that he and other Neonationalist artists had championed. While one critic saw the dances as merely a "gymnastic meet in carnival costume," others allied the creation of the "unholy triumvirate" of Russian artists with similar contemporaneous movements in the visual arts and literature.[98]

Jacques Rivière, Maurice Touchard and Jacques Jary all referred to the "musical Cubism" of Stravinsky's score. Jary noted that composers, painters, sculptors and authors were following parallel paths, and that the attempt by Stravinsky to "render" solids could be found in all their works.[99]

Several critics recognized that the choreography of *Le Sacre* was a significant departure from the "dizzying virtuosity" of classical ballet. Louis Schneider lauded Nijinsky for trying to discover "new forms of movement, to imagine poses and gestures which had not yet found a place in the history of dance."[100] Others, including Jean Marnold and Octave Maus praised the choreographer for his dramatic, even heroic struggle to "liberate" the art of dance.[101]

The first London performances of *Le Sacre du printemps* took place on 11 July 1913, at the Theatre Royal, Drury Lane. Mindful of the uproar the ballet had created in Paris, Diaghilev made efforts to make the ballet more acceptable to London audiences—or, at least better understood. Edwin Evans, the distinguished English music critic, appeared in front of the curtain before the start of the ballet to explain the music and the intention of the new work.

Pierre Monteux later wrote to Stravinsky that "the London public are better students" than the Parisian, and that the ballet had "considerable success," receiving six or seven curtain calls.[102] The critical response indicates that while Le Sacre's London reception was more sedate than the Paris premiere's, the ballet's impact was no less controversial. The Daily Telegraph thought the work "a whirlwind of cacophonous, 'primitive' hideousness," while The Standard felt "the subject—primitive man—is ugly, and his movements are ugly as the ugliest duckling."[103]

In an effort to categorize Nijinsky's choreography, Richard Capell, in the Daily Mail, repeated someone's observation that Le Sacre was akin to "Cannibal Island Dancing." He deduced, however, that the dancing was "allied to recent manifestations in the other arts, and may be called 'Cubist dancing.' (According to a recent definition—'twenty-four dances performed by twenty-four dancers to twenty-four tunes played simultaneously.')"[104]

In London, too, Le Sacre was associated with modernism—French modernism, according to the critic of The Sketch, thus divorcing the arts of music and dance "from beauty as we conceive beauty."[105] Some of the English artistic vanguard agreed. Lytton Strachey termed Le Sacre "one of the most painful experiences of my life," while Charles Ricketts stated that the ballet made him want to "howl like a dog."[106] For the most part, London received Le Sacre with somewhat bewildered restraint, a decided contrast to the French battage. For one young American poet, John Gould Fletcher, Le Sacre was a revelation. He found the score "perfectly futurist" and felt that the performance of the ballet "more than anything else I have ever seen in life confirmed me in my determination to risk everything in order to become a modern artist."[107]

With Le Sacre du printemps, Stravinsky and Nijinsky resolutely declared themselves modern artists. The ballet itself was both a summing-up and a beginning; it was, in Jean Cocteau's phrase, a "work which opened and closed an epoch."[108] Its creators shared a cultural heritage, and each artist made his individual contribution to this paean to their homeland. Roerich's knowledge of ancient Slavic rituals and cultures, Stravinsky's use of Russian folk tunes, and Nijinsky's abstraction of Russian folk dances combined to make Le Sacre a potent metaphor for the ultimate revelation of âme slave in the prewar Ballets Russes repertoire. Yet beneath this evocation of primitive rites, Jacques Rivière saw something more profound, "more secretive and more hideous. This is a biological ballet. It is not only the dance of the most primitive man, it is also the dance before man."[109] Florent Schmitt saw, prophetically, a "dying humanity staggering once more through all the actions of life. Or perhaps of humanity being born from chaos and beginning the rhythm [of life] and all its actions."[110] The year after the premiere of Le Sacre du printemps, the world was engaged in the war to end all wars and a generation who had thrilled to Stravinsky's hurricane of sound became accustomed to the whine of zeppelins and the rattle of guns.

Diaghilev and Nijinsky were growing increasingly estranged and after Le Sacre du printemps, it became clear that the two were no longer seeing eye to eye. The Ballets Russes sailed for South America in August 1913, without Diaghilev. On the Atlantic crossing, Nijinsky met Romola de Pulszky, whom he married in Rio de Janeiro that September. Thus began his final separation from Diaghilev, and his decline into mental illness began shortly afterward. His mind began to disintegrate in 1917 and his condition was diagnosed as schizophrenia in 1919.

Although the Diaghilev company performed in Europe and America during World War I, Nijinsky and his wife were interned as prisoners of war in Hungary from 1914 to 1916. Le Sacre du printemps, that big, complex, controversial ballet, was never again performed with Nijinsky's original choreography. When Diaghilev wanted to revive Le Sacre in 1920, no one could remember the steps, although five dancers who had performed the ballet were still with the company. Perhaps recalling the difficulty of learning Nijinsky's choreography and how strange and uncomfortable they found the movement, no one wished to remember. Seven years after its creation, Le Sacre du printemps became a "lost" ballet.

Over the decades following the ballet's premiere, Le Sacre du printemps acquired the patina of legend. The drama enacted at the Théâtre des Champs-Elysées has acquired all of the embellishment, contradiction and mythology that tend to envelop unexpected moments in history. The story of the riot has been recorded and retold by many who witnessed or participated in the event and Stravinsky's monumental score has become a landmark in twentieth-century music. The extant artifacts connected with the ballet—the few photographs, sketches and costumes—remain pieces of an incomplete and mysterious puzzle. The original production of Le Sacre du printemps was mythologized as soon as it appeared, an extraordinary tribute to its impact on this century's cultural history.

5

Counterpoint

In the summer of 1914, few people foresaw the lengthy agony of the world war which lay ahead. But when the British Foreign Secretary, Lord Grey, gazed at the lights of London from his Whitehall window, he grimly prophesized that "the lamps are going out all over Europe; we shall not see them lit again in our lifetime."[1] A war of unprecedented dimensions erupted, and when the armistice was signed on 11 November 1918, "la belle époque" had ended. A generation of artists and intellectuals looked toward the touchstones of civilization—literature, art, music, drama and dance—for stimulus and inspiration.

Serge Diaghilev had succeeded in the gigantic task of keeping the Ballets Russes intact during the years of the Great War. Few people in 1915 thought the war would be a long one, and Diaghilev might well have bided his time and "allowed his Ballet to fall into abeyance."[2] The impresario had, however, good reasons for reassembling whatever company he could and continuing to work. Along with the everpresent need for money, Diaghilev knew the importance of maintaining the company's repertoire and keeping the Ballets Russes in the public eye. Moreover, he had an unending supply of new ideas.

After Nijinsky's departure in 1913, the Ballets Russes needed a *premier danseur* and choreographer to fill the void. New ballets had to be created to satisfy the appetite of a public that had come to expect a sensation every season from the Russian Ballet. With Nijinsky gone, there seemed no immediate alternative but the reengagement of Fokine. His new ballets for the Diaghilev company during the 1914 season, *Les Papillons* and *Midas,* as well as his dances for the Rimsky-Korsakov opera *Le Coq d'or,* were not up to the standard of his prewar works.[3] Although Fokine was also engaged as *premier danseur,* Diaghilev had reserved the right to "employ outside choreographers, after consultation, should the need arise."[4]

The most important work of the 1914 Ballets Russes season was to be *La Légende de Joseph,* with a score especially commissioned from Richard Strauss. Originally it had been intended that Nijinsky would both choreograph the ballet and dance the principal role. Fokine, taking his place, also wanted to do both, but Diaghilev thought that he did not look young enough and decided that someone else should be found. On a visit to Moscow in the winter of 1913, the impresario saw his Joseph.

Diaghilev first spotted the handsome face of Léonide Massine in the *corps de ballet* of the Bolshoi Theater company. Massine had intended to abandon a ballet career in favor of acting, but Diaghilev was determined to cast the young dancer in the title role of *La Légende de Joseph.* Sokolova remembered Massine, age nineteen, as being ''thin, shy and quietly spoken,'' and although his physique was not without its defects, he gave proof of a quick intelligence and a capacity for hard work.[5] Although *Joseph* was ''staggering'' as a spectacle, the ballet on the whole was not exciting, and it was not given for long.[6] Massine, however, had made his mark and Diaghilev soon began the task of educating, molding and encouraging his newest discovery. The impresario discussed his—and therefore his company's—concept of ballet with his new protégé. For his part, Massine was impressed with Diaghilev's almost messianic fervor and conviction.

Massine learned his lessons well, and was soon planning his first work for the Ballets Russes, *Liturgie,* based on the Passion of Christ. He devised ''a succession of angular gestures and stiff open-hand movements inspired by Cimabue's Virgin'' and generally by the style of the Italian Primitives.[7] But the ballet never received a public production, as the music Diaghilev had in mind, a series of ancient Russian liturgical chants, was unavailable from Russia because of the war. Massine's first creation for the Russian Ballet was, therefore, *Soleil de nuit* (1914), to music from Rimsky-Korsakov's opera, *The Snow Maiden.* Diaghilev had played the piano score, which revived memories of childhood singing-games for the choreographer, who was delighted with the music's evocative suggestion of Russian peasant character.

Massine's collaborator for *Soleil de nuit* was the Russian Neo-Primitivist artist Mikhail Larionov. Larionov and his companion, the artist Natalia Goncharova, were leaders in the Russian avant-garde prior to World War I. They spearheaded the Neo-Primitivist movement, which, like the Neonationalist trend before it, brought into focus a ''rediscovery'' of native Russian folk art. The Neo-Primitivists combined the inspiration of their national cultural heritage with a ''new understanding of creative principles,'' and in the process discovered ''formal and conceptual characteristics that coincided with modern conventions of pictoral expression, such as anti-illusionistic, two-dimensional composition.''[8] The Neo-Primitivists, in other words, had done in painting very much the same thing that Nijinsky had done in dance.

Larionov was an unusually gifted designer, as well as a renaissance intellectual with a working knowledge of every aspect of theatrical production. Diaghilev had asked him to supervise Massine's work on *Liturgie*, and, as the choreographer recalled, they went through the ballet's steps together, "paring them down drastically to achieve an organic simplicity."[9] Massine noted that Larionov was intrigued with the idea of basing *Soleil de nuit* on Russian folklore, and it was the designer who suggested that the ballet's libretto should "revolve round the person of the sun-god, Yarila, to whom the peasants pay tribute in ritual ceremonies and dances," fusing this folk myth with the legend of the Snow Maiden.[10] Larionov did not move to Paris until 1914, but it is likely, in view of his involvement with avant-garde artists in both Europe and Russia, and his friendship with Diaghilev, that both the scenario and the choreographic style of Nijinsky's *Le Sacre du printemps* were known to him.

Both Massine and Larionov felt strongly that *Soleil de nuit* must be done in authentic peasant style. Accordingly, the designer used vivid shades of red, purple and green, basing his work closely on Russian folk art. For the dances, Massine drew on childhood memories of the *khorovod* and round games, which Larionov helped him "to embellish with suitably primitive, earthly gestures."[11] The ballet was successful enough for Diaghilev to seriously consider Massine as a choreographer. But however encouraged he felt by the praise for his choreography, Massine knew that *Soleil de nuit* "had been only partially successful in translating *Liturgie*, the essence of Russian folk-art, into choreographic terms. I felt there was still a rich vein of untapped material in Russian folk-lore, which I might some day use for a richer, more exciting ballet."[12] Subsequently, Massine choreographed *Contes russes* (1917), based on well-loved Russian children's stories about such characters as Kikamora, the ferocious and hideous witch, and the demon Baba Yaga. But it was not until 1920 that Massine was given the opportunity to rechoreograph the masterpiece of Russian folklore and ancient ceremony, *Le Sacre du printemps.* He was to stage three more productions of *Le Sacre*, for the League of Composers in Philadelphia in 1930, for La Scala in 1948, and for the Royal Swedish Ballet in 1956.[13] It is the first two revivals that will be considered here; the former because it was the first revival of *Le Sacre* since its premiere in 1913, and the latter because it marks the ballet's debut as a stage production in the United States.

Lydia Sokolova believed that Diaghilev's decision to revive *La Sacre du printemps* in 1920 was, at least in part, a practical one. Throughout its history, the Ballets Russes was often under the threat of bankruptcy, and the exigencies of running a company during a world war left Diaghilev's financial resources nearly depleted. He contrived to arrange a season at the Théâtre des Champs-Elysées in December of 1920, but could afford no new productions. The sets and costumes of *Le Sacre* were still in the company's possession and the Stravinsky ballet seemed an ideal choice for a revival.[14] *Le Sacre* had always been a special favorite of Diaghilev's, and he undoubtedly cherished the hope that the ballet would finally receive the recognition that it deserved. Concert performances of the work in Paris in 1914 had been received in "a fever of adoration" and Diaghilev judged that *Le Sacre* would no longer strike the public as "revolutionary."[15]

There were only five dancers in the 1920 Ballets Russes company, including Sokolova, who had performed in the 1913 Nijinsky production. None of them could recall the original choreography in sufficient detail to reconstruct the ballet.[16] Massine had, of course, heard innumerable stories about the production and its reception. In the summer of 1920, Massine visited Stravinsky in Switzerland to discuss the score and ideas for new choreography. At that time, the composer admitted to Massine that he had been dissatisfied with the choreography for the first production. Nijinsky, Stravinsky declared, had made an error in following the rhythms of the score too closely. After studying the music, Massine thought he could avoid Nijinsky's mistake—"if mistake it was"—by attempting a counterpoint between the score and the choreography.[17] He demonstrated some ideas for the ballet to Stravinsky, who gave his approval. The choreographer then discussed *Le Sacre* at length with Diaghilev. Massine stated that the impresario felt that Nijinsky had "failed" because he had tried to do too much at once, not realizing that "the eye and ear cannot absorb simultaneously as much as the ear alone."[18]

Massine staged a concerted campaign of research and analysis to attack *Le Sacre*. He returned to archaic Russian icons and wood carvings and found no justification for "the bent wrist and ankle movements Nijinsky had used."[19] Presumably, Massine was referring to the flexion of the joints, which is characteristic of Russian folk dance, especially in the Ukraine. Nijinsky may have chosen to *exaggerate* these gestures for the sake of stylization or to emphasize their importance to the choreography. On the other hand, the dancers who were recalling the ballet for Massine probably remembered the movements that felt most "unnatural" to them and may have overemphasized this element, either in its degree or frequency. In any case, the aesthetic of the bent wrist and ankle, viewed separately from the overall concept and construction of the original Nijinsky choreography, would have made little sense to Massine.

After some consideration, Massine decided to base his production on Russian peasants' round dances, "strengthened when necessary by the use of angular and broken lines" which he had evolved from his earlier study of Byzantine mosaics and "perhaps unconsciously from the captivating spirit of cubism."[20] In this way, Massine felt he could infuse *Le Sacre* with a new vitality, reinforce the impact of Stravinsky's music, and present the Russian theme of the ballet all the more powerfully.

It is clear that Massine, like Nijinsky, looked to antique Slavonic artifacts and art works as sources of inspiration. His work with Larionov on *Liturgie* and *Soleil de nuit* undoubtedly made him familiar with both Russian folk art and the Neo-Primitivist movement, which fused the folk tradition with theories of abstraction in art. Indeed, it seems possible that Larionov served the role of mentor for Massine, just as Roerich had for Nijinsky. Massine's interest in the visual arts was even more pronounced than that of his predecessors. His fascination with Cubism was evident in many of his early ballets, especially *Parade* (1917), on which he collaborated with Erik Satie, Jean Cocteau and Pablo Picasso. But while Nijinsky created his *Le Sacre* during the height of the craze for Cubist art, by 1920 it was the vogue for Dada that was becoming the *dernier cri* of the avant-garde.

Massine had an incisive and analytical musical intelligence and Stravinsky felt it was enlightening for the choreographer to hear *Le Sacre* in concert. "Thus from the first he perceived that, far from being descriptive, the music was an 'objective construction,'" Stravinsky declared.[21] Shortly after the premiere of the new version in 1920, the composer stated that he and Massine chose, by common consent, the composer's original image of pagan Russia. They sublimated "anecdotal or symbolic" details, preferring the concept of "pure" musical and choreographic constructions. Stravinsky's appraisal of the first production changed over the years, and in 1920, he preferred to view the ballet—and the music—as an "architectural" work, not a "story-telling" one.[22] The programme for the 1920 revival at the Théâtre des Champs-Elysées did not carry an extended synopsis, as had the 1913 production. *Le Sacre du printemps* was described as "a spectacle of pagan Russia. The work is in two parts and involves no subject. It is choreography freely constructed on the music."[23]

In planning his choreography for *Le Sacre*, Massine began, as Nijinsky had before him, to work on the "Danse sacrale." The choreographer chose Lydia Sokolova, who had been one of the group of women in the original Nijinsky version, to dance the role of the Chosen Virgin. Sokolova had danced many notable roles in Massine ballets, including Kikamora in *Contes russes*, the American Girl in *Parade* (1917), and the Tarantella in *La Boutique fantasque* (1919). She was sensitive to Massine's ideas and has said that she "responded to his type of movement because the whole system of it seemed part of me. I was always so essentially a character dancer that other people could not be expected to perform all my contortions."[24] For the demanding sacrificial dance, Massine was to test both his creative inspiration and the physical and mental resources of his Chosen One.

As a young soloist with the Ballets Russes, Sokolova was painfully conscious of the honor and "awesome responsibility" that Massine bestowed upon her—much like that of the Chosen Virgin she was to dance.[25] "I was called to rehearse alone with Massine," she recorded. "He tried out some movements with me which seemed to present no difficulty.'' The choreographer had her write down the number of times the first step was to be performed, and the procedure was then repeated with the next sequence.[26] After some reflection on the difficulties of the music, Massine decided to work out parts of the solo with a metronome.

Sokolova called this solo "perhaps the most extraordinary dance ever invented.'' She and Massine worked on the dance, which, she said, proved "so difficult for him to plan and for me to memorise because Stravinsky's music made its own rules and abided by none of them for long.'' First, it was necessary to establish the rhythm of each section and to set the metronome at the tempo marked on the score. After Sokolova had performed the first steps many times over, and was imbued with the beat of the music, she tried the sequences with pianist Rae Robertson, who had been engaged especially to rehearse the "Danse sacrale.'' Sokolova sometimes found that certain steps seemed to have nothing in common with the music, and would "ignore the sound and keep going straight on,'' eventually meeting the music on a given beat. As Massine had arranged the dance so that each step had a separate set of counts, Sokolova found that her primary difficulty was the "execution of the actual steps and remembering how many times to repeat each one.'' She soon found the only way to remember how many times she had performed any given step was to press down a finger each time a new section was begun, a process she dubbed her "finger method.'' Once a movement was worked out rhythmically, Sokolova would go back to the beginning of the solo, methodically adding on the newly learned step. These "string of pearls'' repetitions prepared her for the ordeal of performing such a long and completely exhausting dance on stage.[27] Sokolova recorded the entire solo in a little penny notebook, which she was to use in subsequent years as an *aide-mémoire*.[28]

"Without doubt, the most terrifying experience of my life in theatre was the first orchestra rehearsal of *Le Sacre*,'' stated Sokolova. It took place, as had the ballet's premiere in 1913, on the stage of the Théâtre des Champs-Elysées. Stravinsky was in attendance, "wearing an expression that would have frightened a hundred Chosen Virgins.''[29] The composer paced up and down the aisles, while conductor Ernest Ansermet practiced difficult parts with the orchestra. Sokolova, who had to wait through the entire first act and all the repetitions and corrections that such rehearsals entail, became so frightened that she nearly fled the theater. In the second scene, she took her place on stage with the *corps de ballet*. "I was so stunned that I couldn't hear the music,'' she recalled, "but the girls pulled me through the ensemble dances. When the other dancers retreated to the back of the stage and left me alone I thought I was going to faint.'' Ansermet was a sympathetic conductor, however, and both dancer and orchestra finished together.[30]

Remembering the uproar that greeted the premiere of *Le Sacre* in 1913, the members of the Ballets Russes in 1920 wondered how the revival would be received. Sokolova decided that "a generation which had heard German guns was no longer to be shocked by the explosions of Stravinsky's music." In any case, Massine's *Le Sacre* was, in Sokolova's estimation, "clear-cut and methodical. . . . In Massine's choreography, nothing was left to chance." For Sokolova, the Nijinsky *Le Sacre* remained a vague work, less complex and accurate than Massine's.[31]

Léonide Massine's version of *Le Sacre du printemps* had its premiere on 15 December 1920, at the Théâtre des Champs-Elysées. Diaghilev had decided to use the Roerich costumes and decor, departing from the original production only by having the second scene backdrop serve for both acts of the ballet. After the first section of the ballet, which was greeted by applause, the second scene opened with all of the men seated in a horse-shoe formation around the back and sides of the stage. Sokolova was in one of the three lines of women arranged across the central space, thus giving the coalition of bodies grouped onstage the appearance of an inverted lyre.[32] The women in each of the short files linked hands, so that they formed rows of three abreast, facing sideways, along the length of the stage. According to Sokolova, the two women on the ends of each line sank to the earth with bent knees, and then rose up as the center line went down, giving the women's movement "an undulating effect." The three lines of women then moved slowly into a block formation and performed "a quiet but forceful swaying movement." When they took hands and made an exit, Sokolova was left in the center of the stage. From this moment, the Chosen Virgin had to stand absolutely still for twelve minutes, waiting for the "Danse sacrale" to begin. "My left hand was held across my body, [with] my clenched hand in the air above my head, my right hand was at my waist and my feet turned inward," remembered Sokolova. Forbidden by Massine even to blink, she stared fixedly at the red exit light at the back of the theatre, imagining herself as a heroic victim of fate, at once terrified and pathetic.[33]

While Sokolova stood immobile, the dancers of the "tribe" encircled her solitary form, surging and receding in "a frightening way." For every group of men or women, or both, there were different jumps, gestures and counts, and "the whole crowd counted audibly to themselves." Finally, the entire company converged on the figure of the Chosen Virgin. Two men held hands across her body while the other dancers linked onto them on either side, forming a human chain with Sokolova at its center. Then the line of men and women swayed their bodies from side to side, "gradually opening out like a concertina and closing in again." At length, having performed one whole revolution of the stage with Sokolova as an axis, the dancers were again back in their line parallel to the footlights. "The two

Lydia Sokolova as the Chosen Virgin in Léonide Massine's 1920 Production of
Le Sacre du printemps
(*Photo courtesy of the Dance Collection, The New York Public Library at Lincoln Center, Astor, Lenox and Tilden Foundations*)

men on either side of me then broke hands,'' Sokolova recalled, ''and everybody slowly sidestepped upstage'' to twenty counts as the music lowered to a whisper.[34]

Sokolova began with ''a crashing step'' on the first beats of the ''Danse sacrale.'' As she danced, the forty members of the ''tribe'' remained motionless at the back of the stage, their hands arched over their brows, watching the ritual of death. ''The watchers beyond the footlights seemed to be echoing with their opera glasses this ancient gesture,'' observed Sokolova.[35]

The solo proved an exhausting ordeal for the young dancer, who noted that ''whatever it did to the audience it nearly killed me.'' Indeed, Sokolova thought she gave the impression of ''a creature galvanized by an electric current.''[36] The hardest thing for her to remember was the number of times she had performed one of the complex steps. When the sheer length and physical demands of the dance made it impossible for Sokolova to keep count by her ''finger method,'' Leon Woizikovsky, who led the *corps de ballet,* was allowed to call out the counts.[37] The climax of the solo was a final series of spinning jumps around the stage. Sokolova described these as ''*grand jetés en tournant* . . . but between each, on landing, I had to bend down sideways and place one hand on the stage while I raised the other in the air and beat my breast twice. Coming to a sudden halt in the middle [of the stage], I pulled myself up on my toes, waiting for the curtain to begin to fall. I dropped to the ground and lay backwards, raising my body in a taut arch, like a victim meeting the knife, resting on my shoulders, elbows and toes. Just before the curtain touched the stage the last chord of music sounded, and I collapsed.''[38]

The ballet was greeted with deafening applause. After the devastation of a world war, the ancient cycle of sacrifice, death and rebirth seemed to hold a deeper, more personal significance for audiences. The reviews were more analytical and less emotional than those of the first production, although by no means all favorable. The *régisseur* for the Ballets Russes, Serge Grigoriev, thought that Massine's choreography was ''highly expert'' but lacked the pathos of the Nijinsky version. ''It was as if Massine paid greater heed to the complicated rhythms than to [the score's] meaning,'' he wrote. ''The result was something mechanical, without depth, which failed to be moving.''[39] Many critics who had seen *Le Sacre* in 1913, including André Levinson and Emile Vuillermoz, compared the Massine production with the earlier Nijinsky ballet.

Levinson recalled the first performance of *Le Sacre*—the ''battle of 'Hernani' of the Ballets Russes''—and admitted that he preferred ''the old pandemonium and hand-to-hand combat'' to the benign approbation which greeted Massine's effort. In the ''new'' version, Massine had eliminated all historical references, all pretention to ethnology. ''I am not quarreling with this," Levinson declared, because "the theater is not a museum. But the void is filled with a succession of movements without logic, with a collection of exercises devoid of expression. Nijinsky's dancers were *tormented* by the rhythm. Here, they must simply keep time and, more often, it escapes them." For Levinson, although Nijinsky's *Le Sacre* was destined to be incomplete and fragmentary, it was nevertheless illuminated by flashes of genius.[40]

Emile Vuillermoz was angered by Stravinsky's statement that Massine understood "the true sense" of the ballet better than the composer's original collaborator, Nijinsky. Massine's version, wrote Vuillermoz, was not fundamentally different from the ballet's first conception, "despite the ambitious declarations." The new *Le Sacre* was, "quite simply, without innovation and without personality. If you call the rounds and games Nijinsky devised 'anecdotes' and 'symbols,' what names would you give, in the Massine version, to the bout of wrestling where the dancers clasp themselves and burrow into the earth, while their colleagues form themselves into symmetric groups . . . as if on a tennis court, casting their eyes back and forth to follow the match, their hands joined in the form of a lorgnette?"[41]

For critics and audiences—and most certainly for the dancers—Massine's choreography was much less "revolutionary" than Nijinsky's. Vuillermoz felt that the allusions to the "shimmy" which spawned Massine's choreography could not really pass for progress over the discoveries of Nijinsky.[42] But, in fact, Nijinsky had used a similar device. It is possible that some of the dancers who had performed the original ballet recalled the "mechanical shakes" included in Nijinsky's choreography and that Massine reused these "ritual tremblings" in his revival.[43] And, because the origins of the "shimmy" can be traced to such African dance roots as the Shika dance of Nigeria, both Nijinsky and Massine were closer in evoking "primitive" ritual dance movement than some of their critics might have realized.

A number of reviewers noted that while Massine's "tribe" were recognizably "primitive," they were "without doubt, already human."[44] One critic judged that Massine had replaced Nijinsky's "ugly and inadequate" work with clearer choreography that "made concessions to a familiar aesthetic. While they stamp readily, these people no longer turn their feet inward; they gesture without grace, but not in a deliberately grotesque manner." The men, for example, mimed striking movements with their fists to imitate their labors, sparred playfully with the women or carried them ("like plunder") on their backs.[45] It was not "a question of ballet," asserted another observer. "Léonide Massine dictates a sacred ceremony. Only instinct—no longer science or 'taste'—is his master, his demon." In the "implacable realism" of his choreography, Massine recalled "the descendents of our civilized souls from the depths of the ages."[46]

The critical response was mixed. The *Times* reported that there was "no drama, no story, only a passionless ritual, in which men lunge and spar at one another and lift the women on the shoulders." Richard Capell, in the *Daily Mail*, now mourned the Nijinsky production which he had once deplored. "They have tried something new and this time they have taken the wrong turning. . . . They have spoiled a perfectly good ballet. . . . The Stone Age, new version, is a bore."[47] Richard Terry, writing in the *Queen*, declared: "The arrangement of the dances was less illustrative and carried less conviction, than the production of 1913."[48] But neither Massine's choreography nor Stravinsky's score provoked the furor engendered by the first London performance of Nijinsky's *Le Sacre*. The elements of shock, surprise and novelty were now gone.

Massine was a precise and methodical choreographer who believed in striving for two ideals in the production of a ballet: "the highest power of expression possible to obtain" and "the attainment of a perfect balance between dynamic movement and pure *plastique*, and an interesting counterpoint of mass movement as opposed to that of the individual."[49] *Le Sacre* offered him the opportunity to apply these ideals to fresh rhythmic problems, not all of which were ultimately solved to his satisfaction. Like Nijinsky, Massine preferred to work with modern music, comparing his choreographic methodology with the process of musical composition. "I regard solo dances as melodies written for a single instrument," he stated, "just as group dances correspond to a piece orchestrated for a given number of instruments."[50]

Massine wanted to invest his group and mass dances with color and contrast similar to musical orchestration. In his *Le Sacre*, he felt that the music was the predominant element, and that the theme of the ballet became a secondary consideration. Both the music and the theme had moved Nijinsky; for Massine, *Le Sacre* was an interesting choreographic puzzle rather than a work of emotional significance. The choreographer himself noted that "as some people who saw both versions said, mine may have lacked the inner fire, the intensity of the pathos that characterized the original."[51] Perhaps Massine's disavowal of the "magnificently human ground plot of the work" weakened the impact of the rhythmic counterpoint which he hoped to make plain in his choreographic construction.[52]

For his movement patterns for *Le Sacre*, Massine, like Nijinsky, returned to traditional dances such as the *khorovod*. As in the original version, the sacrificial victim was chosen from among the maidens in the magic circle. The solo which Massine created to depict the ritual dance of death of the Chosen Virgin was the ballet's most intensely dramatic moment and, in this respect, provided a striking contrast to the controlled, disciplined sensibility that pervaded the rest of the work.

Although the solo originally was choreographed for Sokolova, it was performed by Bronislava Nijinska in 1923 and became one of her greatest roles. Sokolova's description of the "Danse sacrale" needs little embellishment. While both she and Nijinska performed the dance with equal success, their interpretations of the solo seem to have varied. Levinson described Nijinska as "dramatic." In the long moment before the "Danse sacrale," he noted she stood "immobile, the left elbow supported on the right palm, the cheek leaning on the other palm in the familiar manner of a female slave, she is the very image of anguish." But even Nijinska's performance of this vehement dance, with jumps "which burst forth like a whirlwind" could not erase the image of Maria Piltz, the original Chosen Virgin, from the critic's memory.[53] Florence Gilliam, who reviewed *Le Sacre* in 1923 for *Theatre Arts Monthly*, contrasted the impressions made by Sokolova and Nijinska. "La Nijinska danced the role with terrible macabre intensity," wrote Gilliam. "Sokolova makes the part more voluntary, more spiritual, more exalted. She is less the victim and more the martyr. La Nijinska's was a dance of spasmodic hysterical terror in the face of an inevitable fate; Sokolova's is rather the fanatic ecstasy of the dervish who dances until overtaken by unconsciousness or death."[54]

Whatever the dancer's interpretation—tragically resigned or dramatically heroic—the death-dance of the Chosen Virgin remained the focal point of the ballet. Massine had avoided specific references to the various games, rituals and choreographic images that Stravinsky had detailed in his original "musical-choreographic" conception of the work. Despite Massine's professed desire to "Russianize" the ballet, his *Le Sacre* seemed less an evocation of the rites of a pagan Russian tribe than Nijinsky's ballet had been. Massine's dancers were a universal tribe, entrapped by the ancient decrees of tradition, compelled to reenact the ceremonial formulas of their ancestors to ensure their survival. Massine's *Le Sacre*, then, was moving away from the depiction of a particular primitive society in a specific place. This new *Le Sacre* began to reveal the significance that the work would come to have as a universal drama.

Poet and essayist T. S. Eliot, in his review of the Massine production for the *Dial*, identified two key issues that would confront subsequent choreographers of *Le Sacre*. "The music," wrote Eliot, "struck me as possessing a quality of modernity which I missed from the ballet which accompanied it. . . . Music accompanied and explained by an action must have a drama which has been put through the same process of development as the music itself. The spirit of the music was modern and the spirit of the ballet was primitive ceremony."[55] In 1913, Nijinsky's choreography had broken through the established conventions of ballet technique.

Although Russian folk dance was his initial inspiration—as it was to be Massine's—Nijinsky's use of the vernacular had been uncompromisingly modern. When Massine essayed *Le Sacre* in 1920, he discarded the most extreme archaic movements adapted by Nijinsky and chose a more conventional ballet-based vocabulary for his choreography. Nijinsky's "Danse sacrale," for example, unlike Massine's, had no movement that critics and audiences could identify as a *grand jeté en tournant*.

With this decision, Massine may have lessened the impact of the original *Le Sacre*'s synthesis of traditional Russian folk forms and a modernist aesthetic. By 1920, too, Stravinsky's score had been widely heard and, while still somewhat controversial, it was generally recognized as a pivotal creation of the pre-World War I era. Emile Vuillermoz expressed the opinion that Stravinsky's score would always dominate the ballet's choreography; the intentions of a ballet master, he believed, would always be reduced to a mere trifle in comparison to the tempest of the music.[56] This observation has often been echoed over the years, and many critics and choreographers have termed the score "undanceable."[57]

Massine's production of *Le Sacre du printemps* was performed off and on during the 1921–24 seasons of the Ballets Russes, and was revived again for the company in 1928 and 1929. The Berlin premiere of *Le Sacre* in 1929 was enthusiastically received, and Sokolova, who again danced the role of the Chosen Virgin, recalled that the ovation was colossal "and I had never known anything like it before in my life."[58]

The Ballets Russes completed its final season at London's Royal Opera House in 1929. Diaghilev, whose health had been deteriorating, appeared at the theater unexpectedly to see two of his favorite ballets, *Le Lac des cygnes* and *Le Sacre*. The performance went well and Sokolova's performance was called "a triumph."[59] The *Times* waxed eloquent: " 'Le Sacre' is 'absolute' ballet, and we are assured that it will come to be regarded as having a significance for the 20th century equal to that of Beethoven's choral symphony in the 19th."[60] Grigoriev recalled Diaghilev speaking to him of *Le Sacre* at the time of this last performance of the ballet by his company. "So the public has accepted it at last. It has taken sixteen years to persuade them!"[61]

Nine years after the premiere of *Le Sacre du printemps* at the Théâtre des Champs-Elysées in Paris, the flamboyant conductor Leopold Stokowski led the Philadelphia Orchestra in the American concert premiere of the score. "Without description or program," wrote the critic of the *Philadelphia North American* in March 1922, "the work might have suggested a New Year's Eve rally of moonshine addicts and the simple pastimes of early youth and maidens." Another critic simply termed the score "Paleozoic."[62] But Stokowski was a champion of contemporary music, and was determined to introduce his audiences to contemporary music.

His friend and biographer, Oliver Daniel, notes that the conductor was close enough to the times of violent negative reactions to the works of such composers as Strauss, Debussy, Ravel, Schoenberg and Stravinsky to realize that repeated performances of their music would be needed before it could become part of the accepted repertoire of the orchestra. He had begun to shock his audiences as early as 1915, with performances of Strauss' *Alpine Symphony* and Schoenberg's *Kammersymphonie*. After a performance of Scriabin's *Poème de l'extase,* one critic noted that "conspicuous use was made of the exit doors."[63]

Stokowski, however, was adamant that his public give such new music a hearing and he was not above delivering a lecture to concert-goers on the subject of proper audience etiquette. Certainly he was the ideal candidate to introduce *Le Sacre du printemps* to America.

A successful stage production of Stravinsky's *Les Noces* at the Metropolitan Opera House in April of 1929 encouraged Stokowski to consider presenting *Le Sacre* as a full-scale ballet. *Les Noces* was the first cooperative venture of Stokowski and Claire Reis, who had founded the League of Composers in Philadelphia. Reis had assembled a formidable board, including the designer Norman Bel Geddes, Martha Graham, Doris Humphrey, Charles Weidman, Richard Hammond (an old friend of Stokowski's), Léonide Massine, Nicholas Roerich and Agnes De Mille.[64] Stokowski greatly admired Graham's work, and both he and Roerich agreed that she should perform the role of the Chosen Virgin. Graham had begun to experiment with her own new style of movement—spare, elemental, blunt and percussive—and Roerich and Stokowski asked her to consider doing the choreography for *Le Sacre*, but she demurred. Graham was entering what she has called her "long-winter-underwear period" and felt she did not have the experience, especially in handling large groups. She was, in fact, still developing her personal choreographic creed.[65]

Performing in *Le Sacre*, however, meant a new kind of recognition for Graham. Bessie Schönberg, a member of her all-female "Group" in 1930, felt that the ballet represented an enticing proposition. "Graham was very young . . . and this represented all the glamorous trappings of the theater—Stokowski, the orchestra, the Metropolitan Opera."[66] Whatever her motivation, she accepted the offer to dance the role of the Chosen Virgin, but declined to act as choreographer. The next, and more logical, choice for a choreographer was Massine, who had come to the United States in 1928.

When Massine and his wife, ballerina Eugenia Delarova, first arrived in New York, he discovered that American interest in ballet was no greater than it had been a decade earlier when he had made his first visit to the States. After months of looking for work, Massine met S. L. Rothafel, the entrepreneur responsible for the Roxy Theater in New York. Rothafel had begun staging live shows between the films shown at the theater, and he offered Massine a contract to choreograph a few ballets. The Roxy productions were vaudeville-type spectacles, razzle-dazzle affairs with endless rows of "sequined and high-kicking chorus girls" moving on and off the vast, raked stage. Massine, grateful for the opportunity, devised Easter Ballets, Christmas Ballets, Halloween and Thanksgiving Ballets for "a well-trained company" of about thirty dancers, as well as performing four times a day himself—and five times on Saturday. The offer to choreograph *Le Sacre* for Stokowski and the League of Composers came just as his Roxy contract expired and proved to be, as he later wrote, "the only bright spot" in a difficult year.[67]

In an interview before the 1930 League of Composers production of *Le Sacre*, Stokowski said that he had discussed the work with Stravinsky during the previous spring. The composer had made some changes in rhythm and orchestration, and the new edition of the score that resulted would be used for the upcoming performances. "Although the creators of the work, Stravinsky and Roerich, are both Russian," declared Stokowski, "we are not aiming to make this production of the work essentially Russian because we felt that the ideas and feelings it expresses are universal."[68] Their decision was predicated on practical as well as aesthetic considerations. Nearly everyone involved in the League production was American, and only Massine and Roerich were familiar with *Le Sacre* as a fully-staged ballet.

Stokowski and Reis realized that another work would be needed to fill out the proposed program. Accordingly, Stokowski, in keeping with his campaign to present the music of contemporary composers, settled on Arnold Schoenberg's *Die glückliche Hand,* which was termed a "Drama mit Musik." Reis assembled another impressive team to mount this "pantomime ballet with a voice in it."[69] The experimental one-act work was to be directed by Rouben Mamoulian, and the set and lighting were entrusted to Robert Edmond Jones. The dance/mime roles were choreographed by Doris Humphrey, who performed the part of The Woman, with Charles Weidman as The Stranger and Olin Howland cast as the mysterious Chimera. The only "voice" part, that of Everyman, was sung by the Russian baritone Ivan Ivantzoff. Reis and the manager of the Philadelphia Orchestra, Arthur Judson, arranged two series of performances for the resulting double bill. The League would assume full responsibility for the productions, which would first be presented to the Philadelphia Orchestra's regular subscriber audience, and then at the Metropolitan Opera House in New York.[70]

Rehearsals for *Le Sacre* took place in the gymnasium of the Dalton School in New York. The forty dancers needed for the ballet were drawn from a variety of sources. There were three women from the Humphrey–Weidman company—Rose Yasgour, Helen Strumlauf and Eleanor King—as well as twelve members of Graham's all-female "Group," including Lily Mehlman, Anna Sokolow, Mary Rivoire, Lillian Shapiro, and Sylvia Wasserstrom. Some of the dancers were members of the Roxy ballet company and the remainder of the cast was hired *ad hoc*.[71] Bessie Schönberg, then a member of Graham's company, took part in the early auditions and rehearsals which Massine held for the women from Graham's troupe. Although an injury prevented her from actually dancing in the ballet, Schönberg took part until the final rehearsals.

"For us," recalls Schönberg, "Massine represented BALLET—in large letters. Working with a ballet choreographer was an unique experience for us, but we felt it was a rather ridiculous situation." He spoke to the dancers about the idea of the ballet, and told them it would be rhythmically difficult. "That didn't worry us particularly," Schönberg asserted. "He talked about 'primitive movement' and showed us a few steps. He wanted us to 'toe-in,' which we thought rather gauche, but . . . entertaining and amusing." All in all, Schönberg felt that Massine was very pleasant and charming—"an extremely sensitive director."[72]

Claire Reis reported that warfare broke out at the first rehearsal. There were arguments between Massine and Stokowski over matters of tempo, and between Graham and Massine over questions of dance style.[73] Graham had her own ideas—"as she always had," noted Reis. "Massine wanted it just as it had been done in Paris and they crossed swords and neither one would give in."[74] The stories surrounding the Massine–Graham feuds are dance-world legends. Dance critic John Martin declared there was "considerable bloodshed on both sides" and Agnes De Mille says that Massine accused Graham of "not trying."[75] Richard Hammond, who was deeply involved in the production, said that "Martha did not like Massine for one minute."[76] Both Eleanor King and Bessie Schönberg have detailed rehearsal incidents which corroborate the accounts of tension between the choreographer and his Chosen Virgin. King recalls Graham sitting in a corner during rehearsal, with a shawl over her head. "When she did move, it was with condescension," observed King. "It was hard on Massine and the forty dancers supporting her."[77] Schönberg remembers another instance which occurred soon after rehearsals had begun. "When he had finished working with us, Massine turned to Graham, who had been watching, and said, 'Miss Graham, anytime that is convenient, I will teach you your dance.'" An absolute silence, which Schönberg declares "seemed to stretch for days," followed this invitation. Finally, Martha stood up and drew herself up to her full height—"she seemed taller than she could possibly be—and stormed out and slammed the door." Schönberg's explanation of Graham's temperamental behavior is disarmingly logical. "Martha simply wasn't used to having someone teach *her* a dance. She had nearly always done her own choreography. Now, here was a *ballet* choreographer who was going to teach *her* [the choreography for] his solo!"[78]

In his autobiography, *My Life in Ballet*, Massine calls Graham "a most subtle and responsive dancer to work with" and says that her powerful performance as the Chosen Virgin "added considerable strength to the production."[79] He makes no allusions to the fabled battles. Graham, too, denies the conflict and told Oliver Daniel that she had made up her mind to follow Massine's direction completely. "I never argued with any of them because I felt they were dealing with something I was not ready to deal with choreographically or musically." She recalls there were certain "balletic" things that she changed slightly, but she insists that Massine was usually very generous and would say, "We'll keep that." "But," adds Graham, "my style was beginning to develop at that time and I would do the thing the way I would do it."[80]

Graham, apparently, was indeed very determined to do the thing the way she would do it. Bessie Schönberg believes that Graham learned her solo "exactly as Massine directed her . . . every step exactly as he taught it. Then she took [the dance] into the studio and worked on it and rehearsed it until it was her own." The solo underwent a metamorphosis. "Massine had created it, but Graham transformed it," declared Schönberg. "Certainly Massine could never say she wasn't doing the *steps* he'd set."[81] In handling Massine's choreographic style, Graham was faced with new challenges, testing her technical range, dramatic aptitude and stamina. She had never been noted, for example, for her *ballon*, that is, for great elevation in jumps. On the contrary, much of her work just preceding *Le Sacre* had been very much concerned with the development of a floor technique that was to become one of her hallmarks. Massine, however, demanded that she leap, as Don McDonagh notes, not "out of capriciousness," but because the choreography demanded it.[82] It is understandable, then, that Graham preferred to wrestle with this unfamiliar choreography alone rather than in full view of her company, colleagues and peers.

As the day of the premiere drew near, Graham's reluctance to rehearse with the rest of the dancers began to cause considerable anxiety for all concerned. Someone suggested to Stokowski that he approach Russian ballerina Tamara Geva to replace Graham. The conductor had made an appointment to see Geva when Richard Hammond suggested to Stokowski that the news of this imminent meeting be "leaked" to Graham. The information, accordingly, "came back to Martha and the next thing she was right with it," said Hammond.[83] Eleanor King recalls that at one point a desperate Massine told Graham that he thought the part might be "too difficult" and suggested giving the role to Anita Bay, who was dancing the role of the Witch.[84] Even Graham herself concedes that, halfway through rehearsals, Massine requested that she resign because she would be "a failure." When Graham asked if this was Stokowski's view as well, Massine replied that it was. Graham then confronted the conductor, who replied, "I don't understand you. What are you talking about? Do you want to quit?" "I said no," remembers Graham. "So I stayed and I finished the performance but I did exactly as he said."[85]

Massine conducted rehearsals in a mixture of French and Russian, occasionally punctuated with a few words of English. Lily Mehlman, another member of Graham's "Group" who danced in *Le Sacre,* recalls how startled the Graham dancers were to have the choreographer show them their steps in minute detail. "He demonstrated!" recounts Mehlman. "It was all so artificial after working with Martha. With her, one felt as though the movement . . . grew out of oneself. Rather like it was organic. Massine would take one step here, two steps there."[86] At this point, the dancers were working to a piano reduction of the score, played by Graham's music director, Louis Horst.

While Massine was the titular head of the choreographic side of the League's *Le Sacre* production, Stokowski often offered advice to the dancers, suggestions which would sometimes bleed over into actual alterations in the movement. In fact, the dancers received more dramatic direction from Stokowski than from Massine. According to Eleanor King, the choreographer never gave advice on interpretation to the dancers. They were taught steps "as abstractly as mathematics." One did as one was told with no questions asked, a system King attributes to ballet masters in general.[87] It is likely, however, that Massine's tendency to demonstrate the choreography repeatedly, as well as his seemingly meager verbal directions, can be attributed as much to his difficulty with the English language as to any traditional balletic methodology. In any case, Stokowski's flamboyant personality more than made up for the laconic Massine, and his presence gave the rehearsal process an added zest.

The women in the Graham company, used to the suggestions and directions of Louis Horst, were less taken aback by Stokowski's unorthodox contributions than were the members of the Humphrey–Weidman troupe or the "ballet people." "Stokowski saw that we were moving like automatons, with no feeling for what we were doing," said Eleanor King. Disregarding the choreographer, Stokowski would demonstrate gestures and movements to the dancers. While Massine looked on, the conductor changed the final lift of the Chosen Virgin, rearranged the dancers' spacing for the ending, "and in other ways tightened up the mass design."[88] King felt Stokowski had a nearly infallible theatrical instinct, and whatever changes he made were for the better. Whether lecturing the dancers on the emotions behind Stravinsky's music or putting on a pyrotechnic display of temperament for the benefit of the wealthy members of the League of Composers board, Stokowski proved equally effective. At the first stage rehearsal of *Le Sacre,* Stokowski chose to conduct the score seated in a saddle attached to a sawhorse with his feet in the stirrups. But his musicians were aware that he knew the score perfectly and responded absolutely to his direction.[89]

The dancers, for their part, had to grapple with a different type of score. In the ballet's formative stages, recalled Lily Mehlman, Massine would sit on the floor with stacks of notebooks spread out in front of him.[90] Reams of paper covered with drawings, notes and sketches— Massine's personal version of Stepanov notation—frequently accompanied the choreographer to rehearsals. He kept detailed journals throughout his career and therefore it is likely that some sections of his 1920 version of *Le Sacre* were incorporated into the production. Before the ballet's New York premiere, John Martin wrote that the 1930 work would not be "an exact reproduction of his former version for several reasons, one of which is that he does not remember the details and they were not recorded."[91] Although the "details" of the work were reportedly not chronicled by Massine, he may well have made general notes regarding certain steps, images, gestures, floor plans and the like. Furthermore, his first *Le Sacre* was a major feature of the Ballets Russes repertoire during the 1920s. While Massine left the Diaghilev company in 1920, he returned in 1924, remaining with the Russian Ballet until its penultimate season. Thus he had a number of opportunities to see and perhaps rehearse his 1920 version of *Le Sacre.* It therefore seems likely that some movements were carried over from the earlier work to the League of Composers production.

Massine said that his 1920 *Le Sacre* had evolved from a combination of influences, including Russian peasant round dances, Byzantine mosaics and Cubism. Throughout his life, the choreographer was inspired by a surprisingly broad range of stimuli, from modern art and ancient Greek sculpture to popular music, dance and theater, including jazz, flamenco dance and the *commedia dell'arte.* His solo as the Barman in his ballet *Union Pacific* (1934), was based on a compendium of "American folk-dances," which always fascinated him.[92] Massine's interest in folk and popular dance forms dove-tailed with the development of his choreographic vision. In a 1919 interview with English music critic Edwin Evans, he declared that choreography should include "every form of regulated movement, such as that of a religious ceremony or a State function. As raw material, it includes even the undisciplined movements of daily life. There is no scene of human beings in motion that cannot be adapted to the purposes of choreography."[93]

Massine was an inveterate diarist and kept notes and journals on his myriad interests throughout his career. As early as 1916, during the Diaghilev Ballets Russes' tour of the United States, he recorded ideas for ballets in his personal notebooks. "Having seen an American Indian for the first time," reported the *New Mexico Telegraph*, "Leonide Massin [*sic*] . . . has an inspiration, a new one and all . . . American in theme and idea." During the company's engagement in Washington, D.C., Massine had watched a Sioux Indian tribe perform its war dances on the stage of the National Theater. "Here was born Massin's [*sic*] inspiration for an American Indian ballet à la Russe," declared the *Telegraph*. Before leaving the city he visited the Smithsonian Institution with Ernest Ansermet and together they made a study of the musical instruments of the war dance, the moon dance, the pipes and tom-toms used on feast days and other ceremonies and rites.[94] The ballet was to be based on the story of Pocahontas, and Ansermet was said to be at work on the libretto. The *Telegraph* also asserted that between the Ballets Russes performances at the Metropolitan Opera, Massine worked nightly at his "little desk in the dressing room on his figurantes and charts, which, by the dance expression, are to carry out his scenario."[95] The proposed ballet never materialized, but it is interesting to speculate on whether some of Massine's impressions of this experience might later have become part of the choreographer's evocation of a primitive tribe enacting a sacred rite in *Le Sacre du printemps*.[96]

Whatever his source of inspiration, Massine's 1930 *Le Sacre* proved as great an ordeal for the dancers as his 1920 production had been. The final full-stage dress rehearsals with orchestra were grueling. "The violence of the Round Dance of Spring closing the first part was so consuming," recalls Eleanor King, "I had to suck on a lemon in order to swallow and ease my burning throat. Most of the dancers fell flat to the floor in sheer exhaustion between parts one and two."[97] Stokowski made last-minute suggestions regarding Roerich's costumes, which he thought hid the dancers' movements. Although the artist had modified his original designs, the performers still found some of the "accessories" a handicap. King remembers that the strings of heavy wooden beads which the women wore tended to break, "ricocheting in minor thunderclaps" as they rolled about the stage. As a result, at Stokowski's insistence, animal skins were substituted for the beads.[98]

The first American performance of *Le Sacre* took place at the Academy of Music in Philadelphia on 11 April 1930. Oscar Thompson, writing for *Musical America*, noted that the "pre-war modernity" of Schoenberg and Stravinsky "still smacks strange in the mouth of American audiences."[99] Strange or not, the Philadelphians were impressed—as much with the spectacle of Stokowski conducting without a baton as with the ballet. One critic decided that the sight of bare-legged dancers "whirling madly and

Kitty Reece and Lillian Shapiro in Léonide Massine's 1930 Production of *Le Sacre du printemps* (*Photo courtesy of the Dance Collection, The New York Public Library at Lincoln Center, Astor, Lenox and Tilden Foundations*)

stamping upon the stage to an orgiastic fury of sound . . . scenically and symphonically shattered all historical precedent of Philadelphia Orchestra performances."[100] Thompson discovered that the performance of the ballet tended to demystify Stravinsky's score. The "convulsions of shuddering nature" became largely "the calisthenics of vigorous dancers." The stage activity seemed to rob the music of some of its "hairy-ape characteristics," in Thompson's view, and he concluded that, all in all, the rite was a colorful, virile and aggressive spectacle, "but by no means a horrendous or appalling one. Primitive Russia was no such terrifying place, after all."[101]

The production opened at New York's Metropolitan Opera House, on 23 April 1930. The Shoenberg-Stravinsky evening was considered "one of the most significant occasions in the musical annals of New York," and the theater was completely sold out for all performances.[102] A. Walter Kramer, writing for *Musical America*, felt that *Le Sacre* had already begun to wear thin. As for the choreography, Kramer decided that Massine's work was sufficiently Muscovite, but somewhat disappointing. "The ballet was well trained but much too small," he complained. "They tell me Diaghileff had two hundred dancers in his 'Ballet Russe' when he produced the work."[103] Thus, twenty-six years after *Le Sacre*'s Paris premiere, the legend of the Nijinsky ballet continued to grow. The critics of the *Musical Leader*, Marion and Flora Bauer, wondered whether "in this day of over-sophistication and neurotic over-civilization" the experiment of asking that a ballet produce "the illusion of the primitive" was demanding too much of an audience. But they concluded that this production of *Le Sacre* was remarkably successful.[104]

John Martin, the dance critic for the *New York Times* and an admirer of Graham's choreography, wrote about the ballet at length. Massine, Martin observed, had effectively conveyed the mystery of the earth's annual vernal equinox, and asserted it was possible to speak about the choreography with enthusiasm. He emphasized that some sections of the work ranked at the very top of modern dancing. "Through its complicated visual counterpoint and its terrific energy there shines the barbaric passion of elemental human beings," Martin observed. "The movements of the dancers were colored with hieratic suggestions, and imbued with a tremendous muscular vigor which at the same time was to be inhibited by the mental limitations of a crude people." Significantly, however, Martin felt that the women in the piece were sometimes less than impressive in their dancing, appearing too soft and sweet. Considering the strength and power of Graham's latest dances for her "Group," Massine's choreography for the female *corps de ballet* may well have seemed pale in comparison with the male dancers in *Le Sacre*, who emerged "most triumphantly."[105]

Although Massine had stated that his choreography for this *Le Sacre* was not an exact reproduction of his 1920 version, some of Eleanor King's description of the opening section of the 1930 work is strikingly similar to accounts of the earlier production. She recalled stylized movements of "plucking vines and beating grain," dancing "in place with vertical leaps" and "hands and bodies swept low to the floor."[106] King's account recalls the first part of Massine's fragmentary work film of his 1948 production of *Le Sacre*, for La Scala, Milan.[107] In another section of the 1930 *Le Sacre*, probably "The Dance Overcoming the Earth," King says that Massine arranged six groups of dancers moving, on alternate phrases, in figure eight circles. Her set, she remembers, "stamping along, began with eight beats of elbow thrusts, then nine to fifteen progressive gallops with arms curvetting in the air; sixteen to twenty-one counts on the knees, clapping the hands, swinging the arms from side to side. Each group started on a different beat." This "dizzy round" continued until the curtain fell on the first scene, and was undoubtedly part of the intricate mass movement which Martin described as closing that act.[108]

An extraordinary moment preceding the "Danse sacrale" is chronicled by King and appears in the work film as well. As King describes it, the dancers of the ensemble link up on both sides of the Chosen Virgin. They stand shoulder to shoulder, the men facing one way, the women another, "vibrating in place, then alternately shuffling to make a "sun-circle" of the stage in a mystical, frenzied adoration of the lifeforce."[109] Thus, it would appear that both the "shimmy" movement and the "sun-circle" used in the 1920 production appeared again in Massine's revised version a decade later. The work film shows the section just before the victim is chosen from within "the magic circle." A small group of women begins performing a large jumping step, a kind of a pitched-forward *grand jeté*, which they perform around the Chosen Virgin. Their arms are first held rigidly and well behind their bodies; then the dancers reach forward as if to pull their reluctant mortality into space.[110]

The "Danse sacrale" was, once again, the highlight of the ballet. John Martin, who called the dance one of Massine's "most brilliant achievements," praised Graham's performance. He noted that the physical demands of the choreography required elevation, speed, balance and the complete mastery of the body. "Miss Graham compasses these difficulties with supreme ease and authority," wrote Martin, "and instead of allowing them to speak for themselves, she imbues them with her characteristic emotional strength and color."[111] It was Graham's "conquest of the air," her remarkable ability to seemingly devour space, that astounded her colleagues. "We'd never seen Martha do anything like that before," says Lily Mehlman. "She seemed to float above our heads. No ballerina ever leaped the way Martha sailed through the air."[112] Bessie Schönberg

Martha Graham as the Chosen Virgin in Léonide Massine's 1930 Production of
Le Sacre du printemps
(*Photo courtesy of the Dance Collection, The New York Public Library at Lincoln Center, Astor, Lenox and Tilden Foundations*)

remembers Graham doing splits sideways in the air with flexed feet—''like little screams''—but it was the dramatic portrayal of the Chosen Virgin that Schönberg recalls most vividly. ''She moved forward to the edge of the [stage] apron and just stood there, transfixed. One couldn't take one's eyes off her. She had a kind of spiritual aura. She was exotic, wonderful, remarkable and beautiful. I know Massine was very moved by working with Martha.''[113]

The role of the Chosen Virgin marked a turning point in Graham's career. The arcane rites and ceremonial formality of *Le Sacre du printemps* appealed to her sense of the theatrical, the mysterious and the mystical. In fact, Graham's fascination with the language of myth and the symbolic forms of ritual dates from her performance in *Le Sacre.* ''The passionate Russian thing—whether it's Russian or whether it's primal doesn't matter,'' she observes, ''but it was a sacrificial rite and it had nothing to do with the idiosyncrasies of ballet style and modern dance. *Le Sacre* meant spiritually a great deal to me and still does, and people have hounded me to choreograph it but I've said I couldn't.''[114] More than a half century would pass before Graham returned to *Le Sacre du printemps*, finally presenting her choreography of the ballet for the first time on 28 February 1984.

In a curtain speech following *Le Sacre*'s premiere at the Metropolitan Opera House, Stokowski spoke of achieving a synthesis of drama, dance, music and lighting in the hope of evolving a new and unique American art form. The production launched Graham on a new phase of her career and brought Stokowski unprecedented recognition. His picture appeared on the cover of *Time* magazine, the first conductor to be so honored. Massine's choreography was called a masterpiece, and he was to produce the ballet twice more; first for La Scala, Milan, in 1948, and then for the Royal Swedish Ballet in 1956. Commenting on the 1930 League of Composers performances, Massine observed, ''We were all very relieved when *Le Sacre du printemps* was enthusiastically received, and hoped it was a sign that New York was beginning to take ballet seriously.''[115]

The Massine revivals of 1920 and 1930 were the first indications of the ballet's future popularity. Although Massine's productions remained faithful to the original concept and libretto devised by Stravinsky and Roerich, other choreographers were to treat *Le Sacre* according to their individual vision of the ballet's themes of myth and ritual, life, death and rebirth.

6

Epithalamion

Maurice Béjart's production of *Le Sacre du printemps* received its first performance on 8 December 1959, at the Théâtre Royal de la Monnaie in Brussels. The ballet's premiere, noted one critic, was accompanied by outrageous comments, grinding of teeth and accusations of pornography.[1] Forty-six years after *Le Sacre*'s uproarious premiere, Béjart's conception of the work simultaneously raised new issues for debate and old ghosts of scandal and dissent.

In the decades since the ballet's debut, Stravinsky's score had become increasingly familiar—and popular—through concert performances and recordings. Acclaimed as a masterpiece, *Le Sacre* was both a milestone and a classic in the lexicon of modern music. Béjart's production to the now well-known score once again stirred the embers of controversy. It wasn't "Russian"; there was no "Sacrifice of the Chosen Virgin"; some said it wasn't even ballet. It was nothing more than old wine in new bottles. Béjart jettisoned the Stravinsky–Roerich libretto and presented his very personal vision of a spring rite. With his now familiar and much-copied version of *Le Sacre du printemps*, Béjart inaugurated the era of the pop ballet, a genre that has grown increasingly slick, glossy and superficial. Béjart's *Le Sacre* was the progenitor of a style of ballet using monumental scores, hordes of dancers, an eclectic, athletic hybrid movement style that is a mixture of ballet, "modern" jazz and some form of "ethnic" dance, combined with pared down sets and minimal costumes. Although Béjart asserts that he did not see any version of *Le Sacre* before he attempted the work, two earlier productions of the ballet warrant brief consideration in light of the choreographer's idiosyncratic conception.

Seven years after Léonide Massine's production of *Le Sacre du printemps* premiered in the United States, the American modern dancer and choreographer Lester Horton presented his conception of the ballet at the Hollywood Bowl. On 5 August 1937, the Horton Dance Group performed *Le Sacre* with Bella Lewitzky as the Chosen One. Although the theme of the ballet remained a celebration of spring, Horton's individual movement style, his study of American Indian dance, and the costumes and sets designed by the choreographer and William Bowne, combined to give this production a different sensibility from either the Nijinsky or Massine versions.[2] Dorothi Bock Pierre's programme notes for the Horton *Le Sacre* state that this ballet was based "upon the religious Spring Festival of all primitives, not just Russian; and the choreography and movements are modernization of authentic primitive movements."[3]

Horton's youthful enthusiasm for American Indians had led him to study ethnology, in particular the dances and ceremonies integral to Indian life and culture. Bella Lewitzky felt that a number of movement motifs created by Horton were typical of American Indian dance. "The use of the foot on the ground was definitely Indian," she recalls, "both in the stamping movements we used and in the way the foot was flexed and brought up parallel to the floor."[4] Lewitzky also noted that Horton emphasized "a kind of jumping down rather than jumping up," an instruction which recalls Nijinsky's insistence on heavy, uncontrolled descents from leaps. Horton's choreography, as Lewitzky described it, was "very primal. There was nothing in it only for the sake of decoration or simply to please the eye." Angularity was central to the movement design. The line of the body was deliberately distorted. "The hip would be lifted along with the thigh, and the foot would be flexed," Lewitzky remembered. "An arm might be used in a powerful swinging action or held in a right angle position. That produced terrific titters in the audience."[5] The parallels with Nijinsky's choreography are extraordinarily clear, yet Lewitzky believes that Horton did no research on previous versions of *Le Sacre*.

The costumes for the Horton production were strongly reminiscent of American Indian dress. Although Bowne's designs were abstractions rather than literal reproductions of such attire, the earth colors of brown, red and yellow, with touches of white and sky blue, created a vivid picture. The bold striping of the women's skirts and tops emphasized the women's breasts and hips, which, together with their exposed midriffs and frequently glimpsed bare legs, gave an erotic suggestion to the choreography. The men were bare-chested, and most were dressed in leotards with exposed legs or close-fitting knicker-like pants, with boldly patterned stripes.[6]

The brilliant and sensuous effect created by the costumes was accentuated by Horton's choreography, using forward pelvic thrusts, wide second position *pliés* and ecstatic backbends. The ballet's overall visual impact prompted W. E. Oliver to label this *Le Sacre* "hot stuff," although he felt that the choreographer had managed to put "the phallic content in this paean to the primitive far enough into the abstract to avoid the censors."[7] Oliver has here identified an important point about the evolution of *Le Sacre*—the adaptability of its theme. Horton had not only "Americanized" the ballet by abstracting an American Indian motif, but also emphasized the universality of the nature of ritual and highlighted a sensual, even erotic aspect of the work. Both of these ideas would be central to Béjart's realization of *Le Sacre*.

Although the press reaction to Horton's *Le Sacre* was enthusiastic, the audience reception was somewhat mixed. Dance and drama critic Frank Eng observed that when this *Le Sacre* was performed "the little old ladies from Pasadena were outraged," while another reviewer noted that many people in the audience laughed at this unusual exhibition of "strange art." Oliver, who watched a rehearsal, was confident that no riot would ensue. He believed, however, that "this new ballet is almost brutal in its strength, and original enough to provide a new jumping off place for the modern dance."[8] With his production of *Le Sacre*, Lester Horton opened new avenues of possibilities for future choreographers of the work. He had proven that its sensibilities were not exclusively or even specifically "Russian," and that its atavistic theme was universal in its appeal.

Mary Wigman, the great German dancer-choreographer, was invited to stage a production of *Le Sacre* for the 1957 Berlin Festival. In a letter to a friend in March of that year, she confided that "this 'Sacre' is a murderous task."[9] Wigman called the ballet "my hell and heaven, my adoration and exasperation," although she professed to love the music "more than anything else."[10] Realizing that simplicity was the key to handling the complex score, she decided to subordinate the dance creation to Stravinsky's edifice of sound.

Wigman envisioned her *Le Sacre* as "neither ballet nor mimed drama," but rather simply as expressive movement running parallel to the score. She conceived the choreography as a large group piece, the dancers functioning as members of an ancient chorus.[11] The design of the dance used simple and clear spatial forms to symbolize and stand for the idea of community. "The stage was a slanting oval disk before a curtained background—no decoration, no props, timeless."[12] Wigman deliberately jettisoned the idea of presenting a specific "tribe of dancers," preferring her realization of *Le Sacre* to take place, as she said, in "another world."[13] She retained the skeleton of Stravinsky's libretto—the adoration of the earth, the initiation ceremonies and games and, most importantly, the sacrifice of the Chosen Virgin. Jacqueline Robinson described what she recalled as the ballet's most "unforgettable moments: The procession of young girls around the magic circle, spiritual and contemplative; the kiss of the earth by the old sage, who unleashes the delirium among the community; the tender vision of couples entwined in the moonlight; and especially the moment when the Chosen One, livid in her red dress, bound and wreathed, whose fate appears to have been already sealed, is thrown rigid, from one group to another, like a sacred doll."[14]

The costumes were stark and austere—simply long dresses for the women and black tights and a bandeau across the chest for the men. When Wigman's *Le Sacre* premiered on 9 September 1957, with Doris Hoyer as the Chosen Virgin, the ballet was received with "frantic applause." Anne Villiers wrote that "one can speak of primitivism, of modernism, of expressionism . . . in fact, it is of *classicism* that one must speak in this great composition of universal force and purity."[15]

The Wigman and Horton productions of *Le Sacre* gave added dimension to two aspects of the ballet—the universal and timeless nature of its theme and an erotic sensibility underlying the work's emphasis on the continuing cycle of life, death and rebirth. In 1959, Maurice Béjart decided to present his *Le Sacre* as a "Hymn to [the] union of Man and Woman," a celebration of "the essential forces of mankind which are the same all over the world and throughout all periods of history."[16] The Wigman and Horton versions were, in a sense, the choreographer's precedents, although both productions were unknown to him.

For Béjart, then a promising young choreographer of thirty-two, *Le Sacre* was a great opportunity to make his mark. Maurice Béjart was born in Marseilles, the son of writer and philosopher Gaston Berger. He studied ballet at the Marseilles Opera Ballet School and was a dancer with the Opera company until 1945. After the war, he travelled to Paris, studying technique with Lubov Egorova and choreography with Leo Staats. In 1948, Béjart joined Roland Petit's Les Ballets de Paris, and the following year he became a member of Mona Inglesby's International Ballet in London. While in London, he worked with the Russian master teacher Vera Volkova and with Nicholas Sergeyev, formerly the ballet master and *régisseur* of the Maryinsky Ballet. Béjart performed with the Royal Swedish Ballet in the early 1950s, and choreographed his first ballet in Sweden, a version of Stravinsky's *L'Oiseau de feu*.

Returning to Paris in 1953, Béjart founded a small ensemble company, Les Ballets de l'Etoile, in 1954, with writer and critic Jean Laurent. He continued to choreograph, finding much of his inspiration in literature. Pierre Schaeffer, a composer of *musique concrète*, urged Béjart to to do a ballet using this "new" music.[17] The result, *Symphonie pour un homme seul* (1955), to a score by Schaeffer and Pierre Henry, was the choreographer's first major work. Its theme was "Man as prisoner: of himself, of a woman, of 'the others', prisoners of all the pressures of modern life." The ballet's psychological overtones reflect Béjart's view of the postwar "Age of Anxiety." Even the decor, ropes hanging on an otherwise bare stage, was abstract and symbolic.[18]

In *Symphonie*, too, Béjart began to work in the movement style that would become his hallmark. Although he uses classical ballet as a foundation technique, he also borrows stylistic elements from other dance forms; for example, the modern dance contraction or hand gestures (*mudras*) from Hindu dance. The finished product can be a more or less contemporary-looking work such as *Nuit obscure,* or quasi-Oriental, such as *Bhakti.* The more recognizable ''balletic'' of Béjart's works (*Romeo et Juliette, Serait-çe la mort?*) are aggressively athletic, emphasizing what dance critic Deborah Jowitt describes as ''a kind of voluptuous forcefulness, a pressurized, high-protein muscularity.''[19]

One of Béjart's favorite themes is that ''dance is a rite . . . a language: primitive, elementary, direct, of mystic source rather than intellectual attitude.''[20] His fascination with ritual and folklore, with symbol and metaphor, made *Le Sacre* an irresistible challenge. After producing *Symphonie pour un homme seul,* Béjart met Maurice Huisman, then Director of the Belgian Center of International Cultural Exchange, as well as Director of the Brussels Opera House, the Théâtre Royal de la Monnaie. Béjart remembers Huisman as a ''devil of a man,'' who, when he decided on a project, made it happen.[21] Huisman wanted to present ballet as an art form capable of appealing to young people, as well as attracting an international audience. To accomplish his goal, Huisman chose to present the ballet that had caused a ''revolution'' in Paris in 1913, *Le Sacre du printemps,* with choreography by Maurice Béjart.[22]

Béjart began work on *Le Sacre* by listening to the music from morning to night. He subsequently read the Stravinsky/Roerich libretto printed on the record jacket and decided that spring ''would have nothing to do with some ancient Russians.''[23] He tried instead to create a scenario that would convey what the idea of ''Spring'' meant to him. ''Spring is something very positive, very youthful and very strong,'' he observed.[24] He based his conception of the ballet on the presentation of the masculine and then the feminine side of the universe. ''It's rather like the Yin and the Yang; two complementary powers that are equal, yet different.'' Most importantly, Béjart decided not to end the ballet with the sacrificial death of the Chosen Virgin. Although, for him, the powers of life and death were inherent in *Le Sacre,* Béjart chose ''to put more emphasis on 'Eros'—the power of life—than 'Thanatos', the power of destruction and death.'' The focus of this *Le Sacre,* then, was to be ''the positive power [represented by] the reproduction of life.''[25]

First, the choreographer jettisoned the idea of an ancient tribal rite. ''When you try to make a reconstruction of primitivism,'' he explained, ''it always looks like those (Victorian) Gothic buildings which pretend to be '*moyen âge*' and then are just something false.'' Instead, he drew on the cycles of nature for his initial inspiration—the disappearance of the snow, ''the earth burned by the cold, harsh winter,'' and the tremendous force needed to bring the trees, the grass and the flowers to life once again. Béjart then transformed this poetic vision of the ''orgasm of nature'' into a universal human rite. "I planned the meeting of a man and a woman," he recalled, "then the act of love as a ritual; something religious, even something very violent."[26]

To highlight the ritual mating of the man and the woman, Béjart decided to use a full ensemble and have large groups of men and women. Like Nijinsky, Béjart also wanted to create a work of masses rather than of individual effects. He combined his own company, now called Le Ballet-Théâtre de Paris, with the dancers of the Théâtre de la Monnaie, and members of the English experimental company, Western Theatre Ballet, thus giving him a *corps de ballet* of more than forty dancers. *Le Sacre* offered Béjart the opportunity he needed to begin working with large groups of dancers.

With the images he wanted to evoke firmly in mind, Béjart again turned his attention to the Stravinsky score. In the choreography he tried to present a simple concept, "to just choreograph music and form and form and music." The dancers, he asserts, had no difficulty in coping with the score. "Now for the dancer, it's just like dancing *Coppélia*," he observed. "It's not difficult to count, to remember, or to feel the rhythms."[27]

At the time of *Le Sacre*'s creation, Béjart felt that his choreography and his use of music had been increasingly and consciously contemporary in sensibility. (*Orphée*, created in 1958, had a *musique concrète* score by Pierre Henry.) In the music of *Le Sacre* he recognized a classic. "It is so rich, so new, so amazing," he remarked, "and at the same time it is terribly simple. It is important when a work is both rich and simple; it is those attributes which make it a great classic." Consequently, Béjart decided to use simplicity as the key to his choreography. Rather than trying to interpret every note of the score, as Nijinsky intended, or to use complex counterpoint, as Massine had done, Béjart chose to "orchestrate" his movement to highlight the broad rhythmic phrases of the music.[28]

The choreographer began work on the second part of the ballet, the "feminine half" of his rite. His primary inspiration for the work's movement style was African dance. "African people concentrate on their contact with the earth," he explained, "and that's why they still have dance in their hearts and in their bodies. They dance *on* the earth, while Europeans try to dance 'in the air.'"[29] Béjart chose Tania Bari, with whom he had worked on *Orphée*, for the role of "She." Recalling a favorite phrase from his readings on ethnology—"I have a neolithic intelligence"—he created the opening tableau for the second part of *Le Sacre*. As Béjart describes it, Bari stands in the center of the stage, with her left arm along her body and her right hand hiding one eye. "The women lie around her, their arms and legs thrown wide apart, lifting their pelvises like buds that are about to open."[30]

Rehearsals did not go smoothly. The choreographer confesses that he was nervous, and the company was not "knit together" by any past endeavors. "I would arrive [for rehearsals] knowing better what I did not want than what I did," Béjart remembers. The choreographer felt it was necessary to prevent the dancers from expressing their personal feelings. He wanted them to have an animallike appearance, to push them beyond their own powers of endurance. In the ritual combat between the two male "tribes," Béjart demanded that the men fight "like savages" and not like "the knights of the Round Table . . . or Robert Taylor in *Ivanhoe*." He was determined to create images not of men, but of "thighs, fists, sudden throwing [movements] of heads."[31] Here, too, the choreographer's conception shows parallels to Nijinsky's attempts to abstract gesture and fragment the observer's perception of the human body.

It was crucial to Béjart's evocation of this union of the sexes that there be an equal number of men and women enacting this rite. In his finale for *Le Sacre*, he explained, "I needed couples because everyone makes love; to show the fundamental force that incites the race to reproduce."[32]

In keeping with the elemental nature of his theme, Béjart had the dancers costumed in tights and leotards; skin-toned for the women and earth tones of brown, green and yellow for the men. In the original 1959 production, the only decor was a monolithic totemlike sculpture, scenery that Béjart later decided was superfluous and discarded in subsequent revivals.

Béjart has said that in folk dancing "the real dancer is always the man."[33] Although he choreographed the "female" section of *Le Sacre* first, the ballet opens with an all-male hosanna. As the first chords of the music are heard, the dim stage light reveals a vast checkerboard of recumbent male bodies, their legs curled under their torsos and their arms splayed wide. Overhead spots illuminate several figures, who raise their upper bodies slowly, warily, expectantly. As they rise, one by one, to begin their ritual dances and games, the men become aware "of the life-blood coursing through their veins [and] of the power of their limbs."[34]

The men's movements are alternately gymnastically athletic and deliberately coarse, "primitive," even grotesque. Béjart uses signature motifs to convey an atavistic image of the male animal "*en rut*." They spring up and down on all fours, or, in a wide stance in second position *plié*, pulse convulsively, alternately lifting a leg to one side and then the other. The men's hands, too, take on a canine aspect, dangling like paws in front of their bodies. In other moments, Béjart shapes the men's arms and torsos to resemble predatory birds—eagles, falcons or hawks in search of prey. These aviary images are reinforced by the shuntlike hops which the men perform in fragmented patterns of circles and arcs, and in jagged lines.

The Male Ensemble in Maurice Béjart's *Le Sacre du printemps*
(*Photo © William Dupont*)

The spatial formations gradually become more formal, and the men begin to coalesce into long diagonal lines and files, large squares and concentric circles. Here, Béjart introduces a different stylistic inflection. The flexed feet, wide-open arms, and characteristic movements of the Russian *hopak* and *prissyatka*, appear, perhaps, as the choreographer's homage to the ballet's origins.

In a commentary on primitive man's "imitation" of animal movements and behavior, the "Games of the Rival Tribes" becomes a ritual of stylized combat. Jean-Claude Dienis describes the images evoked by the action as "aerial clashes, chest-to-chest," the combat of "fighting rams, horn to horn, or of stags, antler to antler."[35] The figure of the Chosen Man, "He," emerges from the conflict and performs a solo, using the "bird of prey" motifs: facing directly downstage, he establishes a wide second position *plié*, allowing his body to pulse with the music's accents. His arms, flexed winglike at the elbow, pump rhythmically like the movement of a bird in flight. He then opens his arms in a wide arc and circles his right leg around to the back to support his body, bringing it into sharp profile. Drawing his arms in sharply toward his hips and throwing back his head, the Chosen Man appears to be preening, glorying in the very physicality of his body.

The initiate is surrounded by the rest of the men, who sometimes echo or mirror his actions. This section has the ominous, mysterious quality of a ceremonial rite of passage. As the music builds to the climax of the first half of the ballet, "The Dance Overcoming the Earth," the atmosphere grows more violent. The men's movements become increasingly frenzied and percussive. They stamp and paw the ground with their feet, like bulls preparing to charge. Three members of the group capture the Chosen Man, kick him and tear at his hair. Suddenly, a shaft of amber light appears from the upstage right wing. The men cluster in the opposite downstage corner, seemingly mesmerized by the glow. Still banded together, they move cautiously toward the light and then retreat. Finally, to the last galvanic chords of music, the men, performing froglike jumps, leap offstage in an Indian-style single file line, in the direction of the gradually fading illumination. The Chosen Man, with "less power and physical strength than the rest," follows last, slithering and crawling like a reptile.[36] The stage is then blacked out.

The second half of the ballet begins, as Béjart has described it, with the Chosen Virgin, "She," standing alone with the community of women around her. They lie face upward, with their arms and legs splayed apart, hugging the ground. To the section of the music entitled "Pagan Night," the women gently release their legs, their arms and their pelvises, as though trying to nudge the sleeping earth to life.

"He" with the Male Ensemble in Maurice Béjart's *Le Sacre du printemps*
(Photo © *William Dupont*)

Béjart devised "The Mystic Circle of Virgins" as a lyrical contrast to the aggressive male rituals which precede it. The women's dance has a somnambulistic quality. There is an ever-present sense of submission and fatalism in the maidens' chains of circles, lines and processions. Their movements and gestures suggest introspection and fragility. Arms are held close to the body or folded across the torso; hands cradle and frame the face, bringing to mind the images that Nijinsky borrowed from Russian folk dance. This chorus of women is bound together both physically and spiritually. In one stiking moment, they form a single vertical file behind the Chosen Virgin, each woman extending her arms outward at shoulder level. To the elegiac eight-note melody of the "Mystic Circle," they first lean slowly to the right and then to the left, repeating the motif while kneeling and then with a leg extended to the side. Béjart uses this communal genuflection in a variety of rhythms and spatial patterns throughout the women's dances.

From the opening moments of the second section, it is clear that the Chosen Virgin has an unique status in the female group. The women kneel to her, softly stroke her arms and surround her in protective circles. "She" is distinguished from the group not only, as Dienis notes, because she dances alone. It appears that the Chosen Virgin has ascended to a plane of superior knowledge, and that she is entrusted with a special mission.[37] It is her actions in the dance of the maidens that define the spatial boundaries for the ritual; it is her movements that consecrate the ground for the rite. While the women stand passively in two files, "She" walks slowly between them, cleaving the air before her in a sweeping arc, first with one arm, then the other. As she does this, the maidens in her path fall away, lunging precipitously toward the earth.

Toward the end of "The Naming and Honoring of the Chosen One," the women have a last moment of quiet reflection. Béjart highlights their vulnerability by showing them relaxed and off-guard—standing, sitting and kneeling—before the strident chords herald the entrance of the men and the beginning of "The Evocation of the Ancestors." This is the first moment in the ballet when both the men and women are onstage together and Béjart effectively portrays the sexual tension which this confrontation initiates. The women huddle protectively around the Chosen Virgin while the men, linking arms at shoulder level, encircle them in two concentric chains, allowing no escape. To the throbbing beat of drums, each of the rings of men, moving in opposite directions, wheels around the hub formed by the females. "The Ritual of the Ancestors" has become, in accordance with Béjart's concept of *Le Sacre,* a dance metaphor for erotic foreplay in a mass fertility rite.

Unexpectedly, the Chosen Virgin rises from the center of this eddy of humanity. At her appearance, the women fall away and turn their backs,

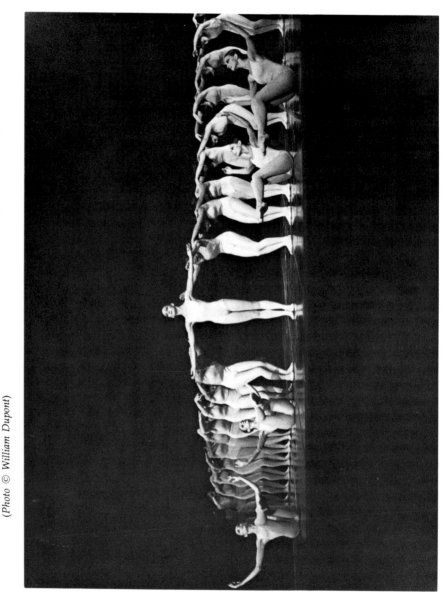

Tania Bari as "She" with the Female Ensemble in Maurice Béjart's *Le Sacre du printemps*
(Photo © William Dupont)

in concert with the men. Both groups peel away and gather in a semicircle on the ground behind the Chosen Virgin. "She" begins her solo to the "Danse sacrale," repeating her male counterpart's "bird of prey" movement. Her second motif, however, is different from the Chosen Man's. Rather than an opening of arms and body, she draws her legs together and squeezes her arms close to her body. With her open palms framing her hips, she still allows the steady rhythmic vibration to flow through her body. As she moves from her position center stage, she looks increasingly remote from her fellow celebrants, as though her movements had initiated a rite of transfiguration.

Béjart's solo for the Chosen Virgin is less strenuous and overtly dramatic than those created by Nijinsky and Massine. Fragile and resigned, "She" wraps her arms close around her body. Flexing her left leg at every joint, she executes a fitful kicking motif, hopping backwards in an erratic circuit around the stage. This is one of the same hieratic images that Béjart used in the "Mystic Circle" section, now magnified in solo performance. Many of the movements which Béjart devised for this "Danse sacrale" are remarkably simple and "unballetic." In one instance, the choreographer uses the classical *pas de chat* and has the Chosen Virgin perform it moving backwards, with her legs turned parallel instead of *en dehors.* Each jump is accompanied by a convulsive inward sweep of the arms which, coupled with a subtle contraction, draws attention to the Chosen Virgin's womb—and to her fears. Another hopping motif, which "She" executes squatting close to the earth, is simultaneously childlike and primal. By alternating these motifs with traditional steps from the ballet vocabulary, Béjart evocatively suggests a rite of passage from adolescence to womanhood.[38]

The final section of Béjart's *Le Sacre* is the completion of the mating ritual. When the chosen couple is brought together, "He" stalks his mate, slowly walking in a circle around her. The group then teases the two initiates—first pulling them apart, then pushing them towards one another—in a sexually charged game of "keep away." The final duet, watched by the entire tribe, is gymnastic and explicit. The Chosen Virgin slides over her partner's neck and shoulders, is pulled through his legs and wraps her thighs around his loins. At the moment of consummation, the stage becomes a hive of couples, repeating the strategic moments of the love duet. At times their movements recall the well-known steps of the jitterbug. They tug and grasp one another's limbs, emulating the rite of their chosen leaders. On the final chords of the score, "He" and "She" are lifted above the commune of bodies gathered *en masse* around them.

It is this final moment that provides the most powerful image in the ballet. A community of men and women come together in a "magic" circle—a *Reigen*—to regenerate mankind, and from this ring emerges, liter-

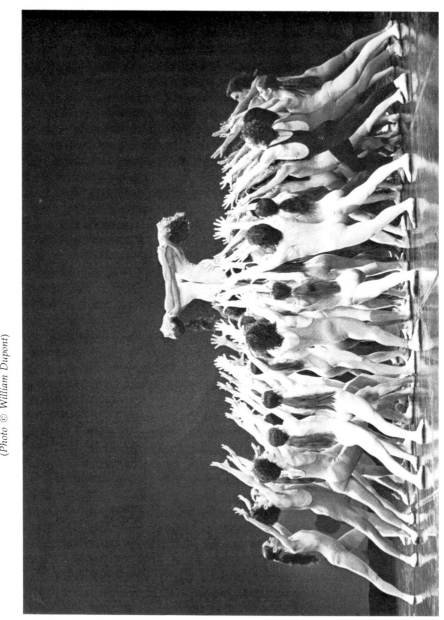

The Final Tableau of Maurice Béjart's *Le Sacre du printemps*
(Photo © William Dupont)

ally, the chosen couple. For Béjart, it was not death, but ''the renewal, the reconstruction of life'' that is the focus of his rite of spring.[39] Béjart's ritual does not attempt to depict a specific ''tribe,'' nor is it ''primitive'' in the antediluvian sense. As his programme notes reveal, the choreographer wanted to ''avoid folklore that is not universal and only retain the essential forces of mankind which are the same all over the world and throughout all periods of history.'' His *Le Sacre* focuses on spring as ''an immense primordial force which . . . bursts forth new life in all things.''[40]

This statement recalls Nijinsky's description of the ballet as ''the incarnation of Nature,'' as well as Stravinsky's remark that the music's ''Prelude'' should represent the awakening of nature. While Béjart's interest in Stravinsky has been mentioned, it is notable that the choreographer has long been fascinated by Nijinsky. From his youth, the character of Nijinsky greatly impressed the choreographer. ''When I was twenty, I thought about him a great deal and I was very touched and moved by him,'' he recalled.[41] In a 1972 interview, Béjart describes himself as ''a primitive. I am not a civilized man. Deep inside I am a savage.''[42] These statements, too, recall Nijinsky, who asserted that *his* inclinations were ''primitive.'' It is extraordinary that the first production of *Le Sacre*—its music, its choreographer and, increasingly, its mythology—so strongly influenced both the work and sensibility of a choreographer who had never seen *any* production of the ballet.

Béjart's production of *Le Sacre du printemps* was an immediate popular success, and has been a feature in the repertoire of the ''Ballet of the Twentieth Century'' for twenty-three years. The ballet's critical reception, however, was mixed, although a number of reviewers trace the phenomenon of ''pop dance'' to the premiere of Béjart's production.

When the Théâtre Royal de la Monnaie brought Béjart's *Le Sacre* to London in the summer of 1960, many English dance critics were skeptical, but some expressed frank admiration for a dance work that ''proved effective on its own terms.'' A. V. Coton decided that this new version showed a distinctly mid-twentieth-century view of primitiveness. ''With no clear race or place indicated the action celebrates the fact of Man then Woman, discovering movement and dance, and through these incentives discovering the raptures of sex,'' he wrote.[43] The *Times* critic felt that Béjart's work was not simply a new interpretation of the ballet, ''but a fresh conception altogether,'' and that the ballet might have been choreographed to another piece of music without loss of effect.[44] Oleg Kerensky feared that some people would be as shocked by Béjart's *Le Sacre* as audiences in 1913 had been by Nijinsky's. ''He [Béjart] depicts primitive men little better than savages, emerging from their animal state, engaging in brutal tribal fights, and greeting the spring by jumping lustfully upon their women.'' Kerensky concluded, however, that while this *Le Sacre* might not be what audiences were used to in terms of traditional ballet, it was a striking and original work that "nobody searching for excitement or novelty should miss."[45]

Clearly, it was this very novelty and lack of resemblance to "normal ballet" that bemused some observers. Clive Barnes saw the choreography as "a brilliantly monotonous selection of grotesque movements and erotic gestures," but found the ballet significantly less effective on subsequent viewings. He attributed this phenomenon of diminishing impact to the superficial sexuality that Béjart had made the focus of the ballet's theme. While Peter Williams found some of the movements interesting, he decided that "in spite of the fact that the choreography was very musical there seems something 'démodé' about these mass movement ballets."[46] The critic for the *Guardian* expressed the view that much of the ballet was "merely strenuous gymnastics rather than expressive dramatic art," an assessment with which many critics agreed.[47]

Two critics, however, could perceive a new trend in Béjart's depiction of the rebirth of human desire. A. V. Coton connected this *Le Sacre* with the emerging sensibility of the "pop culture" of the sixties. "Where pornography might have been feared," he wrote, "there was displayed a smooth woven pattern of writhings, falls, rolling and jerking, which spoke tellingly to a generation familiar with jive and other social dance developments." Not only did Coton see the influence of popular dance forms in Béjart's work, but he declared that "new notions of choreography are thick in the air around us."[48] Clive Barnes made an even more far-seeing prophesy. Noting that Béjart had a sincere desire to extend the frontiers of ballet, Barnes noted that the choreographer's "serious quest for immediacy, heightened drama and contact with contemporary life and art, may well be signposting the way others might follow."[49]

And follow they did. On 3 May 1962, as part of an eightieth-birthday tribute to Igor Stravinsky, Kenneth MacMillan presented his version of *The Rite of Spring*. The choreographer worked in close collaboration with Australian designer Sidney Nolan. Nolan felt that Stravinsky had written "the best dance music ever" for *Le Sacre*.[50] In the "primeval pulse" throbbing through the score, the designer found an affinity with his native Australia. As a result, both the costumes and sets of *The Rite* reflect a synthesis of images inspired by Stravinsky's score and Nolan's recollections of his native land.

Like Béjart, MacMillan and Nolan elected to present *The Rite of Spring* as an expression of "universal primitivism."[51] The dancers wore body-stockings in a variety of earthy brown, orange, red and yellow hues, as well as white face masks, an idea of MacMillan's, possibly inspired by African or Aboriginal ritual masks. This effect was intensified by painting the dancers' faces with colored greasepaint to "break the contours" and add to the remote effect engendered by the music.[52]

MacMillan chose to retain the concept of a sacrificial rite, and selected South African dancer Monica Mason to portray the Chosen Virgin. In an unconscious echo of Béjart's attraction to African dance, Mason recalled her ability to relate the feeling of her solo to her youthful memories of native African dances. "The feeling of contact with the earth, and the power and intensity of the rhythm," she said, "was very like the [African] rhythm of 'feet against the earth.'"[53] This theme of "the earth as the home of life" is a connecting thread that runs through the productions of *Le Sacre*— from the ancient Slavonic tribes in the Nijinsky and Massine versions to Horton's American Indians and the atavistic tribes in the Béjart and MacMillan productions.[54] As mythologist Joseph Campbell notes, "the idea of death-and-rebirth, [and] rebirth through ritual . . . is an extremely ancient one in the history of culture."[55] Béjart chose to focus his *Le Sacre* on the latter concept, thus reinforcing the status of the ballet as a seminal work.

Maurice Béjart's *Le Sacre du printemps* has remained one of the most popular and successful works in the repertoire of his Ballet of the Twentieth Century. During the "dance revolution" of the late 1960s and 1970s, a number of young "contemporary" choreographers—notably two Americans, John Neumeier and Glen Tetley—adapted Béjart's brand of dance eclecticism. The versions of *Le Sacre* produced by these two choreographers strongly reflect the influence of Béjart's more original, idiomatic concept. Paradoxically, the abundance of Béjart imitators, coupled with the choreographer's own later, more theatrically grandiose and ponderous ballets, has convinced many critics that *Le Sacre* was one of Béjart's finest works. Arlene Croce notes that the work was composed at a time when the choreographer "was still able to make a dance about ritual without turning dance itself into a ritual." while Anna Kisselgoff asserts that Béjart "never created a better ballet than his 'Rite,' one in which ideas and choreographer were well matched."[56]

The creation of Béjart's *Le Sacre* was not only an instance of well-matched choreography and ideas, it was an archetype for the nonnarrative, physically virtuosic, sensationally glossy ballets of the dance boom era. At a time when ballet was gaining increasing recognition, and increasing popularity, as an art, Béjart matched his glorification of "dance as rite"—young, athletic, technically accomplished dancers who are "celebrants of some mystical rite of perfection"—with the theatrical presentation of dance as ritual—the mass fertility drama he envisioned as the rite of spring.[57]

7

Movieola

Le Sacre du printemps was not performed as a ballet in the Soviet Union until 1965. While both *L'Oiseau de feu* and *Petrouchka* were produced in Russia in the early post-Revolutionary years, *Le Sacre* received only one performance on a concert program in 1926. Socialist realism was the aesthetic favored by political hierarchy and Stravinsky's works proved less than acceptable to its canons. Consequently, the composer's works disappeared from public performance. It was not until the reform of official attitudes after Stalin's death that Stravinsky's music was more favorably viewed in his native Russia.[1]

The cultural exchanges between the Soviet Union and the West in the late 1950s and early 1960s brought myriad new ideas to Russian audiences and artists, especially in the field of dance. American Ballet Theatre had performed in Russia in 1960, and the following year England's Royal Ballet made its first tour of the Soviet Union, presenting a production of Fokine's *L'Oiseau de feu*.[2] Konstantin Boyarsky, ballet master and choreographer for the Maly Opera, revived *Petrouchka* that same year, and produced both *L'Oiseau de feu* and Stravinsky's *Orpheus* in 1962.[3]

The resurgence of interest in Stravinsky in Russia coincided with the emergence of a new generation of Soviet choreographers, anxious to declare their artistic tenets. Two young members of the Bolshoi Ballet, Natalia Kasatkina and Vladimir Vasilyov, presented their conception of *Le Sacre du printemps* at the Bolshoi Theater on 28 June 1965. Although the choreographers devised a scenario somewhat different from the original—setting the ballet in "the second millenium B.C."—the look of the work was decidedly contemporary. The sets, by A. D. Goncharov, included rocklike flats and totem figures scattered about the stage, while the costumes were simple flowing tunics for the women and tights, tunics and soft boots for the men.[4] This *Le Sacre* bore little resemblance to the pagan rituals performed by the strange troglodytes of the Nijinsky–Stravinsky–Roerich ballet.

The impact of the choreographic styles of such masters as Balanchine, MacMillan and even Alvin Ailey, all of whose work had recently been seen in the Soviet Union, can be gauged by the critics' impressions of the ballet by the two fledgling choreographers. Hungarian ballerina Zsuzsa Kun wrote that Kasatkina and Vasilyov brought an entirely new style to this ballet, "departing from the classical rules and combining Russian character dance motives with what we call free dance movements." Kun noted that "free dance" meant the use of "almost every possible movement of the human body, including jumps, twisting and turns."[5]

When the Bolshoi Ballet brought its *Le Sacre* to the United States in April 1966, it was the ballet's libretto rather than its choreography that caused a controversy when the ballet was presented in New York.

For the purposes of their ritual drama, the choreographers provided the Chosen Virgin with a Shepherd lover. The Maiden is to be sacrificed to the hideous tribal god, Dazh-Bog. Before her lover's eyes, the Chosen One is murdered by the leader of the Wise Old Men and thrown on the sacerdotal fire. The enraged youth then plunges his dagger into the totem-like god for whom she was sacrificed. The tribe, horror-stricken, waits for retribution for his action, but nothing happens. Swift notes that this *Le Sacre*, as portrayed at the Bolshoi, "was a dramatic blow against religious superstition."[6] Among the American critics, Jack Anderson examined arguments pro and con in his discussion of the inclusion of a love interest. "Some viewers thought this added an unnecessarily sentimental touch to the otherwise grim conception. The ballet's defenders claimed that the changes were in keeping with the general theme and permitted increased audience identification with the protagonists."[7] Doris Hering found that the love interest "shifted the emphasis of the ballet from the ritualistic to the dramatic," a point which is important in the context of changing perceptions of narrative drama in dance.[8]

The emphasis of most versions of *Le Sacre* had been on the ritual aspect of the ballet, including the work of Horton, Wigman, MacMillan and Béjart. The Russian production, however, used an elaborate dramatic framework, proving once again the ballet's adaptable durability. In the 1960s and 1970s a production of *Le Sacre* became, in effect, a mark of originality, a badge of modernity; for many choreographers, *Le Sacre* became their personal manifesto.

Brian MacDonald choreographed a version for the Harkness Ballet in 1964 based on Shirley Jackson's short story, "The Lottery." Eric Walter, John Taras and John Neumeier devised productions of the ballet, à la Béjart, for the Deutsche Oper am Rhein in Düsseldorf (1970), La Scala, Milan (1972), and the Hamburg Ballet (1976), respectively. Glen Tetley's *Le Sacre*, first danced by the Bavarian State Opera Ballet in Munich in 1974, made the Chosen Maiden into the Chosen Man. Tetley's vision of the work concerned "the sacrifice of a . . . youth who is the incarnation of men's hopes and sins and sufferings. He is killed as a scapegoat, but is reborn with the spring and represents the hope and promise of a new life."[9] Like other choreographers, Tetley could not resist choreographing an erotic mass fertility rite for the work's climax. Marcia Siegel characterized Tetley's *Le Sacre* as "a locker room ballet." She found the choreography "violent; his bodies lash out and thrust in distorted shapes, knot together in agonized copulations, or stiffen in a rigor of ecstasy. His dance has no line, only mass. It has not rhythm, only the pounding of the blood."[10]

Modern dance choreographers also began experimenting with *Le Sacre.* Joyce Trisler, formerly a student and company member with the Lester Horton Dance Theatre, produced a *Rite of Spring* for her company in 1954. One of the most unusual and controversial versions of Stravinsky's masterwork was created by German avant-garde choreographer Pina Bausch. Bausch trained at the Essen Folkwangschule with Kurt Jooss and Lucas Hoving. She later came to the United States, and studied with Antony Tudor, José Limón and Paul Taylor, performing for a time with the Taylor company in the early 1960s. She became ballet mistress for the Wuppertal State Opera Dance Theatre in 1973, and staged *Le Sacre du printemps* for that company in 1975.

In 1980, choreographer Paul Taylor, the *"enfant terrible"* of American modern dance, created *Le Sacre du printemps (The Rehearsal)* for his company. The ballet, which critic Anna Kisselgoff termed an *"anti-Sacre,"* is a three-tiered rite.[11] It is a mystical marriage of Nijinsky's evocation of ancient Slavonic rituals, a grotesque cartoon of a "Runyonesque gumshoe story" and the daily drama hidden beneath the routine of a dance company's ritual of daily rehearsal.[12] Ever practical, Taylor decided to use Stravinsky's four-hand piano arrangement of the score because it was in the public domain, more portable, more affordable and he could "hear the rhythms better."[13] The final product of Taylor's efforts is a *Rite* that is a complex saga of good guys versus bad guys, of the needs of the individual struggling against the power of the group; a tale of greed, duplicity and personal sacrifice twisting and turning through the work like a malignant growth.

As Arlene Croce suggests, Taylor's version is a *Rite* "without ceremony," but it is as graphic a depiction of the power of ugliness as Nijinsky's primitive "biological" ballet.[14] Taylor's *Rite* speaks to some of the choreographer's favorite themes—the celebration of the crippled, cruel strength inherent in the human condition and the depiction of evil as a mordant agent in society. With an alchemist's recondite skill, he has concocted a detective yarn, based in the 1930s, combining the improbable elements of cinema, melodrama, vaudeville, ritual and dance. The choreographer insists, however, that he was not trying to satirize the original *Le Sacre*. Instead, he simply did what he thought was logical. While his *Rite* may seem unintelligible or odd to some, Taylor declares that "to me it makes perfect sense."[15]

The prehistory of Paul Taylor's *The Rite of Spring (The Rehearsal)* is as multifaceted and complex as the choreographer's own career. Taylor discovered dance in college, comparatively late in life. He was an art major at Syracuse University, where the art department "was teaching everybody to paint like Matisse."[16] His interest in movement was reinforced by an aptitude for swimming, for which he was awarded a scholarship. Dissatisfied with his painting, he began to attend dance concerts and realized that he was making comparisons between painting and dance. While painting created an illusion through the use of color, depth and space, Taylor discovered he preferred to experiment with "real space, real bodies, real movement. I saw more dance and that seemed much closer to meeting my needs. That's how I got into dance."[17] His fascination with images and movements in two dimensions is a constant in his choreographic invention and a key ingredient in a number of his works, including *The Rite of Spring (The Rehearsal)*.

While at Syracuse, Taylor saw performances of the Ballet Russe de Monte Carlo, which prompted him to explore the college library's collection of dance books. He was particularly impressed with photographs of Nijinsky and Martha Graham. In quick succession, Taylor took a crash course in Graham technique from Ethel Butler, won a scholarship to the American Dance Festival at Connecticut College in the summer of 1952, and another to Juilliard the following autumn. After a year, he decided to study at the Graham school full-time and, by 1955, was a member of her company. During that period, Taylor continued to pursue his own vision of dance, studying and performing with Merce Cunningham, taking ballet class at the Metropolitan Opera school, and becoming involved with a group of young dance "experimentalists." Although he created a number of important leading roles while in the Graham company, including Tiresias in *Night Journey* and Aegisthus in *Clytemnestra*, Taylor also began to choreograph his own pieces, working with a "fly-by-night" group of dancers whenever his schedule allowed.[18]

Robert Coe has observed that the choreographer's "earliest dances were fantasies impenetrable to the uninitiated." Taylor's friend and collaborator, artist Robert Rauschenberg, remembers that "you didn't know whether to laugh or cry."[19] Controversial from the outset, one of Taylor's early works included the weirdly eccentric *Four Epitaphs* (now *Three Epitaphs* and still in the Taylor company repertoire) with costumes by Rauschenberg and a score of traditional brass band music of the sort once played at funerals in New Orleans. Rauschenberg termed the piece "either the funniest or the saddest thing you had ever seen."[20] Taylor's ability to mix pathos with humor, to leaven even the most grotesque and macabre themes with unexpected wit, remains a hallmark of his work.

While developing his own dance style and movement theories, Taylor had the opportunity to work with a stellar group of American choreographers—Charles Weidman, Doris Humphrey, Anna Sokolow and James Waring—and even appeared in a Broadway production of *Peter Pan,* with choreography by Jerome Robbins. In 1959, George Balanchine and Martha Graham collaborated on a new ballet entitled *Episodes,* a two-part work with music by Anton von Webern. Graham's half of the evening was a dance-drama about Mary Queen of Scots, with New York City Ballet dancer Sallie Wilson; Balanchine's contribution was an abstract ballet with a solo for Taylor, in which the dancer's convoluted athleticism made him resemble, in Balanchine's words, "a fly caught in a glass of milk." Indeed, Lincoln Kirstein's nickname for Taylor was "the Geek."[21]

By 1962, although he was still dancing "mythic roles in the psychodramas of Martha Graham," Taylor realized that his own choreography was his priority.[22] He had also come to believe that even abstraction couldn't obviate feeling. In 1962, Taylor created *Aureole,* a dance of "old-fashioned lyricism and white costumes," to music by Handel. The piece was well received by the critics, and Taylor left the Graham company to form his own permanent dance group.[23]

The following year, Taylor created a work that was, indirectly, an indication of his preoccupation with *Le Sacre du printemps.* If *Aureole* was representative of the choreographer's developing neoclassic sensibility, *Scudorama* was an early entry in his lexicon of darker pieces. The choreographer was assailed by images of "distress, signals, shrouds and thrashings, a ghastly pile of Grünewald remains, a duet between a corpse and its carrier."[24] Marcia Siegel saw the "strong, distorted movement" as evocative of "empty relationships and shocking images. . . . [T]he dance gave the impression of the futility and isolation of modern life that was at once realistic and abstract."[25]

What is most remarkable about the piece, in terms of Taylor's later creation of *The Rite,* is the fact that he choreographed *Scudorama* to a recording of *Le Sacre du printemps.* Although the piece was actually performed to "railway music," an electronic score by C. Jackson, Stravinsky's music had inspired Taylor to create movement that Siegel describes as "percussive contractions and rotations of the upper torso against the lower, arms and legs flailing in dissonant shapes, energies that shoot out from the center as if they would tear the body apart."[26] Siegel's account of *Scudorama* bears a striking similarity to a section of Rivière's analysis of Nijinsky's *Le Sacre,* in which the critic speaks of the choreographer's use of "bizarre and violated forms." Nijinsky, Rivière says, made his dancers perform "impossible movements and seemingly deformed poses," twisted their bodies as if he would "break them if he dared," working them with "unpitying brutality as if they were things."[27] Thus, the power of the impacted images exerted by Stravinsky's music on movement is clearly demonstrated in Taylor's experiment with *Scudorama*.

A number of Taylor's works are basically dance commentaries, eccentric polemics on mores and communal behavior, glimpses of "the kinds of formalized activity—ritual, myth, art and theater—that can be produced by generically specialized people."[28] These dance fantasies are often combined with references to American popular culture—sometimes gleeful, sometimes dire, and often irreverent. *Big Bertha* (1971), for example, stars an anthropomorphic harridan of a nickelodeon who wreaks havoc on a typically American nuclear family of father, mother and daughter. In *American Genesis* (1974), Taylor created a pageantlike full evening's work, using the fables of Creation, the Fall and the Flood, and presenting them as a parable of American folk history—Noah, for example, is portrayed as a Mississippi riverboat captain. The spectrum of Taylor's creative imagination runs the gamut of social and popular culture; from sports (*Sports and Follies*) to fairy tales (*Snow White*) to social customs (*Cloven Kingdom*). Part of Taylor's fascination with such themes is their link to ceremony and ritual. While a number of his works are bound up with some mysterious and eccentric form of communal activity (the "Black Mass" section of *Churchyard*, for example), it is *Runes* that is most clearly the ancestor of *The Rite*.

Created in 1979, *Runes* is an ensemble work performed to a percussive piano score by American composer Gerald Busby. It is a mystical, haunting work, filled with hallucinatory images. A man and a woman appear to merge to create one human form, bodies seem to grow out of one another and replace each other in a ceremonial "death." One senses that the choreographer has dropped a plumb line to an atavistic root of the collective unconscious; every aspect of the piece, from the dancers' spare, fur-trimmed costumes to the nocturnal moonlight set, places the audience in a mysterious, primeval realm.

Elizabeth Kendall felt that *Runes* elicited "a race memory—and it satisfies our deep hunger to know and re-experience our tribal beginnings."[29] Taylor's ability to transform his troupe into a tribe of dancers, "as if they belong to some community with a history and a local patois," is most strongly evident in *Runes*.[30] Nijinsky's *Le Sacre* and Taylor's *Runes* share a number of concepts, both in terms of movement characteristics and theme. Both choreographers were intrigued with the deliberate reordering of perception of the human body, and both works center on the idea of a mystical ritual of birth, death and rebirth. But it is the aura of fraternity, the sense of an arcane society performing a perpetual enigmatic rite, that Taylor would bring to his version of *Le Sacre*.

Taylor began to consider the possibility of choreographing a production of *Le Sacre* in 1979. He had been commissioned to premiere a piece for the American Dance Festival that summer and had begun work on the movement style he intended to use in the ballet. He was unable to complete *The Rite* in time and a shorter work, *Profiles*, was the result. Taylor has called the ballet an experiment in working in two dimensions.[31] *Profiles* is an abstract chamber piece, a quartet of two women and two men. Kendall describes its atmosphere as "dense and gloomy" and describes the movement as "stark, taut motions, bodies in profile with heads thrown back, bodies held up in swastika shape."[32] The dancers are dressed in all-over body tights, covered with an almost pointillist dot design. The effect is of a moving frieze.

Ruth Andrien, a member of the original cast, recalls that dancing *Profiles* "was like performing a ten minute pushup. It was all the movement [we were working on] for *Le Sacre*, but in a different context."[33] Danced to an original score by Jan Radznski, *Profiles* is the link between *Runes* and *The Rite of Spring (The Rehearsal)*; it is Taylor's formalist essay on his own technique of "stylized gesture." The torsion of the body—its confinement in a two-dimensional form—is the governing principle of *Profiles*. This basic profiled body posture, with its reverberations from Nijinsky's *Faune*, is a recurrent motif in Taylor's choreographic canon. The choreographer has said that "we as American contemporary dancers owe a great deal to Nijinsky, and I'd like to see that acknowledgement made."[34] With his production of *Le Sacre*, Taylor pays homage to his revolutionary predecessor.

The Taylor *Rite* is not about vernal equinox, the fertility rites of ancient tribes, or ritual sacrifice—at least not overtly. Rather than depicting a primeval society, Taylor has contrived a more contemporary theme for a work that he terms an "exercise in style." The choreographer has a great interest in the original production, and has read about and studied pictures of the Nijinsky version.[35] Ruth Andrien, who created the role of the Girl in Taylor's *Rite*, recalls that "when we started work on *The Rite*, we were never allowed to come out of the two-dimensional plane. We were very uncomfortable and Paul was very uncomfortable, but I think he was determined to have that frame of reference. I think he was very touched by that idea and by the pictures [of the Nijinsky production] that showed the boundness [of the movement]." Andrien feels that Taylor's insistence on the flat, two-dimensional style of movement helped to give the ballet a three-dimensional impact.

Andrien also asserts that, in rehearsal, Taylor "doesn't do a lot of talking, but he does enough to give you what he needs to give you." When he worked on *The Rite*, his primary exhortation was, "commit yourself to the twist," a reference to the profile body posture he demanded. Although

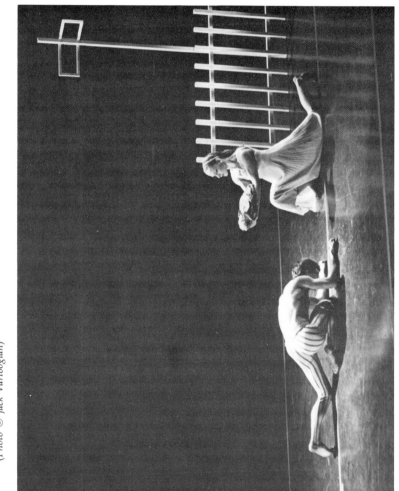

Christopher Gillis and Ruth Andrien in Paul Taylor' *The Rite of Spring (The Rehearsal)*
(Photo © *Jack Vartoogian*)

working on *The Rite* made the Taylor company feel unified, the physical strain of the piece told on the performers. ''The dancers just want to throw up before that dance,'' says Andrien, ''but they really come together over it too.''[36]

In his *The Rite of Spring (The Rehearsal)*, Taylor presents his troupe first as a ''tribe of dancers'' in rehearsal and then assigns them specific roles in a modern allegory. In the Taylor version, a bizarre detective yarn, ca. 1930, the basic plot is of a ballet in rehearsal. ''There are numerous correlations between what happens in the 'rehearsal' and the private-eye plot,'' he notes. ''Some of it has to do with the use of mirrors and mirror images . . . and at the end, mirrors descend in a way that may remind people of a dance studio.''[37]

The emphasis on stylization in Taylor's reductionist *Rite* extends to every aspect of the production. The libretto of the work is a vintage cops and robbers tale, with allusions to the Chinatown atmosphere of Hollywood's popular Charlie Chan films. The dancers in rehearsal double as the cast of characters—a gangster, his oriental mistress, his stooge and various henchmen, floozies, policeman, an innocent young girl, a private eye and a baby. The minimal settings by John Rawlings suggest rather than depict changes of place. A few vertical bars indicate a jail cell, while a bench and a picket fence evoke a park.

As the ballet begins, a dance company is going through the daily ritual of warming up; exercising their limbs, flexing their individual and collective muscle. Presiding over the proceedings is the Ballet Mistress, dressed in a somber gray and black Cossack outfit, complete with boots and a tall black Astrakhan hat. A ladder provides a physical support for some of the troupe—this often used backstage *barre* becomes an onstage prop. Seated atop the ladder is a woman, posed à la Rodin's *Thinker*. She is the sultry Mistress of the story. Wearing a short, shiny dark sheath, she stares ahead, impassive and bored. Meanwhile, a tender duet is playing out downstage. The young Private Eye and his Girl coo over a baby wrapped in a red blanket. The bright scarlet of the blanket is one of the few patches of color in the white-gray-black spectrum of costumes and props. Its color is arresting and ominous. One can already smell the blood.

The rehearsal progresses and the scene shifts to a bar—the *barre*/ladder hung with a large sign—where two Maidens and their escorts are whooping it up. The courting rituals of the two couples are observed by the Mistress and her smarmy Gangster protector. After the Private Eye and the Girl, carrying the child, enter the bar, the Gangster and his Mistress launch into a violent, seething Apache dance. Their gestures are vituperative and combative, with manic ferris wheel lifts, and tense, stalking evasions and pursuits. This is an antagonistic love-rite of two experienced adversaries. They are tough and street-smart, like Barbara Stanwyck and

Christopher Gillis and Ruth Andrien as the Private Eye and the Girl in Paul Taylor's *The Rite of Spring (The Rehearsal)*
(Photo © *Jack Vartoogian*)

The ''Bar'' Scene in Paul Taylor's *The Rite of Spring* (*The Rehearsal*)
(*Photo* © *Jack Vartoogian*)

George Raft in a 1930s potboiler. A minor altercation erupts in the bar and the two "escorts" take on the roles of policemen and drag off the Private Eye, as well as their former "dates," now presumably "informants." The Mistress takes advantage of the melee and kidnaps the baby. As in the Nijinsky version, the "Games of the Rival Clans" have been played out and the "Mock Abduction" has taken place. The stage has been set for the sacrifice.

The Mistress brings the baby to her "hideout" and stashes it in a hole under her dressing table. As she sits down to "fix her face," she confronts not her own image but that of the Ballet Mistress. In an eerie *Döppelganger* sequence, the two women mirror one another's every move and gesture. Ballet Mistress, Gangster's Mistress—they are both subject to another power, an overwhelming force which they cannot quite understand. Dance is as jealous a mistress as the Gangster is a master.

The Gangster returns from a successful jewel heist, carried in atop a human pyramid of his "henchman" like a returning warrior. He showers his Mistress with the shiny tributes of his latest conquest, but she rejects the gems and fondles the child instead of her man. Incensed, the Gangster grabs her, and another torrid duet ensues. Although the movements are essentially the same as in their earlier dance, this pairing has an added dimension of struggle and conflict. Now the lifts explode like expletives. The Gordian knot of their relationship emerges in an intricate web of precarious maneuvers: a declivitive fall caught at the penultimate moment, slow-motion sparring that ends in a reluctant embrace. The dancers never fully free themselves from one another's support. The two "bar couples" suddenly appear to rehearse the Gangster-Mistress duet with the star couple. The fantasy world of the detective yarn and the workaday reality of the dancers' regime seem momentarily to come together. The effect is cinematic, as though the stage had been turned into a triptych-split screen.

Suddenly, the Ballet Mistress is carried onstage on the shoulders of the dancers; a mirror image of the Gangster-henchmen motif. From the same red bag that held the Gangster's booty, she doles out money to the dancers. Is it loot, rehearsal pay or blood money? Or a little of all three?

In the next scene, the Private Eye, stuck behind prison bars, is thinking of his girl. We see his dream as a love duet which, in contrast to that of the Gangster and his Mistress, is softer and more lyrical. The Private Eye is gentle and consoling. Each time he lifts the Girl, she curls her legs and flexes her feet, like a weary child cradled by loving arms. The two dancers hardly look at each other, but a sense of loss and desperation is revealed in achingly sustained poses and in their remote emptiness in moments of stillness.

When the dream duet ends, the Private Eye breaks out of prison, determined to rescue the child. He returns the baby to the Girl, and the three enjoy a moment's respite on the park bench. The Gangster's *âme damnée*, who has been charged by his master to do away with the child, stalks the trio, rehearsing his death-thrusts with ritualistic precision.

Here Taylor momentarily and unexpectedly interrupts the action. The Ballet Mistress appears with three "Graces"—a trio of female dancers carrying a garland of flowers. They dance in a somewhat ironically flavored balletic style, encircling the Ballet Mistress, who acknowledges their labors with a gracious *port de bras*. Perhaps this is the choreographer's wry hommage to Diaghilev, Nijinsky and the legend of the Ballets Russes.

Now the ballet's plot resumes and becomes even more twisted. It is concerned with revenge, retribution and sacrifice. The Private Eye rescues the child, but he will pay the price. The Gangster plots with his Stooge to murder his Mistress. Although the Stooge is designated to execute the dirty deed, both Master and Mignon will meet final retribution. The Mistress must die for yielding to maternal instincts—for betrayal in the eyes of her lover. She has stepped outside the bounds of her role, and by breaking the stereotyped two-dimensional structure of this grotesque community, she has created a fundamental imbalance.

The Private Eye's act of mortal courage, love and sacrifice in returning the child to its mother restores equilibrium. The child too is killed, a death of purity and innocence. Only the Girl remains to mourn, to remember, to renew. She vents her emotions in a dance of electrifying frenzy. Her solo is a vision of grief and horror. Like the wail of a mourning mother, the movements pour out in a paroxysm of despair. The Girl is joined in the last moments by the rest of the dancers. Under the implacable gaze of the Ballet Mistress, the ballet closes as it begins—with the perpetual rehearsal.

Taylor has said that he hoped his *Rite* would have some cross reference to the Nijinsky production, especially in the flat, two-dimensional use of the body.[38] He has chosen to have the upper and lower parts of the body torqued in opposition, increasing the feeling of mechanical tension and superhuman control—or subhuman perversion. Nijinsky's use of body weight as a positive implosion into gravity underlined the affinity of a primal society with the rocks, trees and inanimate objects of the earth. One of the hallmarks of Taylor's choreographic style, however, is its light and buoyant quality. In his *Rite,* the absence of an emphatic use of weight gives a remote, cinematic gloss to the movement. Ruth Andrien recalls that Taylor was particularly concerned with the moments of stillness in the duet between the Private Eye and the Girl. "That whole section is done very much on the pattern of 'move,' 'stop,' syncopation and silence. It was like an aside, a whisper."[39]

In contrast to the elegiac duet, the Girl's solo, to the music for the "Danse sacrale," is a "delirium of precision."[40] The dance is less bound and more fluid than the movement in the rest of the ballet; "it's more like

Christopher Gillis, Ruth Andrien, Elie Chaib and Lila York in Paul Taylor's *The Rite of Spring (The Rehearsal)*
(Photo © Jack Vartoogian)

a human being," in Andrien's words. As a dancer, Andrien found that the problem of matching the music's inexorable rhythms with Taylor's choreographic demands was one of the solo's greatest challenges. "In order not to race on with the passion of the music, the movement must constantly pull itself back, rein in, to the body. I think it's that double pull that gives [the dance] the [sense] of frustration and, somehow, the emotional feeling that it has. The movement doesn't just release and it doesn't hold in, but it fights back and forth between those two things."

When Taylor selected her to portray his Girl cum Chosen Maiden, Andrien was immediately aware of the weight of her responsibility. "I already felt there was all this history attached to the idea of being a character like that. Although Paul didn't ever put any pressure on me, he always believed that I was going to be able to achieve whatever he wanted." Andrien believes that Taylor chose her for the role because of her strength and her quality of vulnerability. Her powers of physical endurance were especially crucial. "The first and middle parts [of the solo] were the sections where I had to push through it, and, finally, when I got to the end, sheer will power would take over. When I got that far, I knew, somehow, that I could make it."

Like many of her predecessors, Andrien had a sense of foreboding about the "Danse sacrale." "Every night I would think 'this is a dance of *death*,'" she recalls, "and I felt like I was really going to die. If I were really to do it, do it the way it should be done, I should never be able to do it again."[41] She believes that in creating the "Dance of the Chosen Virgin" for her, Taylor was making a very personal statement. "It was the sort of solo he might have wanted to dance himself," she observes. But Andrien thought of her performance as an offering, something special she could do both for herself and for her choreographer. "It wasn't too much to ask."[42]

The critical reception of Taylor's *The Rite of Spring (The Rehearsal)* was enthusiastic. Alan M. Kriegsman called the ballet "deliciously berserk," noting that the choreographer divined "heretofore invisible qualities" in the Stravinsky score.[43] Arlene Croce felt that the element that made Taylor's *Rite* a comedy was the music. "Taylor isn't funny at the music's expense; he works with the music and is twice as funny in his straight-faced way as a consciously irreverent parodist would have been," she observed. When the choreographer reaches the climax of the "Dance of the Chosen Maiden," Croce noted that the audience is suddenly reminded of the ballet's historical connections.[44] Anna Kisselgoff observed that "the savagery of the mother's solo . . . comes as a shock after the light-hearted spoofing until this point. And yet the mother's choreography is so broken up into separate movements and so controlled that its stylization prevents the kind of Romantic deluge that would drown everything in sentimentality."[45]

The Ritualistic "Murders" in Paul Taylor's *The Rite of Spring (The Rehearsal)*
(Photo © Jack Vartoogian)

Many critics commented on Taylor's stylization of movement and its allusions, not only to his own earlier work, but to Nijinsky's. Croce saw the dancers' "blunt, thick bodies" as "dense with impacted energy." By condensing and restricting the body's range of movement, the observer's attention was concentrated on the body's core. "As with all theories of polar opposition," she noted, "this anti-classicism makes a classical statement—it gives us the irreducible essence of expression."[46]

Taylor's bold silhouettes, combined with his economical, schematic, almost cinematic movement sequences, give the choreographer's images a larger-than-life impact. By borrowing elements from the tradition of popular melodrama, Grade B Hollywood movies (many of which took their motifs from that source), and comic strip characterizations, Taylor freed *Le Sacre* from its historical context. Although the mythology of the Nijinsky production permeates this *Rite*, Taylor has created a uniquely American artifact; a work that belongs as much to our American dance heritage and cultural sensibility as Nijinsky's arcane rites belonged to his.

Finally, however, Taylor's *Rite* is double-edged. Nijinsky created an ancient ritual in which a chosen virgin danced herself "out of humanity" under the impassive gaze of her ancestral clan.[47] The ritual murders which Taylor depicts are more numerous, calculated and chilling. The "good guys" face the "bad guys" and slowly and deliberately, one by one, each plunges a knife (visible or imaginary) into an adversary. The baby, held in the Girl's protective embrace, is stabbed last, in a final jolting moment, by the poor little Stooge.

The violence of primitive man had a practical motive or a ritualistic significance. Taylor seems to be saying that the drive to destruction of modern man is more terrifying in its indiscriminate victimization of innocent and guilty alike. The purposeful carnage of the choreographer's methodical murders presents a disconcerting perspective on the larger society outside the closed communal world of the dancer, the company and the theater. The audience sees that, when the rehearsal of the detective story is complete, the dancers resume the daily ritual of their classes. Their images are reflected in the mirrors and their efforts are criticized or applauded by their ballet mistress. Taylor himself has described his dance troupe as "a society in miniature, and we are both victim and product of our stage habitat. We dwell in a house that demands that clamor be transformed into music, heated gestures into steps, dreams into choreographic fact, and offstage chaos into onstage order."[48] It is a unique community, united by individual effort, mutual support and a common goal. Here, there is a kind of sanity after all, a sense of order, a view of life. That is, if we trust the teller, and not the tale.

8

Pictures of Pagan Russia

When choreographer Richard Alston asked Dame Marie Rambert to watch one of the first rehearsals for his *Rite of Spring*, Rambert confessed that she was "really very nervous."[1] Nearly seventy years after her close collaboration with Vaslav Nijinsky on the original *Le Sacre*, Rambert was again "present at the creation." In the long gap between these two landmarks in her life, Rambert had become a national monument in British ballet.

Rambert remained as a member of the Diaghilev Ballets Russes until the outbreak of World War I when, after a brief hiatus in Paris, she moved to London. There she met and married British playwright and producer Ashley Dukes in 1918. Rambert soon settled down in her adopted country, teaching not only in her own studio in Bedford Gardens, but at a number of ballet schools in and around London. She had studied with the great Italian ballet master Enrico Cecchetti while with the Diaghilev company and she now transmitted her knowledge of and enthusiasm for the classical *danse d'école* to her students, who soon included Diana Gould, Andrée Howard, Antony Tudor, William Chappell, Maude Lloyd, Walter Gore and Frederick Ashton.

In 1927, Ashley Dukes purchased a church hall in Ladbroke Grove, eventually transforming the building into the Mercury Theatre. The Mercury became a hothouse for the first ventures of Rambert's fledgling ballet troupe. The Marie Rambert Dancers gave short seasons at the Lyric Theatre in Hammersmith in 1930, and by 1931 Rambert and her husband had founded the Ballet Club. Their seasons, made up of Thursday and Sunday evening performances and the odd matinee, are legendary. The list of subscribers read like a *Who's Who*: Anthony Asquith, Arthur Bliss, Lady Cunard, Diana Cooper, Jacob Epstein and Charles B. Cochran represent only a few of the 1,700 who subscribed. The ballets, like the ambience of the Mercury Theatre itself, reflected the taste, sophistication and elegance that were the hallmarks of the Ballet Club.

Rambert had a special gift for spotting and developing choreographic talent in her students. Ashton, Howard, Tudor and Gore all learned and honed their craft on the tiny stage of the Mercury. Early masterpieces of British ballet, such as Ashton's *Les Masques* (1933) and *Mephisto Waltz* (1934), Tudor's *Jardin aux lilas* (1936) and *Dark Elegies* (1937), and Howard's *Lady into Fox* (1939) were all created for the Ballet Club. But Rambert's relationships with her choreographers were sometimes adversarial. Consequently, as David Vaughan notes, "no one seemed to stay with Rambert for long—the pay was ridiculous, two shillings and sixpence per performance and a pound a minute for choreography, and there were always fights."[2] Sir Frederick Ashton recalls that his mentor's tremendous energy was both inspiring and irritating, and Rambert herself once remarked "I need movement always, but calm didn't interest me in any way."[3]

World War II brought an end to the Ballet Club, and the newly reorganized company, now known as Ballet Rambert, gave "Lunch," "Tea" and "Sherry" ballet performances at the Arts Theatre during the first winter of the London blitz. An Equity dispute over low salaries for the dancers forced a disbanding of the company between September 1941 and March 1943. With the financial assistance of CEMA (Council for the Encouragement of Music and the Arts, now the Arts Council of Great Britain), Ballet Rambert again regrouped, touring hostels, service camps and munitions factories, as well as performing for audiences in London and throughout the provinces for the duration of the war.[4]

Over the next two decades, from 1946 to 1966, Ballet Rambert successfully weathered a series of fiscal and artistic problems. However, instead of remaining "a small, experimental company that could perform an essential function in British ballet," Ballet Rambert grew rapidly and was forced to compete with the larger, more conventionally established Royal Ballet for choreographers, dancers and audiences. Clearly, a change of direction was needed.[5]

In 1966, Rambert reorganized the company, sharing its directorship with her senior choreographer, Norman Morrice. Morrice had visited the United States in the early 1960s and was impressed by what he saw of American modern dance. Rather than continue on course producing classical ballet, Morrice and Rambert developed a plan that really proved to be a return to the company's original concept: a choreographers' company that would create its own repertoire. Under Morrice's direction, Ballet Rambert altered course, becoming a small company of soloists who could perform both classical and modern dance styles. New works were commissioned and a generation of choreographers "once again began to emerge from within the company itself."[6] Morrice resigned as director in 1974 and was succeeded by John Chesworth and Christopher Bruce as artistic director and associate director, respectively. In 1986, after five years as resident choreographer, Richard Alston was appointed to direct Ballet Rambert.

While Ballet Rambert was undergoing a renaissance in 1966, British dance enthusiast and patron Robin Howard was establishing the Contemporary Dance Trust. Howard had been impressed by the Martha Graham Dance Company when it first performed in London in 1963 and subsequently financed and organized an exchange program in which British dancers went to New York to study at the Graham school and Graham Company members came to London to teach the famous choreographer's technique. The classes—and the project—soon mushroomed and by 1970 the London Contemporary Dance Theatre was a full-scale part of British dance. A school was opened at The Place on Duke's Road, where dancers could study with such teachers as Jane Dudley, Mary Hinkson and Robert Cohan, the artistic director of the company. One of the school's first students was Richard Alston.[7]

Alston, like Frederick Ashton, is a "public school boy," who attended Eton College before becoming a student at the Croyden College of Art. When, out of curiosity, he went to a summer of performances by the Bolshoi and Royal Ballet in London, including Ashton's *La Fille mal gardée,* Alston decided he wanted "to make something like that."[8] He then saw the Graham and Merce Cunningham companies, which gave him a new sense of direction. Alston now decided that he wanted to "make dance" and sent his application to The Place, where he became one of the school's first twelve students. The intimate, experimental structure of the school allowed Alston to develop his nascent choreographic ideas in a workshop atmosphere.

In 1972, he received one of the first Dance Awards from the Calouste Gulbenkian Foundation to form a small company, a group of dancers/choreographers known as Strider. The enterprise lasted for three years, a time Alston refers to as his "sorting-out period." In order to revitalize his creative energies, Alston next decided to study in New York, feeling there were "things happening in the States" that would stimulate his choreographic ideas. He took classes at the Merce Cunningham studio and, during his two-year stay, presented *UnAmerican Activities,* an amalgamation of works he had created in England.[9]

During his stay in America, Alston was able to see the work of George Balanchine, as well as choreographers such as Tricia Brown, Lucinda Childs and Steve Paxton. "Then of course," he remarks, "there was such a wide range of teaching that one could find the information that was absolutely relevant to oneself: they taught me about my own attitude to dancing and what I had unconsciously been working at for the eight years before I went there."[10]

On his return to England, Alston worked as a free-lance choreographer, creating ballets for London Contemporary Dance Theatre and other companies. Soon the hallmarks of his distinctive style began to emerge. In ballets such as *Soft Verges* (1974), *Blue Schubert Fragments* (1974), *Doublework* (1978) and *The Field of Mustard* (1980), he has combined the finesse and clarity characteristic of Cunningham technique with his own architectural sense of how to design space through movement. The seemingly inevitable quality of his musicality—Arlene Croce has said that Alston "can hear sound as shape"—and his sense of line place him in the lyrical-dramatic tradition of English ballet.[11] What makes Alston's style unique is his ability to allow the formalist precepts of classical ballet to filter through his eclectic modern dance sensibility.

The Rite of Spring: Pictures of Pagan Russia was one of Alston's first creations for Ballet Rambert, premiering on 6 March 1981 at the Sadler's Wells Theatre. The idea of choreographing the ballet had first occurred to Alston when he saw the Royal Ballet's revival of Bronislava Nijinska's *Les Noces*. Stravinsky began composing this moving dance cantata based on the subject of a Russian peasant wedding in the late summer or autumn of 1914. Because of problems with instrumentation, however, the final score was not orchestrated until 1923, the year in which the Diaghilev Ballets Russes first performed the ballet.[12] Alston was "completely bowled over" by *Les Noces* and was convinced that "something of Nijinsky's work [for *Le Sacre*] had crept into his sister's companion piece."[13]

Alston had always loved Stravinsky's piano duet arrangements of *The Rite,* and began to think about his admiration for *Les Noces* in relation to the composer's earlier ballet. "I thought," he explained, "that one of the things that was so wonderful about *Les Noces* was the balance between the music and the movement." His interest in *The Rite* was rekindled and he decided to explore the possibility of choreographing the ballet to the four-hand piano reduction of the score. Alston then discovered that Nicolas Carr, Ballet Rambert's musical director, had made a special study of *The Rite* at Oxford. "Nicolas is one of the company's two pianists," observed Alston, "and suddenly the ballet seemed a good project."[14]

The choreographer discussed the ballet with Dame Marie Rambert, who was both excited and wary. She attended some of Alston's early rehearsals and told him that although Nijinsky's version had "many wonderful qualities," she felt that he had followed the music "too slavishly."[15] But Alston soon discovered that he was, in fact, really more interested in Stravinsky than in Nijinsky. He studied both the original Stravinsky–Roerich scenario and the composer's "choreographic notes" for Nijinsky. Then Alston "scribbled" Stravinsky's instructions and suggested movement images on his own copy of the piano reduction. "I wanted to make a ballet, however, that did not impose any rhetoric on the music," he observed.[16]

Having completed the first part of his research, Alston went to the Theatre Collection at the Victoria and Albert Museum to look at the Valentine Gross drawings of the 1913 production. Here, he felt, was an important clue to Nijinsky's movement language. "I remember looking at those drawings in blue pencil on little sheets. I swear when I looked up I had *seen* the ballet. There was so much movement in those sketches, particularly the ones for the 'Danse sacrale.'"[17] Alston was especially impressed with the sense of angularity in the Gross drawings. He recalled the "curious turned-in, vulnerable image" which was a hallmark of Nijinsky's *Petrouchka*. "I have especially tried to get a sense of the way he used the hands: very strange and expressive," Alston observed.[18]

The number of dancers in the cast was the next problem confronting the choreographer. Ballet Rambert is a chamber dance ensemble and a *Rite* the size of Nijinsky's, Massine's or Béjart's was impossible. Alston reduced his "tribe of dancers" to three Women—"to represent the entire womanhood of the clan"—six Adolescents, six Men and the Sage. Although he kept as near as possible to the Stravinsky–Roerich libretto, Alston was compelled to "pare down" the ballet's complex action. The choreographer noted it was quite a challenge to create a *Rite* on such a small scale, but, in fact, the final choreographic form of the production was determined partly by the restrictions placed upon Alston by force of circumstance.[19]

Alston thought of *The Rite* as "a very wintery piece," and the choreographic images he developed reflected this concept. Struck by Stravinsky's description of the violent beginnings of a Russian spring—"like the whole earth cracking"—Alston wanted the first half of the ballet to conjure up visions of hibernation.[20] "I think of the early part of the ballet as being very 'earthy,'" he said. "The dancers' weight is very much down and they appear quite brittle. There is a great deal of use of the floor and huddled 'sleeping' positions." This emphatic contact with the earth served a dual purpose. The dancers, Alston felt, should fling themselves to the earth "out of fear" as well as for protection.

Alston was particularly determined to evoke the sense of a tribal compound in his choreographic design for the first section of the ballet. "Nobody leaves the [stage] space during the whole first part," he observed. "The dancers are used all the time as part of the design in space."[21] He has created haunting images which recall Nijinsky's assertion that the ballet is the incarnation of Nature, "the life of the stones and the trees." Alston literally made totems with bodies. Tightly curled close to the earth or piled in human pyramids, the dancers become human symbols of the life force of the tribe.

In developing his conception of *The Rite*, Alston found parallels with ancient initiation ceremonies, "especially because it's a young girl who's being sacrificed." He therefore assigned special significance to the role of

Sally Owen as the Chosen One in Richard Alston's *The Rite of Spring*
(*Photo © David Buckland*)

the three Women in the ritual. "I felt they would be quite important and powerful in the tribe's hierarchy," Alston explained. "They are obviously in charge of the young girls [the Adolescents] and they look after and protect them." Having given the Women both a mystical and maternal part in the ceremony, Alston chose to have them begin the dancing in the ballet.[22]

In the original production of *Le Sacre*, in accordance with Stravinsky's instructions, the curtain did not rise until the startling first chords of the "Auguries of Spring." Alston found this theatrically impractical, and chose to have the Women come onto the stage to "The Prelude."[23] He wanted elements of this opening dance to be reminiscent of the Old Witch's "spell conjuring" in the Nijinsky version. The focus of the dance Alston devised for the Women is the still frozen earth; they lunge toward it, fall on it, and huddle together for warmth. Their arms embrace the air as they wrap them around their bodies. Limbs, hips, and shoulders trace curves and arcs in space. As the "Auguries of Spring" begins, the Women run quickly round the perimeter of the space and fall to the earth, facing the huddled group of Men lying upstage.

The Men then dash forward to begin their dance. Their movements are percussive, staccato tattoos; knees and feet flex in small jumps, the bodies are held in profile. In one moment, the Men slowly sink toward the floor at a precarious angle as though resisting the pull of the earth. Then, suddenly, they collapse on the ground. They separate into two groups of three and gather on the edges of the compound. The Women rise to their feet, circle the space, and gently awaken the six young Girls, who have been lying prone at the back of the stage.

The Adolescents then perform an elegiac chain dance to the music for the "Dance of the Young Girls." Their arms are continuously linked, either braided across their bodies or over their heads or shoulders. The Women join the Adolescents and all perform a brief dance, including a reprise of some of the movements from "The Prelude." Now they move with more ease and greater range, as though the ground had become softer and the air warmer.

The Men rejoin the Women and Adolescents for the "Ritual of Abduction." Alston has made this section seem both provocative and civilized. Three pairs of the Men each lift a Woman above their heads, parallel to the floor, forming a scaffolding of human bridges over the huddled bodies of the rest of the tribe. Although the men momentarily encircle some of the women, their gesture is protective rather than threatening. The women's passive use of weight—allowing their bodies to be supported, carried, even dragged by the men—is strangely intimate, even tender. These are images of mutual trust and connection. It is clear that any menace to the community comes from a force "far larger and more uncontrollable" than the tribe can control or understand.[24]

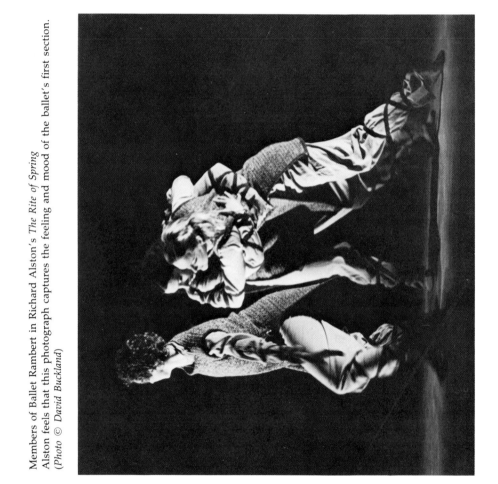

Members of Ballet Rambert in Richard Alston's *The Rite of Spring*
Alston feels that this photograph captures the feeling and mood of the ballet's first section.
(Photo © David Buckland)

The Women and the Adolescents begin the circles and chains of the "Spring Khorovod." The choreographer has developed a modern adaption of this ancient round dance. This section has a hushed, mysterious quality as the women sweep the stage, forming diagonal lines that melt into concentric circles and then evolve into motifs from "The Prelude" and the chain dance. The women now support one another in soft, arcing backbends. At one moment they mass together upstage left, slowly sink to the ground, and finally roll over and stand up, one at a time. It is a strikingly simple image; children waking from sleep after a dream.

The "Ritual of the Two Rival Tribes" is set not as a combative contest, but as a tribal dance that gradually fragments so that groups of dancers are moving in counterpoint. On the orchestral tutti that precedes the "Procession of the Oldest and Wisest One," the community forms a human tunnel as the Sage enters the ritual area. He moves to the center of the space and kneels to bless the earth. The Adolescents are carried to him and then laid, curled up, on either side of his feet. Finally, the tribe members perform "The Dance Overcoming the Earth," which the choreographer envisioned as a "great unison dance," a final hosanna to the gods before the choosing of the sacrificial virgin.[25]

Alston found the second half of *The Rite* "very difficult in terms of theater music, especially in the speed with which the new [musical] ideas tumble one on top of the other." He decided to use part of "Pagan Night," the introduction to the second half of the ballet, as a solo for the Sage. After the climax of the group dance, the Men and Women leave the space and the Adolescents collapse in a line upstage. The solo for the Sage that follows is dignified and restrained, giving the effect of continually changing tableaux. Finally, one by one, each of the young girls gently rolls to her feet and goes to the Sage to receive his blessing. Alston noted that the Sage was simply "an instrument" in the larger context of the ritual. "It may be sentimental," he remarked, "but Madam [Rambert] said that he's not only the oldest member of the tribe, he's the wisest. I felt that a man who was that wise would also be compassionate." Therefore, rather than making the Sage "a big beasty with a beard who would come out and pounce on this little girl and make her kill herself," Alston concentrated on the Sage's ceremonial role in the ritual. "I felt the Sage would be very compassionate towards these young girls; they are like [his own] children to him and he is an old man."[26]

Recalling Nicholas Roerich's description of "young girls playing mysterious games on a sacred hill," Alston used children's games as a choreographic device for the "Mystic Circle of Virgins." "There are elements of 'Ring-a-Ring-a-Roses' or even 'Musical Chairs' in that section," he observed, "little circle dances and formations in which a different girl is left out each time. Without being too much like Alfred Hitchcock about

Yair Vardi as the Sage with Catherine Beque and Members of Ballet Rambert in Richard Alston's *The Rite of Spring*
(Photo © *David Buckland*)

it, I wanted to be unclear to anyone who hadn't read their program which girl would be chosen."[27]

When the games are completed and the victim has been selected, the Sage cradles the Chosen Virgin in his arms and carries her to the back of the stage. The tribe performs a dance in honor of "The Naming and Honoring of the Chosen One," reprising some of the movements from the final section of Part One. Alston used the ritual trembling and shaking for the women in the sections Stravinsky designated as the "Evocation and Ritual of the Ancestors." Just before the "Sacrificial Dance" the Sage carries the Chosen Virgin to the center of the stage. All the dancers form a single line on either side of the old man as he places her on the ground. Finally the tribe slowly walks backwards toward the edges of the compound and lies on the earth to witness the culmination of the ritual.

When Alston began rehearsals for the "Danse sacrale" it would seem that he made himself a participant in the rite of selecting the Chosen Virgin. Like many of his predecessors, he worked on this dance early on "to discover" the movement vocabulary he would use in the ballet.[28] Alston, however, made the unusual decision of choreographing the solo on three Chosen Virgins rather than one. Sally Owen, who danced the role in the premiere of the Ballet Rambert's *Rite* recalls that each girl's version of the dance "turned out slightly differently." Small transitions and linking steps were variously adapted for each dancer. "A lot of the movement for the solo came out in rehearsal, sort of accidently, from something I did, or Quinny [Sacks] or Diane [Walker]," Owen observed. "Richard would then incorporate these individual movement idiosyncrasies into the solo."[29]

Owen had much the same response to dancing the Chosen Virgin as had her predecessors. She discovered that it "took forever" to train herself to perform the entire solo without collapsing. In order to build up sufficient stamina to carry her through a performance, Owen approached the problem in the same way Sokolova had done for Massine's 1920 production. "I'd work full out and nearly kill myself with one short bit and then I'd have to stop," she recalled. "Then the next time through, I'd do a bit more until I could complete the whole solo." Owen found the "Danse sacrale" especially exhausting. "I finally decided I just had to allow what was happening to me, both physically and mentally, to show when I was dancing," she explained. Owen, then, successfully turned what she termed her "paranoia" about performing the dance into her key to the dramatic aspect of the role.[30]

Alston himself admits that the "Danse sacrale" is a tremendous ordeal for the dancer. In it, he has used many of the characteristic hand and arm gestures of Russian women's folk dance, but combined them with his contemporary technical vocabulary so that they take on an unexpected

Sally Owen as the Chosen One in Richard Alston's *The Rite of Spring*
(*Photo © David Buckland*)

Sally Owen as the Chosen One in Richard Alston's *The Rite of Spring*
(*Photo © David Buckland*)

lyricism. Alston often allows the center of the body, the spine and pelvis, to curve with the flow of the movement, giving the solo a sense of inexorable momentum and resignation. The strongest emotional punctuations come with the Virgin's moments of "petrified stillness," one hand held across her mouth in a mute cry of suppressed horror and outrage.[31] As the dance builds to its climax, her movements become increasingly tense and tightly coiled. She repeatedly turns inward, circling around herself, wrapping her arms and legs around her own kinesphere as if trying to protect her body from its fate. When she falters momentarily, the three Women come out to support her, but she pushes them away. After a final convulsive circle of leaps around the stage, the Chosen Virgin collapses and the ritual is complete.

Although there are only sixteen dancers in this production, Alston has created an intimate and poignant ballet, as opposed to the "all-out primitive bash" of many contemporary versions.[32] He has focused on the ceremonial aspect of the work, thus creating an almost paradoxically civilized ritual. "The thing I kept on trying to say to the dancers," Alston explained, "was that if you don't perform this rite, winter's going to go on forever." The choreographer noted that it took some time for the dancers to develop a real "sense of community," and that the rehearsals of the ballet took on a ritual quality in themselves.[33] Owen also recalled *The Rite*'s rehearsal process. "We worked with live piano accompaniment whenever possible, to minimize the shock of the music in actual performance," she said. "But rehearsals seemed endless, just madness and chaos." Despite some difficult moments, however, Owen found that "when everyone was really together, the connection, the cohesive sense of group energy was really incredible."[34]

Alston chose as his costume designer Anne Guyon, who created a contemporary rendering of Russian peasant dress. She devised coarse fibered tunics and jackets worn over loose pants, and skirts in earthy shades of brown, beige and mustard. The trim on the legs and arms was cross-gartered, recalling the original Roerich designs. Peter Mumford's subdued lighting and spare set, consisting of a low wall-like screen upstage and knotted ropes hanging like roots, contributed to the enclosed, self-contained feeling of the ballet.[35] Dame Marie Rambert came to see the final rehearsals and commented that Alston's version had "come out so beautifully" she was carried away when she saw it—"too much so to tell him," she admitted.[36]

When Alston's *Rite* premiered at the Sadler's Wells Theatre in March of 1981, London was also awaiting the revival of Kenneth MacMillan's 1962 production of the ballet. By and large, however, the critics judged the Ballet Rambert version on its own merits. Many reviews cited the choreographer's evocation of the Valentine Gross sketches and photographs of the

Nijinsky ballet as well as the sculptural groupings of Nijinska's *Les Noces*. Mary Clarke noted the contrast between "passages of frenetic dance" and moments of "religious stillness."[37] Alastair Macaulay felt Alston's work reaffirmed Rivière's description of the work as a "biological" ballet, and that the choreographer had created a *Rite* "without crudity of thought or any undue savagery."[38]

The lack of frenzied barbarity appealed to some critics but puzzled others. Jann Parry decided that Alston's celebrants "might be nearing the stage of sophistication where they decide to take the risk of omitting the sacrifice one year, just to see whether spring mightn't return, regardless."[39] It was "the terrible power of quiet" that Stephanie Jordan found compelling, although she concluded that "for all its meat and intelligence," this *Rite* wasn't "tough enough" for Stravinsky's Herculean music and finally didn't make "a convincing whole."[40]

The correlation between the choreographer's use of the four-hand piano score and the subdued quality of the movement was noted by several critics. "The ballet cries out for the richness and density of orchestral colour," declared David Dougill. "This may or may not be the reason why Alston's choreography never reaches any peak of excitement."[41] Clement Crisp found the choreography and the music equally "restrained in colour." The merits of the Alston *Rite*, he concluded, were its "clarity in articulation and rhythmic texture."[42] Although Ann Nugent felt that the choreography "seemed too fluid to ride on the underlying rhythms" of the four-hand piano score, Bryan Robertson thought the ballet seemed to need, at times, the richness of the full orchestration. He thought that the piano reduction of the score offered fresh insight into the music which, "if not totally radical sometimes seemed like the disconcerting equivalent in musical terms of looking at a well-known painting under X-ray conditions."[43]

Jordan and Noel Goodwin both commented that Alston was most successful in the women's dances, where the choreographer, in Goodwin's words, "comes closest to illuminating the musical conception."[44] Alexander Bland considered the "light and fluid" style of the Ballet Rambert company and decided that the general effect of the ballet may have been tentative in consequence.[45] Interestingly, whether or not he noted these observations, Alston later revised sections of the ballet, significantly increasing the action in both "The Dance Overcoming the Earth" and the "Danse sacrale." The latter, he observed, was "just too static," a criticism echoed in a number of early reviews.[46]

The reverberations of the choreography with Russian folk dance were pointed out by a number of critics, although Alston commented that some observers found the movements more reminiscent of Celtic dances.[47] Robertson declared that this *Rite* contained some of Alston's finest dance

inventions, as well as "forging links" with Nijinsky and with Fokine—
"most notably in the way in which movement sometimes flickers like a
whiplash through a long line of dancers."[48] Here Robertson has attempted
to identify the lineage of the idiosyncratic marriage of Alston's fragmented, weighted, asymmetrical style with the lyrical *plastique* associated
with Fokine—the combination, in short, of selected elements of modern
dance and classical ballet.

More importantly, Alston is a product of the first generation of "home
grown" English Postmodern choreographers. Many of the components
that are basic to the aesthetic of Postmodern, or, as it is called in England,
"New Dance"—the sense of detachment, repetition, games structures,
and simple spatial forms and patterns—are also inherent in ritual and folk
dance forms. Alston, then, forged what for him was an inevitable partner-
ship between the contemporary and the traditional, between "New
Dance" and primitive ritual, classical formalism and the iconoclasm of
modern dance. Although his *Rite* pays a sort of homage to the choreographic innovations of Nijinsky and his sister Bronislava, Alston's style is
his own unique alloy. Bryan Robertson concluded that, in *The Rite,* "the
choreographer had reinforced his allegiance to the expressiveness and
discipline of modern dance, but, most decisively, also honors the past by
redefining his approach to tradition."[49]

Alston dedicated his production of *The Rite of Spring* to Dame Marie
Rambert. At the ballet's premiere the past and the future met for a
moment as Rambert clung to Alston's hand during the final curtain call
and performed a few "turned-in" movements from the landmark ballet
she had danced sixty-eight years before.

Epilogue:
The Monster Serpent and the Maiden Sacrifice

When the great Indian dancer and choreographer Uday Shankar saw Martha Graham dance, he pronounced her an avatar. She was, in fact, the very incarnation of her ideal of American dance; a form she once described as characterized by "a simplicity of idea, an economy of means, a focus directly upon movement."[1] Her dance gave shape to the bold, virile rhythms of America; spare, imperative, pared down to the essentials of movement. From the austere ritual of *Primitive Mysteries* (1931), which a distinguished English theatrical producer called "the finest ballet since *Le Sacre du printemps*," to her Greek dance-dramas such as *Night Journey* (1947) and *Clytemnestra* (1958), Graham's fascination with mythology and metaphor has been central to the development of her dance theater.[2]

In December of 1983, shortly before her ninetieth birthday, Martha Graham, whom many have called the high priestess of modern dance, declared she was returning to "hallowed and terrifying ground."[3] Declaring that dancing the role of the Chosen One in the 1930 Massine revival of *Le Sacre* was a turning point in her life, Graham announced the forthcoming premiere of her own production of *The Rite of Spring*. "I started work on [the ballet] with reluctance and fear," she said. "The music is overwhelming."[4] Graham had shut the score out of her mind for more than fifty years, but her associate artistic director, Ron Protas, persuaded her to approach the music once again.[5]

In the early years of her career, Graham was especially influenced by Louis Horst, her musical director and artistic mentor. Horst was particularly sensitive to the affinity between modern art and primal cultures. He made a correlation between the "powerful simplicity" of primitive societies and the inspiration their civilizations provided for pioneers of modernism. Indeed, in an uncanny echo of Nijinsky, Horst asserted that a comprehensive physical awareness is basic "to both archaic style and the modern dance."[6] It was Horst who, in the summer following Graham's performance as the Chosen Virgin in Massine's *Le Sacre* in April of 1930, accompanied the dancer on a trip through New Mexico and the Penitente region of the Southwest. Both were deeply impressed by the customs and rituals of the Indian nature cults of the region. Graham's *Primitive Mysteries*, choreographed the following year, was the first major work to give evidence of a new mysticism which had crystallized on this journey and which was to establish the focus and direction of much of her future work.

In her *Notebooks*, Graham reveals her wide-ranging interest in psychology, philosophy, mythology and poetry. These "work notes" contain extensive quotes from Dante, Rilke and T. S. Eliot, notes on the works of Carl Jung and Ananda Coomaraswamy, and comments on the studies of mythologist Joseph Campbell.[7] She has made numerous notations on primitive dramas which ensure "the fertility of the Earth, the cycles of life and the myth of rebirth."[8] The notebooks provide ample evidence that Graham's dance dramas are the result of nearly as much scholarly research and reflection as creative inspiration. It is therefore not surprising to note striking parallels between Graham's evocation of *The Rite of Spring* and the ancient mythical themes and customs described by several eminent mythologists, most notably by Campbell in his work, *Primitive Mythology*. It is, of course, impossible to document the precise impact of Campbell's study on Graham's *Rite*. However, the choreographer's use of symbolic device, as well as the ballet's theme, make a few instances of correlation noteworthy.

In devising the scenario for her *Rite*, Graham retained the central concept of the original Stravinsky–Roerich libretto—a primordial ritual of propitiation in which a maiden is sacrificed to the god of fertility to ensure a fruitful harvest. Her setting for the ceremony was not, however, pagan Russia, but the stark, primitive landscape of the American Southwest. Ron Protas designed worn stone steps leading to an "abstracted sacrificial mound and a . . . gallows-like structure" modeled after a southwestern plant nicknamed the "devil's claw."[9] The atmosphere created has, as Graham intended, an austerity reminiscent of the art of Georgia O'Keeffe.

Although the Chosen One in Graham's *Rite* is a woman, the choreographer states she did not intend the ballet as a commentary on women as victims, noting that the Chosen One could be either male or female.[10] Graham observes that the concept of sacrifice as an agent of renewal is still part of our system of values. The choreographer sees a corollary between the sacrifices demanded of an artist and the fate of the doomed maiden. "I've always felt that if you become an artist, you are the Chosen One. It's a force that possesses you; it's an exciting and wonderful life, but it's filled with terror, and there's no way, once you accept it, you can escape its sacrificial demands."[11]

Terese Capucilli as the Chosen One in Martha Graham's *The Rite of Spring* (*Courtesy of the Martha Graham Dance Company. Photo © Martha Swope*)

Graham choreographed her *Rite* for an ensemble of eighteen dancers, nine men and nine women. But, in keeping her locale in the American Southwest, she has transformed the part of the Sage into a Shaman, whose role she compares to a Shalako figure, the holy man of the Zuni tribe who is a prominent figure in the propagation ritual. Mythologist Joseph Campbell notes that among planting societies such as the Hopi, Zuni, and other Pueblo dwellers, "life is organized around the rich and complex ceremonies of their masked gods." These are elaborate community rites which correspond to specific events in the religious calendar and are directed by societies of trained priests.[12]

Campbell makes a distinction between the priest of a planting tribe, who holds a specific ceremonial and religious office and fulfills a recognized function in the community, and the Shaman, who, "as a consequence of a personal psychological crisis, has gained a certain power of his own." Campbell observes as well that many tribes also recognized the need to incorporate the Shaman into the complex, group-oriented ceremonial system of their food-growing communities. Graham, exercising some artistic license, undoubtedly wished to focus on the "highly dangerous and unpredictable force" inherent in shamanistic magic as an aspect of community ritual.[13]

Unlike the Sage, the oldest and wisest member of the community in the original Nijinsky production, Graham's Shaman is a young, powerful, charismatic figure. Swathed in an enormous black, white and green cloak, this Shaman seems the incarnation of the cycle of life, death and rebirth. In one of the ballet's most chilling moments, he literally snatches the maiden he has selected for the ritual sacrifice from her partner's back, a frighteningly random and unpremeditated choice. In an ensuing duet, the Shaman enshrouds the maiden in his robe and, assisted by two male acolytes, seemingly prepares the girl to meet her fate in a lurid ceremony laden with necrophilic images and suggestion. Graham, however, defends the erotic nature of this section: "I think all ritual has some element of sexuality in it—in any church, in any belief. . . . That's partly the power of religion over people, our attraction to it."[14]

Here again, Graham's statement is reinforced by Campbell's analysis of similar rites in primordial cultures. A matrix of primitive-village mythology is the understanding of the nature of death, with the intent of making clear that this death is often accomplished by murder. Because the plants on which man depends for existence derive from this act, the world lives on and by death. Indeed, many myths posit the idea that the sexual organs are supposed to have appeared "at the time of this coming of death."[15] Campbell contends that this very interdependence of sex and death, and of the imperative of killing, gives us a powerful, albeit disturbing insight into death as a part of life.

George White, Jr. as the Shaman in Martha Graham's *The Rite of Spring* (*Courtesy of the Martha Graham Dance Company. Photo © Martha Swope*)

Terese Capucilli and George White, Jr. in the Trammeling of the Chosen One from
Martha Graham's *The Rite of Spring*
(*Courtesy of the Martha Graham Dance Company. Photo © Martha Swope*)

Graham has choreographed the climax of the Shaman's preparatory ceremony to the increasingly accelerated rhythms of "The Dance Overcoming the Earth." Here the Shaman releases a long skein of rope from the branches of the "devil's claw" and, circling the transfixed and trembling figure of the maiden, winds it around her. It is a jarring moment, discomfiting and even misogynist in its overtones. Graham, however, is an artist who delights in the theatrical and symbolic use of props. The mythologies of primitive planting tribes abound with legends of the monster serpent and the sacrificial maiden. Certainly snakes and serpents are ancient symbols of eternal life and male fertility. The virgin is emblematic of "the magic door," the vessel through which lives enter into the world. It is the woman, then, who stands naturally "in counterpoise to the door of death," through which the life force must finally leave.[16] If, then, we consider Graham's tableau through the symbology of this myth—the virgin fructified and transformed by the masculine image represented by the "phallic, waterlike, lightninglike" serpent—it becomes a more potent metaphor for the recognition of the cycles of life, of transformation, death and rebirth.[17]

These are the most unusual and original touches in Graham's *Rite.* Although there is the requisite "Danse sacrale," it comes as an anticlimax after the maiden's ritual trammelling.[18] Critic Howard Moss wondered why she was bound at all since she was going to dance herself to death.[19] Tobi Tobias, however, disagreed, and vividly described the moment of epiphany: as the girl dances herself to death, she shudders from "deep in the pelvis, striking out with taut, angled limbs, falling exhausted and rising only to collapse again. When the priest finally displays her inert body to the crowd, lengths of green cloth stream from it—the spring burgeoning assured."[20] Arlene Croce's review was more perfunctory, noting that the Chosen One is wrapped up in thick cable and then unwrapped. "She thrashes and dies under the Shaman's gorgeous cape. More cloth is flung down, and that's the rite."[21]

Some critics found themselves distracted by a spectacle that, in Dale Harris's phrase, "smacked more of high fashion than high drama." Calling the work "Slaughter on Seventh Avenue," Harris dubbed the men's black loin cloths and the women's black and white sarongs designed by Halston "smart tribal outfits."[22]

The technical vocabulary of Graham's choreography offered no surprises. One could catalogue a litany of Graham trademarks: the ubiquitous contraction, the back of the hand pressed to the forehead, the attenuated turning movements that twist first one way and then the other, the celebratory, stationary jumps, the percussive body slaps. Harris, noting the dearth of sustained dance energy or coherent movement phrases in the choreographer's style, decided that instead of a ritual,

The Martha Graham Dance Company in *The Rite of Spring*
(*Courtesy of the Martha Graham Dance Company. Photo © Martha Swope*)

Graham "turned out a neat little gymnastic display, filled with long stretches during which the leading characters gaze significantly at one another while breathing hard."[23]

Many critics cited the seemingly insurmountable problem which the score poses for any choreographer. Moss, agreeing with Emile Vuillermoz's statement at the time of the 1920 Massine revival, decided that it was impossible for the human body to sustain the excitement, violence and intensity of the music.[24] In fact, during her choreographic process, Graham worked out the phrasing of much of the movement before actually setting it to the score. She insisted that the choreography and the music " 'marched side by side—the intensity, the breathing, was the same.' "[25] Arlene Croce, however, asserted that even if the music and movement were in perfect harmony, "the ritual drama of catharsis could not occur, because the Graham technique—that supreme instrument of theatrical catharsis—has faded to the point of ineffectuality."[26]

Croce's observation raises several interesting points. The Graham technique has indeed lost some of the fierce intensity, the implosive use of weight and percussive angularity that characterized the choreographer's early years of experimentation and discovery. Over the decades, Graham's working vocabulary has become softer, more fluid, elastic and symmetrical; it has become, in brief, more balletic. Her present mode of choreography, more than fifty years after the monolithic austerity of *Primitive Mysteries*, is seen as unsuitable for conveying the ecstatic primal "catharsis" of a primordial rite. In contrast, and ironically, when Nijinsky used exaggeration, abstraction and "stylization" to convey the daring message of his new dance language, his work was judged too "primitive." *Le Sacre*, it would seem, has come full circle.

In the context of traditional mythology, the individual understands his role in society through a spectrum of insights, obligations and sentiments invoked by the symbology of myth and ritual. Joseph Campbell contrasts this thesis with what he terms "creative mythology" in which this hierarchy is reversed. It is the individual's experience "of order, horror, beauty or even mere exhilaration," which he wants to communicate through his own unique system of signs. If his realization has been "of a certain depth and import," notes Campbell, "his communication will have the value and force of living myth."[27] *Le Sacre du printemps* is a powerful combination of these two concepts. Stravinsky's dream of a solemn pagan rite in which a young girl dances herself to death was transformed, through his extraordinary score, into art, and with Nijinsky's visionary choreography, into its own apotheosis.

The subjects of myth and ritual have enormous appeal for the creative artist. Nijinsky, Stravinsky and Roerich were able to realize their concept of *Le Sacre* through the evocation of ancient Slavic rites. But the theme of the ballet, the cycle of life, death and rebirth, is not only universal, it is multifaceted and remarkably adaptable.

The mythology surrounding the first production—the glamour, the scandal, even the very evanescence of the Nijinsky *Le Sacre*—are undeniably fascinating to choreographers. Some feel an affinity with Nijinsky and would, perhaps, like to identify with his indisputable genius as a dancer and his innovation and creativity as a choreographer. While *Le Sacre* remains Nijinsky's most famous, not to say notorious, work, the actual choreography for the ballet has been lost. Subsequent choreographers have, therefore, for the most part been freed from comparison with the original, or have been compared only in terms of the novelty of their approach and their skill in handling the score.

Many choreographers cite the challenge of creating a work equal to Stravinsky's colossus as their initial attraction to *Le Sacre*. Although the composer asserted that he conceived the ballet as a "musical-choreographic" work with a specific libretto, he later recanted and declared *Le Sacre* a purely "architectural" construction. The very lack of definite programmatic detail in the music allows a prospective choreographer significant latitude for interpretation. As has been noted, an adaptation may suggest primitive rites of no determinate people or place, contemporary "tribal rituals" of courtship and mating or even the rehearsal rituals of a dance company. Myriad variations are possible; each unique, each valid, yet none violates the spirit of the score.

Finally, *Le Sacre* may function as a paradigm of the artist as vatic; the seer whose vision is emblematic of man's struggle in the throes of an immutable destiny. In composing a "Danse sacrale" and the climactic ritual that leads to it, the choreographer seemingly conducts the ultimate conjuration—the transmutation of human matter into pure energy. In the sacrificial dance of death, the chosen one, the muse, becomes the dance itself.

As an epochal work, *Le Sacre* remains both symbol and paradox. At its premiere, perceptive observers greeted the ballet as the *Zeitgeist* of its era, the fierce voice of Modernism not yet pacified by familiarity. *Le Sacre* reopened the doors of perception to a realm of powers made palpable through the language of myth and the symbolic forms of ritual. Only seven years later, audiences haunted by the phantoms of a devastating holocaust were no longer shocked by the music or outraged by the primitivist spectacle.

Subsequent generations, pursued by the psychology of alienation and engulfed by the technological panoply of popular culture, would refashion and reinterpret *Le Sacre*; sometimes returning to its original guise of arcane rites, sometimes choosing to reflect images of contemporary mores, contemporary angst. Yet, remarkably, the essential "presence" of the work, its ineffable mystery, remains unaltered. It may be that *Le Sacre du printemps* is that most rare commodity in twentieth-century culture: a work of art that is enhanced by the passage of time and the catharsis of change.

Appendix 1

Chronology

1911

January

Nijinsky & Nijinska show Diaghilev & Bakst beginnings of *Faune* (3)

Nijinsky & Nijinska show Diaghilev & Bakst *Faune* (4)

Nijinsky dismissed from the Imperial Theaters (4)

March

Nijinsky & Diaghilev meet with Stravinsky at Beaulieu (3)

July

Stravinsky writes to Roerich and goes to Talashkino to work out plan of action & titles of dances for *Le Sacre* (1)

August

Stravinsky goes to Karlsbad, visits Diaghilev, and *Le Sacre* is commissioned (1)

September

Stravinsky writes to Roerich saying he has "begun to compose" introduction for "dudki" and "Divination with Twigs," "Dance of the Maidens" (Stravinsky in Clarens) (1)

Stravinsky at Ustilug, Russia. He composes Part One: "Augures printaniers" (Jeu du Rapt?); "Rondes printaniers"; "Jeux des cités rivales" (5)

November

Stravinsky writes to Benois from Clarens. Played "what I had composed" of *Le Sacre* in Paris for Diaghilev & Misia Edwards (1)

Key

(1) Stravinsky, Vera, and Craft, Robert. *Stravinsky in Pictures and Documents* (New York: Simon & Schuster, 1978)

(2) Buckle, Richard. *Nijinsky* (London: Weidenfeld & Nicolson, 1971)

(3) Buckle, Richard. *Diaghilev* (New York: Atheneum, 1979)

(4) Nijinska, Bronislava. *Early Memoirs.* Translated and edited by Irina Nijinska and Jean Rawlinson. Introduction by Anna Kisselgoff (New York: Holt, Rinehart & Winston, 1981)

(5) Bullard, Truman C. "The First Performance of Igor Stravinsky's *Sacre du printemps.*" Vols. 1-3 (Ph.D. dissertation, Eastman School of Music, University of Rochester, 1971)

(6) Barron, Stephanie, and Tuchman, Maurice, eds. *The Avant-Garde in Russia 1910-1930: New Perspectives* (Cambridge, Mass.: MIT Press, 1980)

(7) Grigoriev, Serge. *The Diaghilev Ballet: 1909-1929* (London: Constable, 1953; reprint ed., London: Penguin, 1960)

(8) Spaulding, Frances. *Roger Fry: Art and Life* (Berkeley: University of California Press, 1980)

(9) Macdonald, Nesta. *Diaghilev Observed: By Critics in England and the United States* (London: Dance Books, Ltd. and New York: Dance Horizons, 1975)

December

Nijinsky continues to work on *Faune* at Bordighera (4)

First All Russian Congress of Artists in St. Petersburg (6)

First exhibition by editors of *Blaue Reiter* in Munich (6)

Gordon Craig's production of *Hamlet* at Moscow Art Theater (6)

1912

January

Stravinsky in Clarens—Completes Part One (1)

End of January, Stravinsky goes to Berlin to see Diaghilev, who says he can't mount *Le Sacre* in 1912 (2)

First "unofficial" rehearsals of *Faune* (4)

Clarens: Part One—Stravinsky completes remaining sections; Diaghilev postpones premiere until 1913 (5)

Publication of Kandinsky's *Über das Geisitige in der Kunst* (10)

February

Nijinsky & Diaghilev visit Dalcroze school in Hellerau (2)

Stravinsky travels with Russian Ballet (5)

March

Stravinsky begins "The Chosen One"; works on intro. to Part Two; continues on Chosen One & intro. to Part Two; plays part for Diaghilev & Nijinsky; to Roerich—completes first tableau; to Benois—*Le Sacre* not performed in 1912 (1)

Ballets Russes go to Monte Carlo to rehearse (2)

Stravinsky in Clarens: Part Two begun; Prelude & sketches for "Danse sacrale" (5)

April

To Calvocoressi—"*Le Sacre* est bientôt fini" (1)

Stravinsky plays piano reduction for Diaghilev & Monteux in Monte Carlo

Nijinsky finishes *Faune* (4)

Clarens: Stravinsky writes letter to Calvocoressi saying work will soon be finished (11 April) (5)

May

Stravinsky returns to Clarens; goes to Paris (1)

Premiere of *Faune* (29 May) (2)

June

Stravinsky plays 4-hand piano arrangement of *Le Sacre* with Debussy, for Laloy at Bellevue (1)

July

Composition continues

August

Lugano—Stravinsky plays *Le Sacre* for Diaghilev, Nijinsky and Benois; Stravinsky & Diaghilev go to Venice (1)

Stravinsky plays *Le Sacre* for Nijinsky, Diaghilev and Benois (3)

April–June

Monte Carlo, Paris, London—Stravinsky joins Russian Ballet; Monteux hears parts of *Le Sacre* on piano (Monte Carlo); Laloy hears parts in Paris, describes it in *La Grande Revue* (5)

September

Stravinsky plays part of "Dance of the Adolescents" for Diaghilev in Venice (2)

October

Nijinsky begins work on *Jeux* in Monte Carlo (4)

Russian artists included in second Post-Impressionist Exhibit, London, October–December 1912 (8)

1913

January
Nijinsky writes to Stravinsky from Leipzig—has choreographed almost everything through the games and dances in the ring. Nijinsky says *"Sacre* will be everything we both want'' (1)

When Stravinsky arrives in Vienna he brings completed orchestral score of *Le Sacre* (4)—completed ms dated 17 November 1912 (4)

Nijinsky rehearses *Le Sacre* at the Aldwych, London (7)

February
Nijinsky interview with *Pall Mall Gazette*; Stravinsky has interview with *Daily Mail*; Monteux letter to Stravinsky re: correction of piano score at Nijinsky's request (1)

Faune premieres in London (2); Nijinsky begins work on *Le Sacre* "in earnest" in London (2)

Stravinsky in London for some of *Le Sacre* rehearsals (4)

New York Armory Show (6); Stravinsky & Nijinsky give interviews in London re: *Le Sacre* (9) Macdonald dates *Faune* London premiere 17 February (9)

March
Monteux requests *Le Sacre* score; Stravinsky inscribes 4-hand piano score to Roerich; Nijinsky telegraphs "finished 1st part, immediately piano score sacred dance''; Monteux writes Stravinsky re: rehearsals of Part One (1)

Nijinsky & Rambert continue to work on *Le Sacre* in Monte Carlo (2)

Rehearsals for *Le Sacre* in Monte Carlo (4)

April
Diaghilev telegraphs programme to Astruc with *Le Sacre* for 29 May (1)

Rehearsals for *Jeux* in Monte Carlo (2) (3)

May
Stravinsky arrives in Paris & directs piano rehearsal with Nijinsky; first rehearsal of *Le Sacre* with dancers on stage; rehearsals with full orchestra; *répétition générale;* premiere of *Le Sacre* (29 May) (1); premiere of *Jeux* in Paris (15 May) (4)

June
Second performance of *Le Sacre*, Paris (4 June); third performance of *Le Sacre*, Paris (6 June) (1)

Mid-year Russian pavilion at Venice exposition (6)

July
Le Sacre has first performance at Drury Lane, London (11 July); second performance (18 July); third performance (23 July) (1)

October
Salon d'Automne includes a section of Russian folk art (6)

December
Victory Over the Sun produced in St. Petersburg (6)

Appendix 2

Léonide Massine's Work Film of
Le Sacre du printemps

Choreography by Léonide Massine

This is an analysis of a rehearsal/work film of Léonide Massine's *Le Sacre du printemps*. The film was made in 1948 for the purposes of recording the ballet as performed by La Scala Ballet. The film is approximately forty-five minutes long and is silent. No other film record of a Massine production of *Le Sacre* is known to exist.

Massine used his work films for the purposes of recording his ballets and as an aid to memory when those works were "revived." Film techniques in the 1930s, 1940s and 1950s were less sophisticated and complete than the more modern methods of videotape and sound recording. This record of *Le Sacre* is therefore very fragmentary, and affords the viewer only a rudimentary sample of Massine's larger vision. Because the film is silent, it is difficult to correlate accurately the movement on the film with the score. Massine kept voluminous notebooks in his own notational system of each of his ballets. It may be assumed that these notes, used in conjunction with the work films, were the means by which Massine revived and reproduced some of his ballets. Due to the incomplete nature of the *Le Sacre* work film, my observations will focus on selected moments and a general discussion of the ballet's movement style.

The film begins with the dancers, dressed in rehearsal clothes, assembled onstage. Sixteen women are seated cross-legged, stage left, facing downstage. Four men sit in front of them. Another group of men stand in a cluster stage right. The scene is completed by the presence of a silent, immobile figure standing upstage center. The men and women seated stage left behind a series of strongly two-dimensional arm movements. Their arms move in angular patterns, their upper bodies bending and twisting in quick percussive thrusts. Their actions are echoed by the men at stage right, and the series of movements soon become a complex canon between the two groups.

As if by a divine command, the seated group rises and breaks into percussive running triplets in a circular formation about the stage. They hold their arms rigidly at their sides. The men standing stage right join the intertwining circles and the stage becomes a pattern of rapidly forming and dissolving arcs and curves. A circle motif is repeated at strategic moments throughout the ballet. In the first section the circles move counterclockwise; in the later sections the direction is primarily clockwise. These circular formations are like a watch spring that is gradually wound and released. The dancers are often linked to one another—by hands, wrists, elbows or shoulders—reinforcing each member's commitment to the larger chain of communal society. The momentary breaks in these circular patterns result in a temporary sense of exhilarating liberation before the links are forged once more.

The dancers ultimately break the chain and form couples, placing themselves to form jagged lines around the stage. The movements in this section take on the coloration of stylized "courting" rituals. The women stand back to back with their male partners, their arms linked to one another through the crook of the elbow. Slowly, almost painfully, the women are lifted onto the men's backs, as though the men were shouldering both a physical burden and moral responsibility. The women are lowered to their feet, and, turning to face downstage, they lean with their full weight upon the men, who slowly drag them sideways across the stage. The women's dependence on their mates is portrayed powerfully through these images. One senses that strong, supportive men upon whom the woman can "lean" is essential to the propagation and survival of the tribe. Both these moments are recorded in photographs of Massine's 1920 production of *Le Sacre*, suggesting that at least some of the details of the choreographer's earlier conception of the ballet found their way into later revivals.

In the next section, the couples clasp one another back to back, alternately hopping and dragging each other around in circles. This appears to be the culmination of a rite of copulation, the movement growing in speed and momentum. The couples splinter apart. Two groups of men engage in ritual combat, the leaders perched on the shoulders of members of their band. The women, seated quietly on the ground, impassively echo the thrust and parry of the men's gestures. The dancers then form into two opposing "tribes," teasing and cajoling, sparring with one another. The mock battle dissolves into a slow processional walk in a counterclockwise circular formation, increasing in speed, until the dancers form a human pinwheel, pounding the earth with a swift, insistent cadence of triplets.

The group slowly forms a cluster around five women, who repeat the men's combat gestures, now more abstracted and refined. Their movements include lightning-rapid hitchkicks forward and back. The leading women then initiate a weaving pattern, first in small circles then gradually expanding to include the other women of the tribe into ever-widening eddies. Their arms are linked overhead, and it soon becomes evident that one of their number has been singled out. She stands solitary and motionless in the midst of the turning, winding stream of bodies.

The entire group of dancers suddenly halt abruptly and rush downstage to form a spraylike line. Imperceptibly, insidiously, the dancers begin to vibrate and tremble violently, as though seized, as critic André Levinson noted, ''by some mystic terror.'' Other critics who saw the 1920 Massine *Le Sacre* made references to his use of popular dance forms such as the ''Shimmy.'' Perhaps it was this ritual shaking that inspired these comments.

Once again, the dancers break apart and form circular patterns around the stage, their focus centering now on the solitary figure of the Chosen Maiden. A small band of women begins a large jumping step, a kind of pitched-forward *grand jeté*, which they perform around the Chosen One. Their arms are first held rigidly well behind their bodies; then they reach forward as if to pull their reluctant mortality into space. If the observer looks carefully, the striking ''signature'' gesture of Martha Graham's *Primitive Mysteries*—the elbows pulled together and held in front of the chest; the upper arms folded back towards the sides of the face, as Marcia Siegel describes it—may be glimpsed as the women begin this section. This gesture is also recorded in the photographs of the 1920 *Le Sacre,* and may be another holdover from the earlier production.

After this jumping section, the film breaks abruptly. The next scene shows the Chosen Maiden, with six women as her ''chorus.'' This, presumably, is a section from the part entitled ''Mystic Circle of Virgins'' in the Stravinsky score. The women do a delicate folk *pas de basque* very much in the style of the peasant dances of Byelorussia. The arms are held in a characteristic pose of this style: one arm across the waist, the elbow of the other arm touching the supporting hand, the head resting on the index finger of the upraised arm. This is a quiet moment in the dance; soft, rounded, and very feminine. With a soft gliding *rida,* an easy sliding step, the women travel across the stage and repeat the *pas de basque.* Once more the film breaks and the next scene shows the same moment—this time in costume, possibly in dress rehearsal or performance.

The next segment of the film shows a short section of the dance of the Chosen Maiden. The other dancers are grouped in a semicircle around the Maiden: some of the men seated cross-legged, some of the women kneeling, the remainder of the group standing, but all watching intently as the Chosen One performs her final dance, one of the most remarkable aspects of this dance is its markedly percussive, strenuous, and powerful movement. Even the Maiden's head takes on a marionettelike characteristic, bobbing and turning on staccato accents. Her movements seem to be controlled by forces outside her own volition. Her arms claw and thrash the air, as if trying to throw off an unseen oppressor.

Two moments of the dance are particularly striking. In the first, the Maiden performs a drumlike stamping simultaneously with both feet moving on a direct horizontal path across the stage. As her arms move in a circular arc around her torso, the Maiden flings her arms above her head on every third accent, finally pulling them down with fists clenched, her head tossed back on her spine.

The final sequence of the Maiden's dance is another example of Massine's use of circular forms and floor patterns. Using a counterclockwise circular path, Massine devised a strenuous sequence of jumps and turns for the climax of the dance. The Maiden performs a *jeté élancé,* spins out of its recovery and quickly drops into a spiral turn, squatting close to the ground. The entire phrase is executed at breathtaking speed and with exacting precision. Seemingly transformed by this mystic rite into a whirling human vortex of rhythm and movement, the Chosen Maiden reaches the end of her frenzied dance.

As a whole, the filming techniques used to record the ballet make the study of detail and subtlety extremely difficult. It is barely possible to see hands, arms and feet clearly because of camera angles, exposure problems and distance. There is one moment when the *corps de ballet* appears to be clapping, encouraging the Chosen Maiden in her efforts. But ultimately, without intimate knowledge of the ballet's original choreographic score, revival from the film alone would be impossible.

Notes

Introduction

1. There were six performances of *Le Sacre* in Paris, including the *répétition générale* on 28 May, and subsequent performances on 29 May, 2 June, 5 June, 6 June and 13 June. The ballet was given in London on 11 July, 17 July, and 23 July. Truman Bullard, *The First Performance of Igor Stravinsky's 'Sacre du printemps,'* vols. 1–3 (Ph.D. dissertation, Eastman School of Music, University of Rochester, 1971).

2. Nijinsky, quoted in Nesta Macdonald, *Diaghilev Observed: By Critics in England and the United States, 1911–1929* (London: Dance Books and New York: Dance Horizons, 1975), p. 90.

3. Just as this book was going to press, dance historian Millicent Hodson's reconstruction of the original 1913 production of *Le Sacre du printemps,* with the Nijinsky choreography, premiered in Los Angeles on 30 September 1987 and in New York City on 28 October 1987. The work was performed by The Joffrey Ballet. Dr. Hodson's extraordinary achievement is the result of fifteen years of research in five countries. Art historian and Roerich scholar Kenneth Archer supervised the recreation of Nicholas Roerich's sets and costumes for this revival. Critic Alan M. Kriegsman called this revival "stupendous," and noted that the ballet has "a *feeling* of authenticity about it." *The Washington Post* (2 October 1987), p. D1, 4. See also Millicent Hodson, "Searching for Nijinsky's *Sacre,*" *Dance Magazine,* vol. 54 (June 1980), pp. 64–75.

4. Igor Stravinsky, *Poetics of Music,* preface by George Seferis. Translated by Arthur Knodel and Ingolf Dahl (Cambridge, Mass.: Harvard University Press, 1942), p. 10.

Chapter 1

1. The company was billed under a variety of names over its twenty-year history, including Ballets Russes de Serge Diaghilev, Saisons Russes, Diaghileff's Famous Russian Ballet, and Ballets (or Ballet) Russes, the title most often used today.

2. A. V. Coton, *Writings on Dance 1938–1968,* with a foreword by Martin Cooper, edited by Katherine Sorley Walker and Lillian Haddakin (London: Dance Books, 1975), p. 16.

3. Prince Peter Lieven, *The Birth of the Ballets Russes,* translated by L. Zarine (New York: Dover Publications, 1973), p. 54.

4. Debra Goldman, "Background to Diaghilev," *Ballet Review,* vol. 6, no. 3 (1977–78), pp. 1–2.

5. Ibid., p. 3. There were other Russian dancers who appeared in the West prior to the Ballets Russes, including Serge Legat and Maria Petipa, who performed Russian national dances at the Opéra Comique in Paris in 1902 and 1903. Natalia Roslavleva, *Era of the Russian Ballet,* with an introduction by Dame Ninette de Valois (New York: E. P. Dutton, 1966), p. 107.

6. Quoted in Roslavleva, p. 66.

7. Goldman, p. 20.

8. Ibid., p. 26.

9. Tamara Karsavina, *Theatre Street* (New York: E. P. Dutton, 1931; rev. ed, Dutton Everyman Paperback, 1961), p. 58.

10. Lincoln Kirstein, *Thirty Years: The New York City Ballet* (New York: Alfred A. Knopf, 1978), p. 303.

11. Goldman, p. 25.

12. John Bowlt, *The Silver Age: Russian Art of the Early Twentieth Century and the "World of Art" Group* (Newtonville, Mass.: Oriental Research Partners, 1979), p. 9.

13. Ibid., p. 31.

14. Ibid., p. 11.

15. Joan Ross Acocella, *The Reception of Diaghilev's Ballets Russes by Artists and Intellectuals in Paris and London, 1909–1914* (Ph.D. dissertation, Rutgers University, 1984), chapter 3, pp. 117–18.

16. Bowlt, pp. 34, 44.

17. Alexandre Benois, *Reminiscences of the Russian Ballet.* Translated by Mary Britneva (London: Putnam, 1947), p. 127.

18. Bowlt, p. 47. Bowlt also notes that, generically, the World of Art was a title that also applied not only to the literary "club" and the journal, but to three cycles of exhibitions and to three distinct societies that ran them.

19. Janet Kennedy, *The "Mir iskusstva" Group and Russian Art, 1898–1912* (New York and London: Garland Publishing, 1977), p. 14.

20. Bowlt, p. 53.

21. The introductory page of *Mir iskusstva,* quoted in Kennedy, p. 115.

22. Quoted in ibid., p. 73.

23. Quoted in Acocella, chapter 3, p. 146.

24. For a comprehensive analysis of International Symbolism in Russia, see Acocella, chapter 3.

25. Acocella, chapter 3, pp. 158–59.

26. Bowlt, p. 159.

27. Arnold Haskell and Walter Nouvel, *Diaghileff: His Artistic and Private Life.* Foreword by Arnold Haskell (New York: Simon and Schuster, 1935), p. 110.

28. For a complete, if one-sided, discussion of the incident, see "The 'Sylvia' Catastrophe," Benois, *Reminiscences,* pp. 210–18.

29. Lieven, p. 42.

30. Bowlt, p. 166.

31. Quoted in ibid., p. 169.

32. Quoted in Richard Buckle, *Diaghilev* (New York: Atheneum, 1979), p. 82.

33. Quoted in Walter Sorell, *The Dancer's Image: Points and Counterpoints* (New York and London: Columbia University Press, 1971), p. 112.

34. Cyril Beaumont, *Michel Fokine and His Ballets* (New York: Dance Horizons, 1981), p. 22.

35. Quoted in ibid., p. 23.

36. Coton, *Writings on Dance*, p. 16.

37. Roland John Wiley, "Alexandre Benois' Commentaries on the First *Saison russes*," *The Dancing Times*, vol. 71 (October 1980), "Alexandre Benois," Oct. 1980, p. 29.

38. Benois, *Reminiscences*, p. 225.

39. Benois, quoted in Wiley, "Alexandre Benois," Oct. 1980, p. 29.

40. Alexandre Benois, *Memoirs*. Translated by Moura Budberg. Foreword by Tamara Karsavina. Vol. 2 (London: Chatto & Windus, 1964), p. 217.

41. Diaghilev, quoted in Bowlt, p. 107.

42. Astruc had extensive experience in public relations, in editing newspapers and art and music journals, and as an impresario when he met Diaghilev in 1906. Between 1904 and 1913, he was the founder/director of the *Société musicale de Paris* and the coordinator of the *Grande saison de Paris*. Beginning with the concerts of Russian music at the Opéra in 1907, "Astruc became the enthusiastic coordinator of the performances by Diaghilev's musicians and dancers for the following six years" (with the exception of 1910). Bullard, vol. 1, pp. 64–65.

43. Buckle, *Diaghilev*, pp. 96–101.

44. Quoted in ibid., p. 111.

45. Benois, quoted in Goldman, p. 46.

46. The group included Benois, Nouvel, Bakst, Serov, Fokine, the ballet critic Valerien Svetlov and Serge Grigoriev, who was to serve as *régisseur* for the Ballets Russes throughout its existence. Buckle, *Diaghilev*, p. 127.

47. The operas to be presented were Rimsky-Korsakov's *Maid of Pskov* or *Ivan the Terrible*, the first act of Glinka's *Ruslan and Ludmila*, two acts of *Boris Godunov*, two acts of Serov's *Judith*, and the "Polovtsian Dance" act of Borodin's *Prince Igor*. It should be noted that the opera repertoire was weighted heavily with works on historical or mythic Russian themes. Ibid., pp. 142–43.

48. Acocella, chap. 5, p. 308.

49. Anna de Noailles, "Adieux des Ballets russes," *La Revue musicale*, no. 110 (1930), pp. 3–4. Author's translation.

50. Serge L. Grigoriev, *The Diaghilev Ballet, 1909–1929* (London: Constable, 1953; reprint ed. London: Penguin, 1960), p. 53.

51. Quoted in Acocella, chap. 4, p. 240.

52. Ibid., p. 241.

53. Beaumont, *Michel Fokine*, p. 94.

54. Acocella, chap. 4, p. 243.

55. Cyril Beaumont, *The Complete Book of Ballets: A Guide to the Principal Ballets of the Nineteenth and Twentieth Centuries* (London: Putnam, 1951), p. 563.

56. Goldman, p. 49.

57. The ballet's libretto was by Benois and Igor Stravinsky, who were, respectively, the designer and composer.

58. Goldman, p. 49.

59. Acocella, chap. 4, p. 279. This chapter is a comprehensive discussion of Symbolism and the prewar Ballets Russes.

60. Quoted in Wiley, "Alexandre Benois," Oct. 1980, p. 29.

61. Ibid.

62. Acocella, chap. 4, p. 1.

63. Ibid., p. 223.

64. Ibid.

65. See Stephanie Barron and Maurice Tuchman, eds., "Kandinsky's Role in the Russian Avant-Garde," in *The Avant-Garde in Russia 1910–1930: New Perspectives* (Cambridge, Mass.: MIT Press, 1980), pp. 84–90.

66. Frances Spaulding, *Roger Fry: Art and Life* (Berkeley, University of California Press, 1980), p. 148.

67. Quoted in Acocella, chap. 5, pp. 330–31. Author's translation.

68. Quoted in Vera Stravinsky and Robert Craft, *Stravinsky in Pictures and Documents* (New York: Simon & Schuster, 1978), p. 75.

69. Quoted in Igor Stravinsky and Robert Craft, *Memories and Commentaries* (Berkeley and Los Angeles: University of California Press, 1981), p. 30.

Chapter 2

1. Benois, *Reminiscences*, p. 347.

2. A. E. Johnson, *The Russian Ballet* (Boston: Houghton Mifflin, 1913), pp. 201–2.

3. Michel Georges-Michel, "Les Deux *Sacre du printemps*," *Comoedia* (11 December 1920), reprinted in his *Ballets Russes, histoires anecdotiques* (Paris: Editions de Monde Nouveau, 1923), pp. 47–50. The composer was accused by some critics of attempting to "rewrite history," especially in light of *Le Sacre*'s success as a concert work. He later modified his statement in an interview for *The Dial* in 1925.

4. Igor Stravinsky, *An Autobiography* (New York: Simon & Schuster, 1936; reprint ed. W. W. Norton, 1962), p. 31. Art historian Kenneth Archer states that it was Diaghilev who sent Roerich to Stravinsky when the composer had completed the score for *L'Oiseau de feu*. Roerich then suggested the idea for a ballet which was to become *Le Sacre*. Lecture at SUNY—Purchase, 20 October 1987.

5. Stravinsky wrote to N.F. Findeizen, editor of *The Russian Newspaper* on 15 December 1912. "My first thoughts on my new choreodrama *Vesna Sviasschennaya* [*Le Sacre du printemps*, Frühling der Heilige] came to me in the spring of 1910 as I was finishing *The Firebird.* I wanted to compose the libretto with N. K. Roerich, because who else could help, who else knows the secret of our ancestors' close feeling for the earth?" Quoted in V. Stravinsky and R. Craft, *Stravinsky in Pictures and Documents*, p. 77.

6. Craft dates this letter 19 June 1910, in appendix 2, "Letters to N. K. Roerich and N. F. Findeizen," in Igor Stravinsky and Robert Craft, *The Rite of Spring Sketches 1911–1913* (London: Boosey & Hawkes, 1969), p. 27, and as 2 July 1910 in V. Stravinsky and R. Craft, *Stravinsky in Pictures and Documents*, p. 77. Craft notes in his preface to the latter, p. 14, that throughout his life, "Stravinsky used both the Old and New Style Russian Calendars, but inconsistently, and frequently without specification." Craft's dates in *Pictures and Documents* are New Style, but, he admits, errors are unavoidable.

7. Quoted in V. Stravinsky and R. Craft, *Stravinsky in Pictures and Documents*, p. 79. The date of the letter, written from La Baule, Brittany, is given as 27 July in *The Rite of Spring Sketches,* appendix 2, p. 29.

8. *The Rite of Spring Sketches,* appendix 2, p. 29.

9. Igor Stravinsky and Robert Craft, *Expositions and Developments* (Berkeley and Los Angeles: University of California Press, 1959; reprint ed. 1981), p. 140.

10. Buckle, *Diaghilev,* p. 186.

11. Quoted in V. Stravinsky and R. Craft, *Stravinsky in Pictures and Documents*, p. 82. "The Great Sacrifice" and "The Great Victim" were two of the early titles for *Le Sacre.*

12. Bronislava Nijinska, *Early Memoirs.* Translated and edited by Irina Nijinska and Jean Rawlinson. Introduction by Anna Kisselgoff (New York: Holt, Rinehart & Winston, 1981), p. 328.

13. Ibid., p. 306. Nijinska records that Benois, Bakst, Roerich, Golovin, Korovin, Glazunov, Meyerhold, Tcherepnine, Sanine and Nouvel attended these meetings.

14. Quoted in ibid., p. 315.

15. Ibid., p. 328.

16. Ibid. Buckle says Diaghilev "was delighted." *Diaghilev,* p. 186. It is likely his reaction was something between apprehension and unalloyed happiness. Nijinska states that Diaghilev suggested her brother begin by mounting *Les Fêtes* or *Les Nuages,* both by Debussy, but Nijinsky was adamant that his first ballet be *L'Après-midi d'un faune.* Nijinska, p. 328.

17. I. Stravinsky and R. Craft, *Expositions,* p. 141. Some of the original costumes are now in the collection of the Theatre Museum, London.

18. Ibid.

19. Robert Craft, "Genesis of a Masterpiece," in I. Stravinsky and R. Craft, *The Rite of Spring Sketches,* p. 17.

20. Benois, *Reminiscences,* p. 347, and Grigoriev, p. 89.

21. N. K. Roerich to Diaghilev. *Sergei Diaghilev and Russian Art: Articles, Open Letters, Interviews, Correspondence. Contemporaries (Write) on Diaghilev.* In 2 volumes. Compiled with author's introductory articles and commentaries of I. S. Zilbershtein and V. A. Samkov (Moscow: Fine Arts, 1982), vol. 2, p. 430. Translation by Suzanne C. Levy.

22. Craft notes that Stravinsky preferred the Russian title of Part One which translates to "A Kiss of the Earth" to the "unspecific" French, which means "The Adoration of the Earth." The composer's preferences as to section headings are detailed by Craft in "Genesis of a Masterpiece," in I. Stravinsky and R. Craft, *The Rite of Spring Sketches,* pp. 20–23. The English headings used here are those preferred by Stravinsky.

23. I. Stravinsky and R. Craft, *Expositions,* p. 141.

24. Ibid., p. 142. The chronology of Stravinsky's composition can be seen in the chart of "Four Chronologies of *Le Sacre du printemps*—Stravinsky, Diaghilev, Nijinsky, Nijinska," in appendix 1. The composer also stated, in *Expositions and Developments,* p. 141, that the composition of the whole of *Le Sacre* was completed "in a state of exaltation and exhaustion," at the beginning of 1912. By all accounts, he is speaking of a two-hand piano score. Stravinsky also later prepared a four-hand piano score for use at ballet rehearsals. Craft, "Genesis," p. 18n.8. Craft dates the completion of the full score as March 1913 (V. Stravinsky and R. Craft, *Stravinsky in Pictures and Documents,* p. 514). The first completed working draft of the score was sold at an auction in London in 1982, and the date on this manuscript was 19 March 1913. John Nordheimer, "Stravinsky Manuscript Sale Sets Auction Record," *New York Times* (12 November 1982), sec. 3, p. 3.

25. I. Stravinsky and R. Craft, *Expositions,* p. 141.

26. Grigoriev, p. 25.

27. Quoted in Buckle, *Diaghilev,* p. 219.

28. Nijinska, p. 405.

29. James Monahan, *Fonteyn: A Study of the Ballerina in Her Setting* (London: A. & C. Black, 1957), p. 72.

30. Ibid. Serge Lifar states that it was Diaghilev "who actually inspired and created this ballet," actually demonstrating angular forms to Nijinsky. Serge Lifar, *Serge Diaghilev: His Life, His Work, His Legend* (London: Putnam, 1940), p. 265. Both Nijinsky's later work and Nijinska's first reactions to the ballet would seem to refute Lifar's claim. Diaghilev and especially Bakst were influential in developing Nijinsky's ideas and aesthetic tastes, but that either of them was responsible for the choreography is difficult to credit. The story, however, was obviously part of the Nijinsky–Diaghilev mythology. Arnold Haskell and Walter Nouvel assert that Bakst and Diaghilev "followed each rehearsal with care, correcting and guiding Nijinsky at every step." *Diaghileff: His Artistic and Private Life.* Foreword by Arnold Haskell (New York: Simon & Schuster, 1935), pp. 244–45. This notion is upheld by Stravinsky, and Grigoriev notes Diaghilev always attended *Faune* rehearsals. *The Diaghilev Ballet,* p. 77. As there were reputedly over ninety, this is difficult to believe. As for Bakst, he was certainly enamoured by ancient Greece, but the concept of friezelike movement was neither entirely "new" nor could it be credited solely to Nijinsky, Diaghilev or Bakst. In Vsevolod Meyerhold's 1905 Symbolist production of Maeterlinck's "The Death of Tintagiles," he attempted to use "sculptural expressiveness": in the description of theater historian Konstantin Rudnitsky, the actors froze in "bas-reliefs." Quoted in Anna Kisselgoff, "Meyerhold, Dance and Avant-Garde Theater in 1920's Russia" *New York Times* (6 December 1981), p. 16. The play was never produced. Lincoln Kirstein also lists Petipa and Alexander Gorsky as "stylistic antecedents" in their use of "Egytian profiling." *Nijinsky Dancing* (New York: Alfred A. Knopf, 1975), p. 125.

31. Nijinska, p. 434. Another case of claim and counterclaim. Nijinska, who points out that she had been working on *Faune* with her brother as early as November 1910, asserts it was Fokine who copied Nijinsky, appropriating the style of *Faune* for his dance of the three nymphs in *Daphnis*. Buckle states that Fokine claimed the plagiarized material was from his Venusburg scene in "Tannhäuser," "which Nijinsky had performed so excellently." *Nijinsky* (London: Weidenfeld & Nicolson, 1971), p. 246.

32. Grigoriev, p. 75.

33. G. Calmette in *Le Figaro,* quoted in Lifar, p. 271.

34. Buckle, *Diaghilev,* pp. 223–24.

35. Ibid., p. 224.

36. Cyril Beaumont, *Complete Book,* pp. 652–53. Interestingly, the look of the ballet had much in common with staging and movement techniques used in French Symbolist theater, which particularly used two-dimensional movements and bas-relief stagings. There was a corresponding decrease of depth of stage; backdrops were pushed forward to create a shallow stage. Gestures tended to be in a line parallel to the proscenium. The atmosphere created in Symbolist theater tied it to the acting style of flat, monotone voices, very little movement, long pauses and dialogue spoken slowly. Michael Kirby, "Lecture on Symbolist Theater," New York University, 14 October 1981.

37. See Buckle, *Nijinsky,* for a complete account of the ballet, its reception and controversies, pp. 239–46.

38. Eugène Belville, "Les Arts décoratifs au théâtre-La Saison russe—Nijinski choreographe-*Pénélope*-Les Nocturnes de Debussy," *Art et industrie* (September 1913), p. 362. Author's translation.

39. Quoted in Macdonald, p. 79.

40. Quoted in Belville, p. 362.

41. Quoted in Macdonald, p. 78.

42. Bullard, vol. 1, pp. 11–12. V. Stravinsky and R. Craft, *Stravinsky in Pictures and Documents,* p. 86.

43. Pierre Monteux, "Early Years," *Dance Index,* vol. 7 (1947), p. 242.

44. Doris G. Monteux, *It's All in the Music* (New York: Farrar, Straus & Giroux, 1969), p. 89.

45. Selma L. Odom, "Lectures on Eurythmics: Experiments in Music and Movement, 1890–1925." New York University, May–June 1983. For a general discussion of the influence of Dalcroze theories and techniques in *Le Sacre,* see André Levinson, "Les Deux Sacres," in *La Danse au théâtre, esthétique et actualité mêlées* (Paris: Librairie Bloud et Gay, 1924), p. 55.

46. Buckle, *Nijinsky,* p. 164. It is possible that Diaghilev and Nijinsky saw these demonstrations.

47. Nijinska, p. 451.

48. Stravinsky, *An Autobiography,* p. 40.

49. Nijinska, pp. 89, 122.

50. I. Stravinsky and R. Craft, *Memories and Commentaries,* p. 37.

51. Nijinska, p. 449. Craft states that by "the first two weeks of February the solo for the Chosen Virgin was not yet choreographed." *Stravinsky in Pictures and Documents*, p. 514. Nijinska, who gives 17 November 1912 as the date of completion for the initial draft of the score of *Le Sacre*, recalls that "it was sometime before that date that Vaslav had already received from Stravinsky a score for part of the music, including the 'Danse sacrale' in the second scene." Nijinska, p. 449.

52. Nijinska, pp. 449–50.

53. Ibid., p. 450.

54. See R. Craft, "Genesis," pp. 20–22. Craft also notes that for *Le Sacre*, Stravinsky, as always, worked with an exact plan of the stage action in mind, which he not only discarded but also denied had ever existed once the ballet had been completed." *Pictures and Documents*, p. 512. This denial occurred at the time of the Massine revival in 1920.

55. "The Stravinsky–Nijinsky Choreography," appendix 3, I. Stravinsky and R. Craft, *The Rite of Spring Sketches*, pp. 35–43. These notations were made on a four-hand piano score, which Stravinsky gave Misia Sert as a gift the day after *Le Sacre*'s premiere. It was "recovered" by Anton Dolin at a London auction in June 1967.

56. I. Stravinsky and R. Craft, *Memories and Commentaries*, p. 37; Nijinska, p. 458. A letter from Monteux to Stravinsky illustrates Nijinsky's musical acumen. Nijinsky had pointed out to the conductor the fact that parts of the piano reduction did not correspond to the orchestral score and requested clarification for his rehearsal score. Letter from Pierre Monteux to Igor Stravinsky, 22 February 1913. Stravinsky Archives, Paul Sacher Collection, Basel, Switzerland.

57. Nijinska, p. 450.

58. Marie Rambert, interview with the author, 10 October 1978.

59. Nijinsky told his sister that "Roerich's art inspires me as much as does Stravinsky's powerful music. Roerich has talked to me at length about his paintings in this series ['The Idols of Ancient Russia,' 'The Daughters of the Earth' and 'The Call of the Sun'] that he describes as the spirit of primeval man. In *Sacre* I want to emulate this spirit of prehistoric Slavs." Nijinska, pp. 449, 450.

60. Ibid., p. 450.

61. Ibid.

62. Rambert, interview. "Kolossal," then a popular slang word for "great," was Diaghilev's nickname for Maurice Steiman.

63. Ibid. Craft notes that between November 1912 and February 1913, "Stravinsky continued to coach the dancers, pianists, conductors (Monteux and Rhené-Baton) and Nijinsky . . . meeting them in all of the larger cities on tour." "*Le Sacre* and Pierre Monteux: An Unknown Debt," *New York Review of Books* (3 April 1975), p. 33. Craft also dates Rambert's account of the *contretemps* as 22 November 1912 (*Stravinsky in Pictures and Documents*, p. 90), but she did not join the Ballets Russes until December 1912. Rambert recalled to this author that this appearance by Stravinsky probably took place in London in early February of 1913. See also Buckle, *Diaghilev*, p. 243.

64. Rambert, interview.

65. The "entourage" included "the balletomanes and critics from prominent Russian newspapers." Nijinska, p. 461.

66. Quoted in V. Stravinsky and R. Craft, *Stravinsky in Pictures and Documents*, p. 95.

67. Quoted in ibid., p. 94.

68. Nijinsky, quoted in an interview, "Nijinsky Choreographe," *Comoedia* 7 (15 May 1913), p. 1. Quoted in Bullard, vol. 1, p. 113. Similar comments, taken from an article by Hector Cahausac in *Le Figaro* the day before *Jeux*'s premiere appeared in "Echoes of Music Abroad," *Musical America*, 14 June 1913, p. 9.

69. Barbara Barker, "Nijinsky's *Jeux*," *The Drama Review*, vol. 26, no. 1 (Spring 1982), p. 54.

70. For accounts of *Jeux*'s conception, see Buckle, *Diaghilev*, pp. 233–34; Jacques-Emile Blanche, "Un Bilan artistique de 1913" in *La Revue de Paris* (1 December 1913), pp. 517–34; Nijinska, pp. 465–69.

71. Quoted in Buckle, *Diaghilev*, p. 234.

72. Barker, p. 53.

73. Quoted in Bullard, vol. 1, pp. 113–14.

74. Nijinska, p. 445.

75. Lydia Sokolova, *Dancing for Diaghilev*, edited by Richard Buckle (London: John Murray, 1960), p. 41.

76. Nijinska did not dance in *Jeux* or in *Le Sacre du printemps*. She had recently married the dancer Alexander Kotchetovsky and became pregnant during the Ballets Russes' London season in 1912. Her role in *Jeux* was performed by Ludmilla Schollar and the Chosen Maiden in *Le Sacre* by Maria Piltz.

77. Nijinska, p. 444.

78. Nijinsky, quoted in Barker, p. 54. "Stylized gesture" was Nijinsky's term for this "new" form of dancing.

79. See also Romola Nijinsky, *Nijinsky*. Foreword by Paul Claudel (London: Gollancz; New York: Simon & Schuster, 1934), pp. 198–201.

80. Barker, p. 54. The original choreography for *Jeux* has not survived.

81. Louis Laloy, "La Musique: Théâtre des Champs-Elysées: *Pénélope* de M. Gabriel Fauré; *Jeux*, ballet de M. Nijinsky, musique de M. Claude Debussy," *La Grande revue*, vol. 79 (10 June 1913), pp. 402–5. Quoted in Bullard, vol. 2, p. 419.

82. Quoted in Barker, p. 59.

83. Henri Quittard in Buckle, *Diaghilev*, p. 251; Debussy, quoted in ibid.

84. Bullard, vol. 1, p. 116.

85. Ibid., pp. 116, 120.

86. Quoted in ibid., p. 122.

Chapter 3

1. Quoted in V. Stravinsky and R. Craft, *Stravinsky in Pictures and Documents*, p. 87.

2. Quoted in ibid., p. 90.

3. Bullard, vol. 1, p. 58.

4. Richard Taruskin, "From 'Firebird' to 'The Rite': Folk Elements in Stravinsky's Scores," *Ballet Review*, vol. 10 (Summer 1982), p. 72.

5. Ibid.

6. Quoted in Buckle, *Diaghilev*, p. 159.

7. Lieven, p. 107. Lieven felt the plot of *L'Oiseau de feu*, "although colorful, was not convincing for a Russian. It was as if Alice in Wonderland were partnered by Falstaff in a Scotch jig." Ibid.

8. I. Stravinsky and R. Craft, *Expositions and Developments*, p. 128.

9. Beaumont, *Complete Book of Ballets*, pp. 710–12.

10. I. Stravinsky and R. Craft, *Expositions and Developments*, p. 129; Buckle, *Diaghilev*, p. 160.

11. I. Stravinsky and R. Craft, *Expositions and Developments*, p. 129.

12. Quoted in Roland John Wiley, "Alexandre Benois' Commentaries on the First *Saisons russes*—Part 4," *The Dancing Times*, vol. 71 (January 1981), p. 250; Benois, *Reminiscences*, p. 304.

13. Taruskin, p. 73.

14. Ibid., p. 75.

15. The "Mighty Five" consisted of Rimsky-Korsakov, Balakirev, Borodin, Mussorgsky and Cui.

16. Taruskin, p. 76.

17. Eric Walter White, *Stravinsky: The Composer and His Works* (Berkeley and Los Angeles: University of California Press, 1966), p. 188.

18. Arthur Berger, "Music for the Ballet," in Minna Lederman, ed., *Stravinsky in the Theatre*, (New York: Pellegrini & Cudahy, 1949; reprint ed., Da Capo Press, 1975), p. 48.

19. Quoted in White, p. 184.

20. *Balagani* means both "fair booth" and, in theater parlance, "farces." Roland John Wiley, "Benois' Commentaries on the First *Saisons russes*—Part 7," *The Dancing Times*, vol. 71 (April 1981), p. 465n.2.

21. Ibid., p. 464. This statement appears in an article on *Petrouchka* that Benois wrote for the St. Petersburg publication, *Rech'*. It was published on 4 August 1911, and predates the account in his *Reminiscences* by thirty years.

22. White, pp. 196–97.

23. The tune was "Elle avait un' jambe en bois." For a fuller documentation of folk sources for *Petrouchka*, see Taruskin.

24. Taruskin, p. 78.

25. Lieven, p. 145.

26. Taruskin, p. 79.

27. Ibid.

28. Ibid., p. 80.

29. Ibid., p. 81.

30. Quoted in ibid.

31. Ibid., p. 80.

32. Ibid., p. 82.

33. Quoted in ibid.

34. A group of Ukrainian dances entitled *Vesnyaki* is currently in the repertoire of the Moiseyev, the Soviet folk dance company. M. Chudnovsky, *Dancing to Fame,* translated from the Russian by S. Rosenberg (Moscow: Foreign Languages Publishing House, 1959), photograph facing p. 33.

35. Zemtsovsky, in Taruskin, p. 82.

36. The Ustilug population, in Stravinsky's time a town of about 4,000, was entirely Jewish. The composer described it as a community "out of Isaac Babel or Chagall and the cosiest and most affectionate community imaginable." I. Stravinsky and R. Craft, *Expositions and Developments,* p. 52.

37. Taruskin, p. 83.

38. Quoted in ibid.

39. Boris Asafiev, quoted in ibid.

40. Eric Walter White, *Stravinsky: The Composer and His Works* (Berkeley and Los Angeles: University of California Press, 1966), p. 212.

41. Ibid., p. 213.

42. Taruskin, p. 84.

43. Quoted in Bullard, vol. 2, p. 9. In his *Autobiography,* Stravinsky has denied that he is the author of the article which appeared in *Montjoie!* on 29 May 1913. The composer states that he gave the journal's publisher, Ricciardo Canudo, an interview. "Unfortunately," wrote Stravinsky, "it appeared in the form of a pronouncement on the *Sacre* at once grandiloquent and naive, and, to my great astonishment, signed with my name." Quoted in Bullard, vol. 2, p. 4. Contemporaneous correspondence between Canudo and Stravinsky indicates some sort of exchange of information and/or ideas took place between the two men prior to *Le Sacre*'s premiere. One note from Canudo states that the proofs of the article would be needed by Tuesday (27 May 1913) or the publisher would be obliged to correct them himself. The article appeared on 29 May and on 5 June, ill with typhus, Stravinsky wrote a letter of disavowal to Canudo, who in turn was surprised at the composer's "violent and hostile protest." V. Stravinsky and R. Craft, *Stravinsky in Pictures and Documents,* appendix B, pp. 522–23. When a Russian version of the "interview" appeared in *Muzyka* in Moscow on 16 August 1913, Stravinsky wrote to the editor that he had read "the translation of my *Montjoie!* article," and found it inaccurate and incorrect. Craft feels this letter establishes Stravinsky's authorship of the article. Ibid., p. 523.

44. V. Stravinsky and R. Craft, *Stravinsky in Pictures and Documents,* p. 511.

45. Quoted in ibid.

46. Craft, in ibid. Stravinsky's *Autobiography* misdates the ballet's premiere (which he gives as 28 May) and contradicts both his public and private statements regarding Nijinsky's work made at the time of *Le Sacre*'s first performance. Ibid., pp. 46–48.

47. Stravinsky gave this score to Misia Sert the day following *Le Sacre*'s premiere, who, in turn, gave it to Diaghilev. Anton Dolin owned the score between Diaghilev's death in 1929 and the composer's purchase of it at a London auction in 1967. I. Stravinsky and R. Craft, *The Rite of Spring Sketches,* Appendix 3, ''The Stravinsky–Nijinsky Choreography,'' p. 35.

48. Nijinska, p. 471.

49. V. Stravinsky and R. Craft, *Stravinsky in Pictures and Documents,* appendix B, p. 511.

50. Quoted in ibid., p. 512.

51. Quoted in ibid., p. 90.

Chapter 4

1. Blanche, p. 521.

2. Ibid. For a discussion of the French critics' preseason publicity, see Bullard, vol. 1, pp. 85–95.

3. Buckle, *Diaghilev,* p. 250; Grigoriev, p. 91.

4. Nijinska recalled that, at the ballet rehearsals, Stravinsky even taught Steiman ''how to read notes'' when they played together on the piano. Nijinska, p. 458.

5. Quoted in Robert Craft, ''*Le Sacre* and Pierre Monteux: An Unknown Debt.''

6. Louis Speyer, quoted in Bullard, vol. 1, p. 98.

7. Quoted in ibid.

8. Quoted in D. Monteux, p. 89.

9. Nijinska, p. 469. Stravinsky later wrote that, at the premiere of *Le Sacre,* ''the dancers knew what they were doing, even though what they were doing often had nothing to do with the music.'' I. Stravinsky and R. Craft, *Expositions and Developments,* p. 143.

10. Quoted in Bullard, vol. 1, p. 98.

11. Quoted in ibid., p. 99.

12. S. M., ''Voici revenir nos amis les russes,'' *Comoedia,* vol. 7 (6 May 1913), p. 1. Quoted in ibid., p. 41.

13. It should be remembered that Diaghilev presented opera as well as ballet in the prewar seasons.

14. See Bullard, vol. 1, pp. 102–10 and Acocella, chap. 5, ''The Reception in Paris,'' pp. 303–61.

15. Stravinsky, *An Autobiography,* p. 47.

16. Quoted in Bullard, vol. 1, p. 132. The notice appeared in *Le Figaro, L'Aurore, La France, Comoedia* and *Le Gaulois.* Ibid., vol. 2, p. 1.

17. Quoted in Buckle, *Diaghilev,* p. 253.

18. Cyril Beaumont, *The Diaghilev Ballet in London* (London: Adam & Charles Black, 1951), p. 13.

19. Truman Bullard's dissertation, "The First Performance of Igor Stravinsky's *Sacre du printemps*," contains a complete description and analysis of the ballet's reception. For other accounts of the "riot" at the premiere, see Buckle, *Diaghilev*, pp. 252–55, Buckle, *Nijinsky*, pp. 299–304, Lifar, pp. 202–3, Haskell and Nouvel, pp. 219–21, Nijinska, pp. 469–70, Jean Cocteau, "Le Sacre du Printemps" in Minna Lederman, pp. 13–20, I. Stravinsky and R. Craft, *Expositions and Developments*, pp. 142–43.

20. Quoted in Buckle, *Nijinsky*, pp. 299–300. Later, Valentine Gross married Jean Hugo, the great-grandson of the poet Victor Hugo, whose *Hernani* had provoked a similar riot in Paris in 1830.

21. Beaumont, *The Diaghilev Ballet in London*, p. 72.

22. Quoted in Buckle, *Nijinsky*, p. 301.

23. Quoted in A. H. Franks, "*The Rite of Spring*," *The Dancing Times*, vol. 52 (May 1962), p. 483. Bullard investigated "the whole question of police intervention at *Le Sacre*. . . . There is no mention anywhere in contemporary documents of police activity; newspapers which carried a daily column of police news had nothing to say about the Théâtre des Champs-Elysées the following day." Vol. 1, p. 143n.93. Both Henri Girard and Marie Rambert denied that the police were involved. Girard in ibid., Rambert in an interview with the author.

24. Buckle, *Diaghilev*, p. 254. See also Carl Van Vechten, *Music after the Great War* (New York: G. Schirmer, 1915), pp. 87–88. Van Vechten also attended the second performance of *Le Sacre*, as did Gertrude Stein, Alice B. Toklas, and Guillaume Apollinaire. Stein called the performance "incredibly fierce." Quoted in James R. Mellow, *Charmed Circle: Gertrude Stein and Company* (New York and Washington: Praeger Publishers, 1974), p. 197.

25. "The Adolescents" in act 1; Rambert interview. "We weren't *ready*, we simply weren't *ready*," she said of the first night of *Le Sacre*.

26. Bullard, vol. 1, p. 148.

27. Quoted in ibid., pp. 149–50.

28. Girard, in ibid., p. 150.

29. Nijinsky, p. 470.

30. I. Stravinsky and R. Craft, *Expositions and Developments*, p. 143.

31. Sokolova, *Dancing for Diaghilev*, p. 44.

32. Gustave Linor, "Au Théâtre des Champs-Elysées: *Le Sacre du printemps*," *Comoedia*, vol. 7 (30 May 1913), p. 3.

33. Stravinsky's account, quoted in Buckle, *Diaghilev*, p. 254.

34. Bullard, vol. 1, p. 160. When Astruc totaled the receipts for the Théâtre des Champs-Elysées for the season, he found the Russian Ballet had brought in the most money, with seventeen performances netting an average of $5,600 each. "Champs-Elysées Receipts," *Musical America* (19 July 1913), p. 31. By the middle of October, however, Astruc was bankrupt.

35. In recent years there have been a number of efforts to reconstruct Nijinsky's original choreography. Millicent Hodson, a choreographer and dance historian, has completed a carefully documented reconstruction and has discussed her project with the author. Her work will be cited later in this chapter.

36. Nijinska, illustration 102.

37. Hodson notes that some of the rumors of the existence of Nijinsky's notations derive from a project of Mme. Nicoliavena Legat, wife of Nicholas Legat, one of Nijinsky's teachers. Mme. Legat wished to make Nijinsky's notation system available to the public. A reviewer for *Dance and Dancers* attended Mme. Legat's lecture on the subject and reported "Although Mme. Legat has Mme. Romola Nijinsky's permission to consult the original manuscripts, her knowledge is not based on these but on a poor French translation." Quoted in Hodson, "Searching," p. 75n.17.

38. In August 1917, French poet Blaise Cendrars wrote to Stravinsky proposing that he negotiate with Abel Gance for a film of *Le Sacre*, but the project never materialized. V. Stravinsky and R. Craft, *Stravinsky in Pictures and Documents*, appendix B, p. 656n.10.

39. Hodson, "Searching," p. 64.

40. V. Stravinsky and R. Craft, *Stravinsky in Pictures and Documents*, appendix B, p. 512. In the first edition of the four-hand piano score, the *mise-en-scène* for *Le Sacre* is credited to both Nijinsky and Stravinsky (Ibid., p. 510). In a document called a "bulletin of declaration" (n.d.) from the Société des auteurs et compositeurs dramatiques in Paris, *Le Sacre* is listed as a "choréodrame." The form also cites Stravinsky as both author and composer. Interestingly, an "s" has been added to the column headed "Auteur" and there is an "et" under Stravinsky's name, but no additional name (or names) appear. Stravinsky Archives, Paul Sacher Collection, Switzerland.

41. Craft, "Genesis," in Igor Stravinsky and Robert Craft, *The Rite of Spring Sketches*, pp. xx–xxiii. Stravinsky's instructions to Nijinsky are those cited in chapter 2.

42. Craft notes that Stravinsky "warns choreographers that it is a Sabine-type mass rape and not an action that can be symbolized by a single pair of dancers." Craft, "Genesis," p. xxi. The composer also noted that a ceremony of young men locking arms in a circle around a young girl survived in country weddings in Russia in this century. Ibid.

43. Craft writes that the Sage is "helped to his knees by two attendants" (Craft, "Genesis," p. xxi), but Rambert recalled the spread-eagle movement in an interview with the author. This description is also confirmed in the review of *Le Sacre* by M. Casalonga, "Nijinsky et *Le Sacre du printemps*," *Comoedia illustré*, vol. 17 (5 June 1913), quoted in Bullard, vol. 1, pp. 150–51.

44. Lydia Sokolova, in a letter to Richard Buckle dated 1 December 1970, wrote "I can also tell you now that the made ending to the first act was planned, if it is of any use after all, it is 57 years ago and so few performances." In the Valentine Gross Sketches File, in the Theatre Museum, London.

45. There are twelve girls listed in the cast for the second scene of *Le Sacre*, Bullard, vol. 1, p. 242, but Stravinsky specifies six, Craft, "Genesis," p. xxii.

46. The Stravinsky–Craft commentary makes no mention of the men and Elders observing.

47. This is a quote from the four-hand piano score. In Craft, "Genesis," p. xxii.

48. Craft states that the "women retire" at this point. There is nothing in Stravinsky's notes to Nijinsky to indicate this, and the women are included in the composer's notations for the "Ritual Action of the Ancestors" section. Craft, "The Stravinsky–Nijinsky Choreography," in I. Stravinsky and R. Craft, *The Rite of Spring Sketches*, p. 42.

49. Stravinsky noted that for the last fifteen bars of the "Danse sacrale," the Chosen Virgin is the only dancer moving. As Craft describes the ending, as Stravinsky originally conceived it, "The Elders stand like witnesses at an execution, and extend their hands to the victim as she falls in time with the flute scale." Craft, "Genesis," p. xxii. The final chords were added before the ballet's premiere.

50. Nijinska, p. 449.

51. Quoted in Macdonald, p. 90.

52. Quoted in ibid.

53. Edward F. Fry, *Cubism* (New York and Toronto: McGraw-Hill, 1966), pp. 70–71; Roger Rosenblum, *Cubism and Twentieth-Century Art* (New York: Harry N. Abrams, 1966), p. 25.

54. Robert Hughes, *The Shock of the New* (New York: Alfred A. Knopf, 1981), p. 20.

55. Ibid.

56. Nijinsky in a letter to Stravinsky, January 1913, quoted in Craft, p. 33. Roger Shattuck, in his discussion of the avant-garde in France prior to World War I, noted that "modernism coincided in a significant fashion with primitivism." *The Banquet Years: The Origins of the Avant-Garde in France, 1885 to World War I* (New York: Random House, 1968; rev. ed. London: Cape, 1969), p. 24.

57. Taruskin, p. 80.

58. Christopher Gray, *Cubist Aesthetic Theories* (Baltimore: The Johns Hopkins Press, 1953), pp. 58–61.

59. Nijinska, pp. 5, 162–63.

60. Rambert called this latter pose "kuluchki" or "fistikins," a diminutive. The position is "not strong, a little relaxed." Interview with the author.

61. Gross' notes are in the collection of the Stravinsky–Diaghilev Foundation, New York. There are over 50 small line drawings in the Theatre Museum, London. A selection of these sketches, including one illustrating the moment described above, are reproduced in Richard Buckle, *Nijinsky on Stage: Action Drawings by Valentine Gross of Nijinsky and the Diaghilev Ballet Made in Paris between 1909 and 1913* (London: Studio Vista, 1971), pp. 134–41.

62. Similar gestures can be seen in a film excerpt of Léonide Massine's production of *Le Sacre* for La Scala, Milan, in 1948, and in Martha Graham's *Primitive Mysteries*. Graham danced the role of the Chosen Virgin in Massine's 1930 production of *Le Sacre* for the League of Composers, Philadelphia.

63. Mme. Maria Fay, who studied character dance with Igor Moiseyev, documents the step as "dotting" in the Russian peasant style and the Hungarian peasant style uses the "rida" which has a similar foot action. In both these examples, however, the upper body is held erect.

64. This action, with the accompanying side-stepping movement, was used by Mme. Tamara Karsavina in the "Russian Dance" she choreographed for the Royal Academy of Dancing Girls Examination Syllabus, Grade 5. Valentine Gross sketched Nijinsky's version of the movement. Theatre Museum—Valentine Gross Sketches, #11.

65. Rambert, interview.

66. Louis Laloy, "La Musique," *La Grande Revue* (25 June 1913), pp. 612–13, quoted in Bullard, vol. 2, p. 177; Emile Vuillermoz, "La Saison russe au Théâtre des Champs-Elysées," *S.I.M. La Revue musicale,* vol. 9, no. 6 (15 June 1913), pp. 49–56, quoted in ibid., p. 169; Jacques Rivière, *"Le Sacre du printemps,"* *La Nouvelle Revue française,* vol. 10 (1 November 1913), pp. 706–30, quoted in ibid., p. 305.

67. Pierre Lalo, "Remarks on the Ballet *Le Sacre du printemps,"* trans. Mrs. Daniel Gregory Mason, *The New Music Review,* vol. 12 (October 1913), pp. 440–43.

68. Rosenblum, p. 20.

69. Rivière felt that Stravinsky and Nijinsky, "because they wanted only to resolve a particular problem, have in fact discovered a general solution. And if, in an attempt closely related to theirs, the cubists until now have been failing, it comes from their having produced first of all an abstract solution, one which they have only thereafter attempted to place, intact and absurd, in their works." *"Le Sacre du printemps,"* (1 November 1913) quoted in Bullard, vol. 2, pp. 301–2. See also Jacques Rivière, "Present Tendencies in Painting," in Fry, *Cubism,* pp. 75–81.

70. Louis Schneider, "Au Théâtre des Champs-Elysées: *Le Sacre du printemps*—La mise en scène et des décors," *Comoedia,* vol. 7 (31 May 1913), p. 2, quoted in Bullard, vol. 2, p. 55. The word "stylization" appeared in four other reviews quoted in Bullard, vol. 2: Gaston Carraud, "Au Théâtre des Champs-Elysées: *Le Sacre du printemps,"* *La Liberté* (31 May 1913), quoted in Bullard, vol. 2, p. 61; Octave Maus, *"Le Sacre du printemps,"* *L'Art moderne* (1 June 1913), quoted in Bullard, vol. 2, p. 73; Lalo, "Remarks," quoted in Bullard, vol. 2, p. 244; Jean Marnold, "Musique," *Mercure de France* (1 October 1913), quoted in Bullard, vol. 2, p. 256.

71. Rivière, *"Le Sacre du printemps,"* quoted in Bullard, vol. 2, p. 300.

72. Ibid., p. 296.

73. Nijinsky, in an interview with the *Pall Mall Gazette,* 15 February 1913, quoted in Macdonald, p. 90.

74. Rivière, *"Le Sacre du printemps"* (1 November 1913) quoted in Bullard, vol. 2, p. 305.

75. Marcia B. Siegel, *The Shapes of Change: Images of American Dance* (Boston: Houghton Mifflin, 1979), p. 50.

76. Rambert, interview.

77. André Levinson, "Stravinsky and the Dance," *Theatre Arts Monthly,* vol. 8 (November 1924), p. 750.

78. Hodson, "Restoring a Lost Work," p. 8. Hodson observes that "this is a very ancient configuration, this forming of a square to represent the human community, as opposed to forming circles that represent the natural community. Ibid., pp. 8–9.

79. Rivière, *"Le Sacre du printemps"* (1 November 1913) quoted in Bullard, vol. 2, p. 305.

80. Quoted in ibid.

81. André Levinson, "Les Deux *Sacres,"* *La Revue musicale,* vol. 4 (1 June 1922), p. 89. Author's translation. The literal translation of *branle* is oscillation or shaking movement. According to Mary Stewart Evans, "the branle [spelled variously bransle, brawl and braul] is a dance type of French origin. Descended from the basse dance, it was originally a rustic dance but later found favor in the fashionable world." Lady Evans is speaking of sixteenth-century fashion. Thoinot Arbeau, *Orchesography,* translated by

Mary Stewart Evans, with a new introduction and notes by Julia Sutton (New York: Dover Publications, 1967), p. 202. It is likely that Levinson was at least familiar with the *branle* as an historical dance form, which usually was performed in a circle and danced moving sideways.

82. Nijinska spoke about the transformation of the Chosen Virgin, her transcendence of death, in the final moments of the "Danse sacrale," whereas most critics spoke about her "death." Rambert, interview.

83. Susanne Langer, *Feeling and Form* (New York: Charles Scribner's Sons, 1953), p. 191.

84. Rambert, interview.

85. Kirstein, *Nijinsky Dancing*, p. 145.

86. Rambert, interview.

87. Valentine Gross Sketches, Theatre Museum, London.

88. Levinson, "Stravinsky and the Dance," p. 750.

89. Rivière, "*Le Sacre du printemps*" (1 November 1913) quoted in Bullard, vol. 2, p. 304.

90. Quoted in Lederman, pp. 18, 13.

91. Quoted in Martin Green, *The von Richthofen Sisters: The Triumphant and Tragic Modes of Love* (New York: Basic Books, 1974), p. 191.

92. For a comprehensive discussion of the critical reception of *Le Sacre* in Paris, see Bullard, vol. 1.

93. Adolphe Jullien, "Revue musicale," *Le Journal des débats*, vol. 125 (8 June 1913), p. 1.

94. Linor, p. 1.

95. Leon Vallas, "*Le Sacre du printemps*," *La Revue française de musique*, vol. 14 (June–July 1913), pp. 601–3.

96. Alfred Capus, "Courrier de Paris," *Le Figaro*, vol. 59 (2 June 1913), p. 1. In July 1913, after *Le Sacre* was performed in London, a parody was presented at the Hippodrome Theater. "Mr. James Watt, it has been said, realises in his creaming parody of the 'Danse du printemps' the difference between rag-time and spring-time. In the former they 'rag' and in the latter they 'spring.' The combination of the two is distinctly amusing." "A Saison russe (i.e., Season's Rush) at the Hippodrome," *The Sketch* (30 July 1913), p. 111.

97. See Hodson, "Searching," pp. 72–73.

98. Paul Souday, "Théâtre des Champs-Elysées: *Le Sacre du printemps*," *L'Eclair*, vol. 26 (31 May 1913), p. 2, quoted in Bullard, vol. 2, p. 67.

99. Jacques Jary, "A travers les revues," *La Renaissance politique, littéraire et artistique*, vol. 1 (6 December 1913), p. 28, in Bullard, vol. 2, p. 340.

100. Louis Schneider, "Le Théâtre des Champs-Elysées, La Saison Russe à Paris: *Boris Godounow, La Khovanchina*, les ballets," *Le Théâtre*, vol. 349 (1 July 1913), p. 24.

101. Octave Maus, in *L'Art moderne* and Jean Marnold in *Mercure de France* in Bullard, vol. 2, pp. 72–76 and 250–68, respectively.

102. Letter from Pierre Monteux to Igor Stravinsky, 31 July 1913. Stravinsky Archives, Paul Sacher Collection, Switzerland.

103. Quoted in Macdonald, pp. 97, 99.

104. Quoted in ibid.

105. S.L.B., "Nijinsky and the Dancing Revolution," *The Sketch* (23 July 1913), p. 96.

106. Quoted in Michael Holyrod, *Lytton Strachey: The Years of Achievement, 1910–1932*, vol. 2 (New York: Holt, Rinehart and Winston, 1968), p. 95; quoted in Acocella, chap. 6, p. 419.

107. Quoted in Acocella, chap. 6, p. 406.

108. Quoted in Rollo Myers, "The Ballet Music of Igor Stravinsky," *The Ballet Annual* (London: A. & C. Black, 1963), p. 27.

109. Quoted in Bullard, vol. 2, p. 304.

110. Quoted in ibid., p. 99.

Chapter 5

1. Edward Viscount Lord Grey. Comment, 4 August 1914, standing at the windows of his room at the Foreign Office as the lamplighters were turning off the lights in St. James' Park.

2. Sokolova, *Dancing for Diaghilev*, p. 67.

3. Sokolova, *Dancing for Diaghilev*, p. 59. Interestingly, part of Fokine's pact with Diaghilev included the agreement that while Fokine was in the Ballets Russes, none of Nijinsky's ballets would be given. Grigoriev, p. 103. Thus, Diaghilev could not have presented Nijinsky's *Le Sacre* in 1914, when the exigencies of war and the later frequent shift in company members had not yet made the production of the ballet impractical.

4. Grigoriev, p. 103.

5. Sokolova, *Dancing for Diaghilev*, p. 60.

6. Ibid., p. 61.

7. Léonide Massine, *My Life in Ballet*, edited by Phyllis Hartnoll and Robert Rubens (London: Macmillan, 1968), p. 45.

8. Magdelena Dabrowski, "The Plastic Revolution: New Concepts of Form, Content, Space and Materials from the Russian Avant-Garde," in *The Avant-Garde in Russia: 1910–1930*, p. 28.

9. Massine, p. 73.

10. Ibid., p. 74.

11. Ibid., p. 75.

12. Ibid., p. 77.

13. The production staged for the League of Composers was also performed at the Metropolitan Opera House in New York. Massine also planned to revive *Le Sacre* for the De Basil Ballets Russes with Nina Verchinina as the Chosen Maiden, but the plans came to nothing. Katherine Sorley Walker, *De Basil's Ballets Russes* (New York: Atheneum, 1983), p. 62. By 1948, *Le Sacre* had been produced by two choreographers: by Lester Horton in 1937, who choreographed a version for his Dance Theatre at the Hollywood Bowl, and by Aurelio Millos, who devised a *Le Sacre* for the Rome Opera

in 1941. Thus, Massine's 1948 and 1956 productions for La Scala and the Royal Swedish Ballet, respectively, were revivals of a work and a theme he had essayed twice before. While the choreography for these two ballets was undoubtedly somewhat different from either Massine's 1920 or 1930 versions, his fundamental concept of the ballet remained unchanged.

14. Sokolova, *Dancing for Diaghilev*, pp. 158–59.

15. V. Stravinsky and R. Craft, *Stravinsky in Pictures and Documents*, p. 107.

16. Sokolova, *Dancing for Diaghilev*, p. 159; V. Stravinsky and R. Craft, *Stravinsky in Pictures and Documents*, appendix B, p. 509.

17. Massine, quoted in Walter Sorell, "On Massine and Cocteau, Scandals and Audiences," *Dance Scope*, vol. 13 (1979), p. 12.

18. Massine, p. 152.

19. Ibid.

20. Ibid.

21. Quoted in Lederman, p. 26.

22. Ibid., p. 24.

23. Programme in the Theatre Museum, London.

24. Sokolova, *Dancing for Diaghilev*, p. 143.

25. Sokolova, Interview with the author, April 1969.

26. Sokolova, *Dancing for Diaghilev*, p. 159. It is possible that Massine had heard the story of Nijinsky's dancers "keeping little notebooks" to record their dancing counts, but Sokolova did not recall telling him about it. Interview.

27. Sokolova, *Dancing for Diaghilev*, pp. 159–60.

28. Sokolova, Interview. The notebook is now in the possession of Sokolova's husband, Ronald Mahon. She stated that the only other person to memorize the solo was Leon Woizikovsky. When this author asked if Massine would have remembered the solo, Sokolova replied that she thought he might recall "some of the difficult bits."

29. Sokolova, *Dancing for Diaghilev*, p. 162.

30. Ibid.

31. Ibid., pp. 162–64.

32. Sokolova, Interview.

33. Sokolova, *Dancing for Diaghilev*, p. 165; interview.

34. Sokolova, *Dancing for Diaghilev*, p. 166.

35. Ibid.

36. Ibid.

37. Ibid. Errol Addison, who danced in the Massine *Le Sacre* after he joined the Diaghilev Ballet in 1921, said Woizikovsky (who counted in Russian) always seemed to be calling out the same four numbers. "I think really it was more moral support than anything," said Addison. Telephone interview with the author, January 1981.

38. Sokolov, *Dancing for Diaghilev*, p. 167. A *grand jeté en tournant* is a leap in which the dancer throws one leg up in front of the body and, making a scissorlike movement with his legs, completes a half or full revolution in the air.

39. Beaumont, *The Diaghilev Ballet*, p. 167.

40. Levinson, ''Les Deux *Sacres*,'' *La Revue musicale*, p. 89. Author's translation.

41. Emile Vuillermoz, ''La Nouvelle Version choréographique de *Sacre du printemps* au Théâtre des Champs-Elysées,'' *La Revue musicale*, vol. 1 (February 1921), pp. 162–63. Author's translation.

42. Ibid., p. 163.

43. Jean Chantavoine, ''Au Théâtre des Champs-Elysées: *Le Sacre du printemps*,'' *Excelsior*, vol. 4 (30 May 1913), p. 6, quoted in Bullard, vol. 2, p. 19; Sokolova, Interview.

44. Jean Chantvoine, ''Premieres: Théâtre des Champs-Elysées: Ballets russe: *Les Sylphides, Le Sacre du printemps, Le Tricorne.*'' *L'Année musicale* (16 December 1920). Theatre Museum, London.

45. ''Théâtre des Champs-Elysées: *Le Sacre du printemps, Les Sylphides, Le Tricorne.*'' Unsigned (n.d.), Theatre Museum, London.

46. ''La Choréographie du *Sacre du printemps*.'' Unsigned (n.d.) The Diaghilev Albums, vol. 4, p. 40. Theatre Museum, London.

47. Quoted in Macdonald, p. 264.

48. Quoted in ibid., p. 266.

49. Quoted in Beaumont, *The Complete Book of Ballets*, p. 842.

50. Quoted in Beaumont, *The Complete Book of Ballets*, p. 841. This concept was developed to the full in Massine's symphonic ballets: *Les Présages, Symphonie fantastique, Seventh Symphony,* and *Choreartium.*

51. Quoted in Sorell, ''On Massine and Cocteau, Scandals and Audiences,'' p. 12.

52. Levinson, ''Stravinsky and the Dance,'' quoted in Lederman, p. 27.

53. Levinson, ''Les Deux *Sacres*,'' *La Revue Musicale*, p. 90. Author's translation.

54. Florence Gilliam, ''The Russian Ballet of 1923,'' *Theatre Arts Monthly*, vol. 8 (24 March 1924), p. 193.

55. Quoted in V. Stravinsky and R. Craft, *Stravinsky in Pictures and Documents*, appendix C, p. 537.

56. Vuillermoz, p. 163.

57. George Balanchine called *Le Sacre du printemps* ''impossible, terrible. Nobody can do it.'' Jonathan Cott, ''A Talk with George Balanchine,'' *Los Angeles Times* (25 February 1979), p. 69.

58. Sokolova, *Dancing for Diaghilev*, p. 276.

59. The date of this performance was 22 July 1929. *Daily Express*, quoted in Buckle, *Diaghilev*, p. 533.

60. Quoted in Macdonald, p. 379.

61. Quoted in Grigoriev, p. 264.

62. Quoted in Oliver Daniel, *Stokowski: A Counterpoint of View* (New York: Dodd, Mead, 1982), p. 225.

63. Ibid., p. 224.

64. Ibid., p. 248.

65. Ibid., p. 252. Bessie Schönberg, a member of the Graham company in 1930, felt that it was Stokowski who "sold" Graham to Massine and the rest of the production group. It was these performances of *Le Sacre*, notes Schönberg, that introduced Graham as "a personage, as a serious artist, to people who were interested in classical music." Telephone interview with the author, January 1981.

66. Bessie Schönberg, interview.

67. Massine, pp. 177-78.

68. Quoted in Daniel, p. 253.

69. Reis, quoted in ibid., p. 251.

70. Daniel, p. 250. The Philadelphia Orchestra usually gave its concerts at the Academy of Music; but the Schoenberg-Stravinsky productions were performed in that city's Opera House.

71. Eleanor King, *Transformations* (New York: Dance Horizons, 1978), p. 58.

72. Schönberg, interview.

73. Daniel, p. 254. Stravinsky wrote to a friend in 1927 that Stokowski had written him regarding making a recording of *Le Sacre*. "Unless this recording has already been made, I am very eager to stop him, not being at all confident of his tempi. . . . You understand that, unlike a concert performance, a recording is definitive." Quoted in V. Stravinsky and R. Craft, *Stravinsky in Pictures and Documents*, p. 59.

74. Quoted in Daniel, p. 254.

75. John Martin, *America Dancing* (New York: Dance Horizons, 1968), p. 195; Agnes De Mille, *The Book of the Dance* (New York: Golden Press, 1963), p. 221.

76. Quoted in Daniel, p. 254.

77. King, p. 60. Hammond states that during rehearsals at the Dalton School, "Martha would just freeze and sit on the floor. . . . Massine would try to get her to rehearse. She would not do it." Quoted in Daniel, p. 254.

78. Schönberg, interview.

79. Massine, p. 178.

80. Quoted in Daniel, p. 255. By "them" Graham means Massine, Roerich and Stokowski.

81. Schönberg, interview.

82. Don McDonagh, *Martha Graham: A Biography* (New York and Washington: Praeger Publishers, 1973), p. 72.

83. Quoted in Daniel, p. 255.

84. King, p. 254.

85. Quoted in Daniel, pp. 255-56.

86. Lily Mehlman, telephone interview with the author, January 1981.

87. King, pp. 59–60.

88. Ibid. In an advance notice of *Le Sacre* for the *New York Times*, John Martin noted that in Massine's 1920 production "realistic emotion" had no part in his scheme, "the effects being gained through aesthetic means." "The Dance: Stravinsky's Ballet," *New York Times* (20 April 1930), sec. x, p. 8. Massine might well have been skeptical of Stokowski's "dramatic" interpretation of the choreography.

89. King, p. 62.

90. Mehlman, interview.

91. Martin, "The Dance: Stravinsky's Ballet."

92. Massine, p. 198.

93. Edwin Evans, "Léonide Massine," *The Outlook*, vol. 44 (November 1919), p. 538.

94. "Massin [sic] Preparing an Indian Ballet," *New Mexico Telegraph*, 10 April 1916, Massine Clippings File, Dance Collection, Library and Museum of the Performing Arts at Lincoln Center, The New York Public Library.

95. Ibid. At one time, Graham also planned a ballet on the Pocahontas theme.

96. In an interview with Eugene Cook in 1961, Stokowski told of an early encounter with Nicholas Roerich. The designer was then living in the Himalayas and Stokowski, knowing Roerich's interest in ethnology, suggested that Roerich return, on his yearly trip to Paris, via the Pacific Ocean. "As you go through America," said Stokowski, "stop at some of the Indian pueblos and see the way they dance." According to Stokowski, Roerich made his next trip through New Mexico and Arizona and "was very impressed" with the costumes, music, singing and sacred dances of the Indians. "Then he saw how he could think of primitive dancing in Russia—the Slavic dance, and that was the beginning [of *Le Sacre*]." Quoted in Daniel, p. 252.

97. King, p. 63.

98. Ibid., pp. 62–63. Publicity photos show Graham barefoot, a departure from the laced sandals and leggings worn by both Piltz and Sokolova. Schönberg believes Graham danced the performances barefoot as well. Reviews also describe bare-legged dancers. It is possible that the company, many drawn from either the Graham or Humphrey–Weidman modern dance groups, put their collective feet down with a firm hand and refused to wear Roerich's cumbersome legwear. Or perhaps the decision came first from the creative triumverate of Massine, Stokowski, and Roerich—no one seems to recall.

99. Oscar Thompson, "Stage Schoenberg Opera and Stravinsky Ballet," *Musical America*, vol. 50 (25 April 1930), p. 5.

100. Quoted in King, p. 63.

101. Thompson, p. 5.

102. Marion Bauer and Flora Bauer, "Success for Shoenberg Opera and Stravinsky Ballet," *The Musical Leader*, vol. 58 (1 May 1930), p. 3.

103. A. Walter Kramer, "Novel Stage Works Close Orchestral Season," *Musical America*, vol. 50 (10 May 1930), p. 10.

104. Bauer and Bauer, p. 6.

105. John Martin, "The Dance: A Novel Experiment," *New York Times* (27 April 1930), sec. 9, p. 8.

106. King, p. 59.

107. See appendix 2 for analysis of the film.

108. King, p. 65.

109. Ibid.

110. These jumps resemble the famous "stalking" leaps in the "Crucifixus" section of *Primitive Mysteries*.

111. Martin, "The Dance: A Novel Experience."

112. Mehlman, interview.

113. Schönberg, interview.

114. Quoted in Daniel, pp. 256–57.

115. Massine, p. 179.

Chapter 6

1. Jean-Claude Dienis, "Maurice Béjart," in *"Le Sacre du printemps," L'Avant-scène: Ballet/Danse* (August–October 1980), p. 68.

2. Naima Prevots, "Dance at the Hollywood Bowl, 1926–1941: Performance, Theory and Practice" (Unpublished Ph.D. dissertation, University of Southern California, Los Angeles, 1984), p. 199. William Bowne was a member of the Horton Dance Group.

3. Dorothi Bock Pierre, "Notes for Lester Horton Ballet," from the Hollywood Bowl programme for *Le Sacre du printemps*. From the private collection of Karoun Toutikian. Copy courtesy of Dr. Naima Prevots.

4. Bella Lewitzky, telephone interview with the author, 2 May 1983.

5. Ibid.

6. Prevots, "Dance at the Hollywood Bowl," p. 201.

7. Quoted in ibid., p. 202.

8. Quoted in ibid., pp. 203–4.

9. Quoted in Walter Sorell, *The Mary Wigman Book* (Middletown, Connecticut: Wesleyan University Press, 1973), p. 181.

10. Ibid.; Mary Wigman, *The Language of Dance*. Translated from the German by Walter Sorell (Connecticut: Wesleyan University Press, 1966), p. 22.

11. Quoted in Marcelle Michel, "Marie Wigman," in *"Le Sacre du printemps," L'Avant-scène: Ballet/Danse* (August/October 1980), p. 65.

12. Letter from Mary Wigman to Genevieve Oswald. Mary Wigman Clippings File. Dance Collection, Library and Museum of the Performing Arts at Lincoln Center, the New York Public Library.

13. Quoted in Michel, p. 65.

14. Quoted in ibid. Author's translation.

15. Anne Villiers, "A Berlin: Triomphe et scandale," *Danse et rythmes,* vol. 35 (October-November, 1957), p. 14. Author's translation.

16. Maurice Béjart, Programme notes for *Le Sacre du printemps, Playbill,* vol. 8 (November 1971), p. 19.

17. Roger Stengele, *Who's Béjart,* ed. J. Verbeeck (Brussels: Théâtre Royale de la monnaie, Opéra National, n.d.), unpaginated.

18. Anatole Chujoy and P. W. Manchester, eds., *The Dance Encyclopedia,* introduction by Lincoln Kirstein (New York: Simon and Schuster, 1967), p. 882.

19. Deborah Jowitt, "The Hybrid: Very Showy, Will Root in Any Soil," in *Dance Beat: Selected Views and Reviews, 1967-1976* (New York and Basel: Marcel Dekker, 1977), pp. 64-66.

20. Quoted in Stengele.

21. Maurice Béjart, *Un Instant dans la vie d'autrui* (France: Flammarion, 1979), p. 133.

22. Marie Françoise Christout, *Maurice Béjart* (Paris: Editions Seghers, 1972), p. 35.

23. Béjart, "*Un Instant dans la vie d'autrui,*" p. 133. Author's translation.

24. Maurice Béjart, interview with the author, 24 September 1983.

25. Ibid.

26. Ibid.

27. Ibid.

28. Ibid. George Balanchine once remarked that Béjart's *Le Sacre* is "the best anyone has done. It has a certain impact and I was amazed how almost right—physically and musically—his version was." Quoted in Cott, p. 69.

29. Béjart, interview.

30. Béjart, "*Un Instant dans la vie d'autrui,*" p. 134.

31. Ibid., p. 135.

32. Ibid., p. 136.

33. Béjart, interview.

34. Peter Williams in Clive Barnes and Peter Williams, "What We Thought of T.R.M.," *Dance and Dancers,* vol. 11, no. 6 (June 1960), p. 22.

35. Dienis, p. 69.

36. Ibid.

37. Ibid.

38. Dancers have interpreted this role according to their individual perception of the ballet. Béjart told the author that Suzanne Ferrall, who usually preferred to discuss her roles in detail, told the choreographer that, for *Le Sacre,* "everything she needed to know was in the movement." Interview.

39. Béjart, interview.

40. Béjart, Programme notes for "Le Sacre."

41. Olga Maynard, "Maurice Béjart: On the Creative Process," *Dance Magazine*, vol. 47, no. 2 (February 1973), p. 58A. In this interview, Béjart mentions the fact that Nicholas Zverev, who had danced in Nijinsky's *Le Sacre,* had been one of his teachers, and that "he showed me all he could remember of Nijinsky's work." This would mean Béjart worked with Zverev around 1958, a year before the premiere of his Béjart's own *Le Sacre.* In an interview with this author, however, Béjart denied that any of Zverev's recollections of the 1913 work had become part of his choreography for *Le Sacre* in 1959. In 1971, Béjart created a dance-drama entitled *Nijinsky: Clown of God,* in which, he stated, the first part of the ballet was "inspired—not copied—by Nijinsky's original choreography for 'Rite of Spring.'" John Gruen, interview with Maurice Béjart, 31 October 1972, transcript, p. 5. Dance Collection, Library and Museum of the Performing Arts at Lincoln Center, the New York Public Library.

42. Gruen, ibid.

43. A. V. Coton, "Stravinsky Brought Up to Date," *The Daily Telegraph* (19 April 1960). Clippings file—Béjart's *Rite of Spring.* Theatre Museum, London.

44. "Artistic Triple Entente: Stravinsky Double Bill at the 'Wells.'" Clippings file—Béjart's *Rite of Spring,* Theatre Museum, London.

45. Oleg Kerensky, "This May Shock, but It's Novel," *Daily Mail* (19 April 1960). Clippings file—Béjart's *Rite of Spring.* Theatre Museum, London.

46. Barnes and Williams, "What We Thought of T.R.M." pp. 23–29.

47. "*Le Sacre du printemps,*" *The Guardian* (19 April 1960). Unsigned. Clippings file—Béjart's *Rite of Spring.* Theatre Museum, London.

48. Coton, "Stravinsky Brought Up to Date."

49. Barnes and Williams, "What We Thought of T.R.M.," p. 29.

50. "Improvisations on a Ritual," *The London Sunday Times* magazine (6 May 1962), p. 13.

51. Monica Mason, interview with the author, June 1978.

52. "Improvisations on a Ritual."

53. Mason, interview.

54. "The Earth as the Home of Life" is the title of a paper by anthropologist Adolph Portmann. As Joseph Campbell points out, "one force that can never have been absent from human life is gravity, which not only works continuously on every aspect of human affairs, but has fundamentally conditioned the form of the body and all its organs." Campbell, *The Masks of God: Primitive Mythology* (New York: The Viking Press, 1959; Viking Compass edition, 1970), p. 57. It is, of course, the manipulation and control of the gravitational force by the human body that is one of the primary principles of dance.

55. Campbell, *The Masks of God: Primitive Mythology,* p. 66.

56. Arlene Croce, "New York Newsletter," *The Dancing Times,* vol. 61 (April 1971), p. 366; Anna Kisselgoff, "How Valid a Symbol Is Béjart's 'Wien' Ballet?" *New York Times* (2 October 1983), p. H10.

57. Arlene Croce, "Folies Béjart," in *Afterimages* (New York: Alfred A. Knopf, 1977), p. 386.

Chapter 7

1. Mary Grace Swift, *The Art of the Dance in the U.S.S.R.* (Notre Dame, Indiana: University of Notre Dame Press, 1968), p. 152.

2. Alexander Bland, *The Royal Ballet: The First Fifty Years,* with a foreword by Dame Ninette de Valois (New York: Doubleday, 1981), p. 130.

3. Swift, p. 153; Roslavleva, pp. 260–61.

4. Roslavleva, p. 298.

5. Zsuzsa Kun, "The Bolshoi's *Rite of Spring,*" *The Dancing Times,* vol. 57 (February 1966), p. 232.

6. Swift, p. 153.

7. Jack Anderson, "A Bolshoi Portfolio," *Dance Magazine,* vol. 30 (June 1966), p. 51.

8. Doris Hering, "The Excesses of Yesterday: The Bolshoi Season Reviewed," *Dance Magazine,* vol. 30 (July 1966), p. 47.

9. Mary Clarke and Clement Crisp, *The Ballet Goer's Guide* (New York: Alfred A. Knopf, 1981), pp. 231–32.

10. Marcia Siegel, "Blight of Spring," in *Watching the Dance Go By* (Boston: Houghton Mifflin, 1977), p. 177.

11. Anna Kisselgoff, "A Radical Inversion of a Modern Classic," *New York Times* (27 April 1980), p. 1.

12. Taylor, quoted in Alan M. Kriegsman, "Paul Taylor Takes on Stravinsky's Challenge," *The Washington Post* (13 January 1980), pp. M1, 8.

13. Taylor, quoted in Anne Marie Welsh, "The Life of Paul Taylor: Creativity amid Adversity," *The Washington Star* (14 January 1980), p. B5.

14. Arlene Croce, "*Le Sacre* without Ceremony," *The New Yorker* (19 May 1980).

15. Quoted in Welsh, p. B5.

16. Quoted in Robert Coe, "A Master of Modern Dance," *New York Times* (5 April 1981), p. 74.

17. Quoted in Lillie F. Rosen, "Talking with Paul Taylor," *Dance Scope,* vol. 13 (Winter/Spring 1979), p. 83.

18. Paul Taylor, *Private Domain: An Autobiography* (New York: Alfred A. Knopf, 1987), pp. 24–55.

19. Coe, p. 80.

20. Jack Anderson, "Choreographic Fox: Paul Taylor," *Dance Magazine,* vol. 54 (April 1980), p. 68.

21. Taylor, pp. 88–91.

22. Coe, p. 80.

23. Taylor, p. 135.

24. Ibid., p. 169.

25. Marcia Siegel, "Spoils of Success," in *At the Vanishing Point* (New York: Saturday Review Press, 1973), p. 203.

26. Ibid., pp. 204–5. This review was written when *Scudorama* was revived by the Taylor company in 1968.

27. Rivière, "*Le Sacre du printemps*" (1 November 1913) quoted in Bullard, vol. 2, p. 297.

28. Siegel, *The Shapes of Change*, p. 301.

29. Elizabeth Kendall, "American Mongrel," *Ballet News*, vol. 1 (April 1980), p. 14.

30. Siegel, *The Shapes of Change*, p. 300.

31. Ruth Andrien, interview with the author, 4 May 1983.

32. Kendall, p. 14.

33. Andrien, interview.

34. Quoted in Tobi Tobias, "Taylor's Domain," *Dance Magazine*, vol. 54 (August 1980), p. 60.

35. Kriegsman, "Paul Taylor Takes on Stravinsky's Challenge," p. M8.

36. Andrien, interview.

37. Quoted in Kriegsman, "Paul Taylor Takes on Stravinsky's Challenge," p. M8.

38. Kriegsman, "Paul Taylor Takes on Stravinsky's Challenge," p. M8.

39. Andrien, interview.

40. Croce, "*Le Sacre* without Ceremony," p. 271.

41. Ibid. In interviews with this author, Bella Lewitzky, Monica Mason and Sally Owen have mentioned feeling similar sensations. Owen, interview, April 1983.

42. Ibid.

43. Alan M. Kriegsman, "Irreverent *Rite*," *The Washington Post* (16 January 1980), D1, D3.

44. Croce, "*Le Sacre* without Ceremony," p. 271.

45. Kisselgoff, "A Radical Inversion of a Modern Classic," p. D12.

46. Croce, "*Le Sacre* without Ceremony," p. 271.

47. Kirstein, *Nijinsky Dancing*, p. 145.

48. Taylor, p. 151.

Chapter 8

1. Alexander Bland, "Creating a New *Rite*," *The Observer* (1 March 1981), p. 34.

2. David Vaughan, "The Evolution of Ballet Rambert," *Dance Magazine*, vol. 54 (October 1982), p. 75.

3. Quoted in ibid.

4. Shelley C. Berg, "Marie Rambert: 1888–1982," *Washington DanceView*, vol. 3 (August–September 1982), p. 18.

5. Vaughan, p. 75.

6. Ibid.

7. Shelley C. Berg, ''Flash in the BAM,'' *Washington DanceView,* vol. 4 (July–August 1983), p. 18.

8. ''Movement and People First: Richard Alston Talks to D & D,'' *Dance and Dancers,* vol. 29 (June 1978), p. 22.

9. Ibid.

10. Ibid., p. 25.

11. Arlene Croce, ''Artists and Models,'' *The New Yorker* (1 November 1982), p. 141.

12. White, pp. 251, 253.

13. Richard Alston, interview with the author, October 1982.

14. Ibid.

15. Alston, quoted in Bland, ''Creating A New *Rite.*''

16. Alston, interview.

17. Ibid. The Theatre Collection is now an autonomous museum, located in Covent Garden.

18. Quoted in Bland, ''Creating A New *Rite.*''

19. Alston, interview. Alston originally cast four women, but shortly after the ballet's premiere reduced the number to three. The Taylor production has a cast of twelve. Alston's may vary from sixteen to nineteen dancers, depending on the resources of the company.

20. Alston, interview; I. Stravinsky and R. Craft, *Memories and Commentaries,* p. 30.

21. Alston, interview.

22. Ibid.

23. The description of the choreography is based on two sources: one rehearsal and one performance of the ballet at Brooklyn Academy during Ballet Rambert's 1982 American tour, and a study of the videotape workfilm of the piece in the Ballet Rambert archives.

24. Alston, interview.

25. Ibid.

26. Ibid.

27. Ibid.

28. Ibid.

29. Sally Owen, interview with the author, 15 April 1983.

30. Ibid.

31. Alston, interview.

32. Alston, quoted in Jennifer Dunning, ''Britain's Oldest Ballet Troupe on Tour,'' *New York Times* (10 October 1982), p. 32.

33. Alston, interview.

34. Owen, interview.

35. Mumford's designs were somewhat modified after the premiere, and Ballet Rambert has since toured with the Alston *Rite,* performing the ballet with little or no scenery.

36. Quoted in Bland, "A New *Rite.*"

37. Mary Clarke, "Ballet Rambert in London," *The Dancing Times,* vol. 71 (April 1981), p. 454.

38. Alastair Macaulay, "Rambert and the *Rite.*" (n.d.) Collection of Richard Alston.

39. Jann Parry, "Spring Sacrifice." *The Listener,* vol. 105 (19 March 1981), p. 390.

40. Stephanie Jordan, "New, Joyful, Sleek," *New Statesman,* vol. 101 (20 March 1981), p. 25.

41. David Dougill, "*Rite of Spring:* The Changing Face of a Modern Classic," *The London Times* (8 March 1981), p. 39.

42. Richard Alston, personal archives.

43. Ann Nugent, "Imaginative and Arousing Premiere" (n.d.), Richard Alston, personal archives; Bryan Robertson, "Fine Fettle," *The Spectator,* vol. 246 (28 March 1981), p. 30.

44. Noel Goodwin, "Stravinsky's *Rite* Is a Fascinating Ritual," *International Herald Tribune* (20 March 1981), p. 6.

45. Alexander Bland, "New Rites and Romeos," *The Observer* (8 March 1981), p. 35.

46. Alston, interview, April 1983.

47. Alston, interview, October 1982.

48. Robertson, p. 30.

49. Ibid.

Epilogue

1. Quoted in Merle Armitage, ed., *Martha Graham* (Reprint ed. New York: Dance Horizons, 1966), pp. 100–101.

2. Quoted in John Martin, "The Dance: Authentic Indian Art," *New York Times* (13 December 1931), p. X4.

3. Quoted in Arlene Croce, "Three Elders," *The New Yorker* (26 March 1984), p. 118.

4. Quoted in Jennifer Dunning, "Martha Graham's Year," *New York Times* (7 December 1983), p. C25.

5. Alan M. Kriegsman, "The Spring of Martha Graham," *The Washington Post* (8 April 1984), p. H1, 6.

6. Quoted in Ernestine Stodelle, "Before Yesterday," *Dance Observer,* vol. 29 (January 1962), p. 7.

7. One of Graham's dancers, Jean Erdman, who joined the Graham company in 1938, is married to Campbell, and Graham undoubtedly is well versed in her knowledge of his work.

8. Martha Graham, *The Notebooks of Martha Graham,* with an introduction by Nancy Wilson Ross (New York: Harcourt Brace Jovanovich, 1973), pp. 191–93.

9. Kriegsman, "The Spring of Martha Graham," p. H1, 6.

10. For a discussion of Graham's *Rite* from a feminist perspective, see Marianne Goldberg, "She Who Is Possessed No Longer Exists Outside," *Women and Performance*, vol. 3 (1986), pp. 17–27.

11. Kriegsman, "The Spring of Martha Graham," p. H1, 6.

12. Campbell, *The Masks of God: Primitive Mythology*, p. 230.

13. Ibid., pp. 230, 238.

14. Quoted in Kriegsman, "The Spring of Martha Graham," p. H1, 6.

15. Campbell, *The Masks of God: Primitive Mythology*, p. 176.

16. Ibid., p. 389.

17. Ibid., p. 390. Graham's *Notebooks* include a reference to "The Serpent's Bride," a chapter in Campbell's *The Masks of God: Occidental Mythology* (New York: Viking Compass edition, 1970), pp. 9–34. *Notebooks*, p. 421.

18. Photographs of the Wigman production also show what the choreographer termed the "shackling of the sacral figure." See photographs in Wigman, p. 25, and Dienis, pp. 66, 67.

19. Howard Moss, "The Rites of Martha Graham," *New York Review of Books* (26 April 1984), p. 38.

20. Tobi Tobias, "Excellent Women," *New York Magazine* (19 March 1984), p. 74.

21. Croce, "Three Elders," p. 118.

22. Dale Harris, "Dance Goddess with Feet of Clay," *Wall Street Journal* (5 March 1984), p. 28.

23. Harris, p. 28.

24. Moss, p. 38.

25. Quoted in Kriegsman, "The Spring of Martha Graham," p. H6.

26. Croce, "Three Elders," p. 118.

27. Joseph Campbell, *The Masks of God: Creative Mythology* (New York: Viking Compass edition, 1970), p. 4.

Bibliography

Acocella, Joan Ross. "Martha Graham Dance Company." *Dance Magazine* 58 (June 1984): 20-21, 24.

——. *The Reception of Diaghilev's Ballets Russes by Artists and Intellectuals in Paris and London, 1909-1914.* Ph.D. dissertation, Rutgers University, 1984.

Alston, Richard. Personal archives.

Anderson, Jack. "A Bolshoi Portfolio: Four Productions, Four Lively Controversies." *Dance Magazine* 40 (June 1966): 44-51.

——. "Choreographic Fox: Paul Taylor." *Dance Magazine* 54 (April 1980): 68-73.

Archer, Kenneth. Lecture on Nicholas Roerich. SUNY-Purchase, October 20, 1987.

Arbeau, Thoinot. *Orchesography.* Translated by Mary Stewart Evans. With an introduction and notes by Julia Sutton. New York: Dover Publications, 1967.

Armitage, Merle, ed. *Martha Graham.* Reprint edition, New York: Dance Horizons, 1966.

"Artistic Triple Entente: Stravinsky Double Bill at the 'Wells.'" Clippings file—Béjart's *Rite of Spring,* Theatre Museum, London.

Astruc, Gabriel. *Le Pavillon de fantômes.* Paris: Grasset, 1929.

Barker, Barbara. "Nijinsky's *Jeux.*" *The Drama Review* 26 (Spring 1982): 51-60.

Barnes, Clive. "Dance: New *Rite of Spring* Version." *New York Times,* 27 April 1966, p. 39.

——. "Massine Revivals for Sweden." *Dance and Dancers* 7 (August 1956): 16-18.

Barnes, Clive, and Williams, Peter. "The Rite of Spring." *Dance and Dancers* 13 (June 1962): 14.

——. "What We Thought of T.R.M." *Dance and Dancers* 11 (June 1960): 22-25.

Barron, Stephanie, and Tuchman, Maurice, eds. *The Avant-Garde in Russia 1910-1930: New Perspectives.* Cambridge, Mass.: MIT Press, 1980.

Bauer, Marion, and Bauer, Flora. "Success for Schoenberg Opera and Stravinsky Ballet." *The Musical Leader* 58 (1 May 1930): 3, 6.

Beaumont, Cyril W. *The Complete Book of Ballets: A Guide to the Principal Ballets of the Nineteenth and Twentieth Centuries.* London: Putnam, 1937; revised with additions, 1951; reprint ed., 1956.

——. *The Diaghilev Ballet in London: A Personal Record.* London: Putnam, 1940; third ed., Adam and Charles Black, 1951.

——. *Michel Fokine and His Ballets.* New York: Dance Horizons, 1981.

Béjart, Maurice. *Un Instant dans la vie d'autrui.* France: Flammarion, 1979.

——. Programme notes for *Le Sacre du printemps. Playbill* 8 (November 1971): 19.

Belville, Eugène. "Les Arts décoratifs au théâtre. La Saison russe—Nijinski choreographe—*Pénélope*—Les Nocturnes de Debussy." *Art et industrie* (September 1913): 359-66.

Benois, Alexandre. *Memoirs.* Translated by Moura Budberg, foreword by Tamara Karsavina. Volume 2. London: Chatto & Windus, 1964.

——. *Reminiscences of the Russian Ballet.* Translated by Mary Britneva. London: Putnam, 1947.

Berg, Shelley C. "Flash in the BAM." *Washington DanceView* 4 (July–August 1983): 16–20.
——. "Marie Rambert: 1888–1982." *Washington DanceView* 3 (August–September 1982): 18.
——. "Taylor's *Sacre.*" *Washington DanceView* 2 (June–July 1981): 28.
Billington, James H. *The Icon and the Ax: An Interpretive History of Russian Culture.* New York: Alfred A. Knopf, 1966.
Blanche, Jacques-Emile. "Un Bilan artistique de 1913." *La Revue de Paris,* 1 December 1913, pp. 517–34.
Bland, Alexander. "Creating a New *Rite.*" *The Observer,* 1 March 1981, p. 34.
——. "New Rites and Romeos." *The Observer,* 8 March 1981, p. 35.
——. *The Royal Ballet: The First Fifty Years.* Foreword by Dame Ninette de Valois. New York: Doubleday, 1981.
Bowlt, John. *The Silver Age: Russian Art of the Early Twentieth Century and the "World of Art" Group.* Newtonville, Mass.: Oriental Research Partners, 1979.
Buckle, Richard. *Diaghilev.* New York: Atheneum, 1979.
——. *In Search of Diaghilev.* New York: Thomas Nelson, 1956.
——. *Nijinsky.* London: Weidenfeld & Nicolson, 1971.
——. *Nijinsky on Stage: Action Drawings by Valentine Gross of Nijinsky and the Diaghilev Ballet Made in Paris between 1909 and 1913.* Chronology by Jean Hugo, introduction and notes by Richard Buckle. London: Studio Vista, 1971.
Bullard, Truman C. "The First Performance of Igor Stravinsky's *Sacre du printemps.*" Vols. 1–3. Ph.D. dissertation, Eastman School of Music, University of Rochester, 1971.
Cahausac, Hector. "Echoes of Music Abroad." *Musical America* (14 June 1913): 19.
Campbell, Joseph. *The Masks of God: Creative Mythology.* New York: The Viking Press, 1959; Viking Compass edition, 1970.
——. *The Masks of God: Occidental Mythology.* New York: The Viking Press, 1959; Viking Compass edition, 1970.
——. *The Masks of God: Primitive Mythology.* New York: The Viking Press, 1959; Viking Compass edition, 1970.
Capus, Alfred. "Courrier de Paris." *Le Figaro* 59 (2 June 1913): 1.
Carraud, Gaston. "Au Théâtre des Champs-Elysées: *Le Sacre du printemps.*" *La Liberté* 48 (31 May 1913): 3.
Casalonga, Marguerite. "Nijinsky et *Le Sacre du Printemps.*" *Comoedia Illustré Supplement Artistique* 17 (5 June 1913).
Chalupt, René. "Le Mois du musicien." *La Phalange* 8 (20 August 1913): 169–75.
"Champs-Elysées Receipts." *Musical America* (19 July 1913): 31.
Chantavoine, Jean. "Au Théâtre des Champs-Elysées: *Le Sacre du printemps.*" *Excelsior* 4 (30 May 1913): 6.
——. "Premieres: Théâtre des Champs-Elysées: Ballet russe: *Les Sylphides, Le Sacre du printemps, Le Tricorne.*" *L'Année musicale,* 16 December 1920.
"La Choréographie du *Sacre du printemps.*" Unsigned (n.d.). The Diaghilev Albums, vol. 4, Theatre Museum, London, p. 40.
Christout, Marie-Françoise. *Maurice Béjart.* Paris: Editions Seghers, 1972.
Chudnovsky, M. *Dancing to Fame.* Translated by S. Rosenberg. Moscow: Foreign Languages Publishing House, 1959.
Chujoy, Anatole, and Manchester, P. W., eds. *The Dance Encyclopedia.* Introduction by Lincoln Kirstein. New York: Simon and Schuster, 1967.
Clarke, Mary. "Ballet Rambert in London." *The Dancing Times* 71 (April 1981): 454–55.
——. "MacMillan's *Rite of Spring.*" *The Dancing Times* 52 (June 1962): 542–45.
Clarke, Mary, and Crisp, Clement. *The Ballet Goer's Guide.* New York: Alfred A. Knopf, 1981.
Coe, Robert. "A Master of Modern Dance." *New York Times,* 5 April 1981, pp. 40, 43, 47, 74, 78, 80, 82–83.

Coton, A. V. "Stravinsky Brought Up to Date." *The Daily Telegraph*, 19 April 1960.

———. *Writings on Dance, 1938-1968.* Foreword by Martin Cooper; edited by Katherine Sorley Walker and Lillian Haddakin. London: Dance Books, 1975.

Cott, Jonathan. "A Talk with George Balanchine." *Los Angeles Times*, 25 February 1979, p. 69.

Craft, Robert. "*Le Sacre* and Pierre Monteux: An Unknown Debt." *New York Review of Books* (3 April 1975): 33.

Croce, Arlene. *Afterimages.* New York: Alfred A. Knopf, 1977.

———. "Artists and Models." *The New Yorker* (1 November 1982): 139-44.

———. *Going to the Dance.* New York: Alfred A. Knopf, 1982.

———. "New York Newsletter." *The Dancing Times* 61 (April 1971): 366-67, 369.

———. "*Le Sacre* without Ceremony." *The New Yorker* (19 May 1980): 137-142.

———. "Three Elders." *The New Yorker* (26 March 1984): 114-19.

"Dancing by Massine Rich in Invention." *New York Times*, 24 April 1930, p. 29.

Daniel, Oliver. *Stokowski: A Counterpoint of View.* New York: Dodd, Mead, 1982.

De Mille, Agnes. *The Book of the Dance.* New York: Golden Press, 1963.

de Noailles, Anna. "Adieux des Ballets russes." *La Revue musicale*, no. 110 (1930).

de Pawlowski, Gustave. "Au Théâtre des Champs-Elysées: *Le Sacre du printemps,* ballet en deux actes de Igor Stravinsky." *Comoedia* 7 (31 May 1913): 1.

Diaghilev Albums, volumes 1-6. Compiled by William Beaumont Morris. Theatre Museum, London.

Dienis, Jean-Claude. "Maurice Béjart." *L'Avant-scène: Ballet/Danse* (August-October 1980): 68-69.

Dougill, David. "*Rite of Spring:* The Changing Face of a Modern Classic." *The Times* (London), 8 March 1981, p. 39.

Dunning, Jennifer. "Britain's Oldest Ballet Troupe on Tour." *New York Times*, 10 October 1982, p. H32.

———. "Martha Graham's Year." *New York Times*, 7 December 1983, p. C25.

Eliot, T. S. "London Letter." *The Dial* 71 (October 1921): 452-53.

Evans, Edwin. "Léonide Massine." *The Outlook* 44 (November 1919): 538.

Franks, A. H. "The Rite of Spring." *The Dancing Times* 52 (May 1962): 483.

Fry, Edward F. *Cubism.* New York and Toronto: McGraw-Hill, 1966.

"The Future of Music and Dancing: *Le Sacre du printemps.*" *The Times* (London), 26 July 1913, p. 8.

Georges-Michel, Michel. "Les Deux *Sacre du printemps,*" Reprinted in *Ballets russes, histoire anecdotiques.* Paris: Editions de Monde Nouveau, 1923, pp. 47-50.

Ghéon, Henri. "Sur quelques ballets de transition (*Daphnis et Chloë, La Tragédie de Salome, Jeux*)." *Nouvelle Revue Française* 10 (1 August 1913).

Gilliam, Florence. "The Russian Ballet of 1923." *Theatre Arts Monthly* 8 (24 March 1923): 191-94.

Goldberg, Marianne. "She Who Is Possessed No Longer Exists Outside." *Women and Performance* 3 (1986): 17-27.

Goldman, Debra. "Background to Diaghilev." *Ballet Review* 6 (1977-78): 1-55.

Goodwin, Noel. "Stravinsky's *Rite* Is a Fascinating Ritual." *International Herald Tribune*, 20 March 1981, p. 6.

Graham, Martha. *The Notebooks of Martha Graham.* Introduction by Nancy Wilson Ross. New York: Harcourt Brace Jovanovitch, 1973.

Gray, Camilla. *The Russian Experiment in Art, 1863-1922.* New York and London: Thames and Hudson, 1986.

Gray, Christopher. *Cubist Aesthetic Theories.* Baltimore: The Johns Hopkins Press, 1953.

Green, Martin. *The von Richthofen Sisters: The Triumphant and Tragic Modes of Love.* New York: Basic Books, 1974.

Grigoriev, Serge L. *The Diaghilev Ballet, 1909–1929.* London: Constable, 1953; reprint ed., London: Penguin, 1960.

Gruen, John. Interview with Maurice Béjart, 31 October 1972. Maurice Béjart Clippings File. Dance Collection of the Library and Museum of the Performing Arts at Lincoln Center, The New York Public Library.

Guest, Ivor. *The Romantic Ballet in Paris.* Middletown, Conn.: Wesleyan University Press, 1966.

Harris, Dale. "Dance Goddess with Feet of Clay." *Wall Street Journal,* 5 March 1984, p. 28.

Haskell, Arnold. *Balletomania: The Story of an Obsession.* London: Victor Gollantz, 1954.

Haskell, Arnold, and Nouvel, Walter. *Diaghileff: His Artistic and Private Life.* Foreword by Arnold Haskell. New York: Simon & Schuster, 1935.

Hering, Doris. "The Excesses of Yesterday: The Bolshoi Season Reviewed." *Dance Magazine* 30 (July 1966): 28.

Hersin, André Philippe. "Au Palais des Congrès: Bravo Béjart." *Les Saisons de la danse* 82 (March 1976): 2–4.

Hodson, Millicent. Lecture on the Choreography of *Le Sacre du printemps,* SUNY–Purchase, 20 October 1987.

———. "Restoring a Lost Work: Nijinsky's *Sacre* and Nijinska's *Les Noces.*" Unpublished transcript of symposium at the 1982 Dance Critics Conference, New York City, New York.

———. "Searching for Nijinsky's *Sacre.*" *Dance Magazine* 54 (June 1980): 64–75.

Holyrod, Michael. *Lytton Strachey: The Years of Achievement, 1910–1932,* vol. 2. New York: Holt, Rinehart & Winston, 1968.

Hughes, Robert. *The Shock of the New.* New York: Alfred A. Knopf, 1981.

"Improvisations on a Ritual." *The Sunday Times* (London), 6 May 1962, p. 13–15.

Jary, Jacques. "A travers les revues." *La Renaissance politique, littéraire et artistique* 1 (6 December 1913): 28.

Johnson, A. E. *The Russian Ballet.* Boston: Houghton Mifflin, 1913.

Jordan, Stephanie. "New, Joyful, Sleek." *New Statesman* 101 (20 March 1981): 25.

Jowitt, Deborah. *Dance Beat: Selected Views and Reviews, 1967–1976.* New York and Basel: Marcel Dekker, 1977.

Jullien, Adolphe. "Revue musicale." *Le Journal des débats* 125 (8 June 1913): 1.

Karsavina, Tamara. *Theatre Street.* New York: E. P. Dutton, 1931; revised ed., Dutton Everyman Paperback, 1961.

Kendall, Elizabeth. "American Mongrel." *Ballet News* 1 (April 1980): 10–14.

Kennedy, Janet. *The "Mir iskusstva" Group and Russian Art, 1898–1912.* New York and London: Garland, 1977.

Kerensky, Oleg. "This May Shock, But It's Novel." *Daily Mail,* 19 April 1960, p. 3.

King, Eleanor. *Transformations.* New York: Dance Horizons, 1978.

Kirby, Michael. "Lecture on Symbolist Theatre." New York University, 14 October 1981.

Kirstein, Lincoln. *Movement and Metaphor: Four Centuries of Ballet.* New York and Washington: Praeger Publishers, 1970.

———. *Nijinsky Dancing.* New York: Alfred A. Knopf, 1971.

———. *Thirty Years: The New York City Ballet.* New York: Alfred A. Knopf, 1978.

Kisselgoff, Anna. "Graham's *Rite of Spring* Is a Creative Triumph." *New York Times,* 11 March 1984, H14, 36.

———. "How Valid a Symbol Is Béjart's 'Wien' Ballet?" *New York Times,* 2 October 1983, p. H10.

———. "Meyerhold, Dance and Avant-Garde Theater in 1920's Russia." *New York Times,* 1 December 1981, p. 16.

———. "A Radical Inversion of a Modern Classic." *New York Times,* 27 April 1980, pp. 1, 12.

Kochno, Boris. *Diaghilev and the Ballet Russes.* Translated by Adrienne Foulke. New York: Harper & Row, 1970.

Kramer, A. Walter. "Novel Stage Works Close Orchestral Season." *Musical America* 50 (10 May 1930): 10.

Krasovskaya, Vera. *Nijinsky*. Translated by John E. Bowlt. New York: Dance Horizons/ Schirmer Books, 1979.

Kriegsman, Alan M. "Joffrey's Stupendous *Sacre*." *The Washington Post*, 2 October 1987, pp. D1, 4.

———. "Irreverent *Rite*." *The Washington Post*, 16 January 1980, p. D1, 3.

———. "Paul Taylor Takes on Stravinsky's Challenge." *The Washington Post*, 13 January 1980, pp. M1, 8.

———. "The Spring of Martha Graham." *The Washington Post*, 8 April 1984, pp. H1, 6-7.

Kun, Zsuzsa. "The Bolshoi's *Rite of Spring*." *The Dancing Times* 57 (February 1966): 232.

Lalo, Pierre. "Remarks on the Ballet *Le Sacre du printemps*." Translated by Mrs. Daniel Gregory Mason. *The New Music Review* 12 (October 1913): 440-43.

Laloy, Louis. "La Musique." *La Grande Revue* 79 (29 June 1913): 612-13.

———. "La Musique: Théâtre des Champs-Elysées: *Pénélope* de M. Gabriel Fauré; *Jeux*, ballet de M. Nijinsky, musique de M. Claude Debussy." *La Grande Revue* 79 (10 June 1913): 402-5.

Langer, Susanne. *Feeling and Form*. New York: Charles Scribner's Sons, 1953.

Lederman, Minna, ed. *Stravinsky in the Theatre*. New York: Pellegrini & Cudahy, 1949; reprint ed., Da Capo Press, 1975.

Levinson, André. *Ballet Old and New*. Translated by Susan Cook Summer. New York: Dance Horizons, 1982. Translation of *Stari i Novyi Balet*. Petrograd: Izdatel'stvo Svobodnoe Iskusstvo, 1917.

———. "Les Deux *Sacres*." *La Revue musicale* 4 (1 June 1922): 89-90.

———. "Les Deux *Sacres*." In *La Danse au théâtre, esthétique et actualité mêlées*. Paris: Librairie Bloud et Gay, 1924.

———. "Stravinsky and the Dance." *Theatre Arts Monthly* 8 (November 1924): 741-54. Translation of "Stravinsky et la danse." *La Revue musicale* 5 (December 1923): 155-65.

Lieven, Prince Peter. *The Birth of the Ballets Russes*. Translated by L. Zarine. London: Allen and Unwin, 1936; reprint ed., New York: Dover Publications, 1973.

Lifar, Serge. *Serge Diaghilev: His Life, His Work, His Legend*. London: Putnam, 1940.

Linor, Gustave. "Au Théâtre des Champs-Elysées: *Le Sacre du printemps*." *Comoedia* 7 (30 May 1913): 3.

Livio, Antoine. "La Creation du *Sacre* de Béjart." *Opéra de Paris* (November 1984): 23-25.

Macaulay, Alastair. "Rambert and the *Rite*" (n.d.). Collection of Richard Alston.

McDonagh, Don. *Martha Graham: A Biography*. New York and Washington: Praeger Publishers, 1973.

Macdonald, Nesta. *Diaghilev Observed: By Critics in England and the United States, 1911—1929*. London: Dance Books, Ltd. and New York: Dance Horizons, 1975.

Marnold, Jean. "Musique." *Mercure de France*, 1 October 1913, pp. 623-30.

Martin, John. *America Dancing*. New York: Dance Horizons, 1968.

———. "The Dance: A Novel Experiment." *New York Times*, 27 April 1930, sec. 9, p. 8.

———. "The Dance: Authentic Indian Art." *New York Times*, 13 December 1931, sec. x, p. 4.

———. "The Dance: Stravinsky's Ballet." *New York Times*, 20 April 1930, sec. x, p. 8.

"Massin [sic] Preparing an Indian Ballet." *New Mexico Telegraph*, 10 April 1916.

Massine, Léonide. *My Life in Ballet*. Edited by Phyllis Hartnoll and Robert Rubens. London: Macmillan, 1968.

Maus, Octave. "*Le Sacre du printemps*." *L'Art moderne* 33 (1 June 1913): 169-70.

Maynard, Olga. "Maurice Béjart: On the Creative Process." *Dance Magazine* 47 (February 1973): 58A-88E.

Mellow, James R. *Charmed Circle: Gertrude Stein and Company*. New York and Washington: Praeger Publishers, 1974.

Michel, Marcelle. "Marie Wigman." *L'Avant-scene: Ballet/Danse* (August–October 1980): 64–67.

Monahan, James. "The Béjart Phenomenon." *The Dancing Times* 68 (June 1977): 504-6.

———. *Fonteyn: A Study of the Ballerina in Her Setting.* London: A. & C. Black, 1957.

Monteux, Doris G. *It's All in the Music.* New York: Farrar, Straus & Giroux, 1969.

Monteux, Pierre. "Early Years." *Dance Index* 7 (1947): 242–43.

Moore, Lillian. "A Triumphant *Rite.*" *New York Herald Tribune,* 20 May 1962, p. 15.

Moss, Howard. "The Rites of Martha Graham." *New York Review of Books* (26 April 1984): 38–39.

"Movement and People First: Richard Alston Talks to D & D." *Dance and Dancers* 29 (June 1978): 22–25.

Myers, Rollo. "The Ballet Music of Igor Stravinsky." *The Ballet Annual.* London: A. & C. Black, 1963, pp. 22–29.

"The National Press on *The Rite of Spring.*" *The Dancing Times* 52 (June 1962): 549–50.

Nijinska, Bronislava. *Early Memoirs.* Translated and edited by Irina Nijinska and Jean Rawlinson; introduction by Anna Kisselgoff. New York: Holt, Rinehart & Winston, 1981.

Nijinsky, Romola. *Nijinsky.* Foreword by Paul Claudel. London: Gollancz, 1933; New York: Simon & Schuster, 1934.

Nordheimer, John. "Stravinsky Manuscript Sale Sets Auction Record." *New York Times,* 12 November 1982, sec. 3, p. 3.

Odom, Selma L. "Lectures on Eurythmics: Experiments in Music and Movement, 1890–1925." New York University, May–June 1983.

"The Old Ballet and the New: M. Nijinski's Revolution." *The Times* (London), 5 July 1913, p. 11.

Parry Jann. "Spring Sacrifice." *The Listener* 105 (19 March 1981): 390.

Pasler, Jann. "Stravinsky's Visualization of Music." *Dance Magazine* 55 (April 1981): 66–69.

Percival, John. "*Rite* Scaled Down to a Harsh and Primitive Picture." *The Times* (London), 9 March 1981, p. 7.

———. *The World of Diaghilev.* Revised ed., London: Herbert Press; New York: Harmony, 1979.

Prevots, Naima. "Dance at the Hollywood Bowl, 1926–1941: Performance, Theory and Practice." Ph.D. dissertation, University of Southern California, Los Angeles, 1984.

———. *Dancing in the Sun: Hollywood Choreographers, 1915–1937.* Ann Arbor: UMI Research Press, 1987.

Propert, W. A. *The Russian Ballet in Western Europe, 1909–1920.* London: The Bodley Head, 1921.

Rambert, Marie. *Quicksilver: An Autobiography.* London: Macmillan, 1972.

Reiss, Françoise. *Nijinsky: A Biography.* Translated by Helen Haskell and Stephen Haskell. London: A. & C. Black, 1960.

Reynolds, Nancy. *Repertory in Review: 40 Years of the New York City Ballet.* Introduction by Lincoln Kirstein. New York: The Dial Press, 1977.

Rivière, Jacques. "*Le Sacre du printemps.*" *La Nouvelle Revue française* 10 (1 November 1913): 706–30.

———. "*Le Sacre du printemps,* ballet par Igor Stravinsky, Nicholas Roerich et Vaslav Nijinski (Théâtre des Champs-Elysées)." *La Nouvelle Revue française* 10 (1 August 1913): 309–13.

Robertson, Bryan. "Fine Fettle." *The Spectator* 246 (28 March 1981): 30.

Roerich, Nicholas. "*Le Sacre du printemps.*" *The Musical Courier* 100 (29 March 1930): 7, 15.

Rosen, Lillie F. "Talking with Paul Taylor." *Dance Scope* 13 (Winter/Spring 1979): 82–92.

Rosenblum, Roger. *Cubism and Twentieth-Century Art.* New York: Harry N. Abrams, 1966.

Roslavleva, Natalia. *Era of the Russian Ballet.* Introduction by Dame Ninette de Valois. New York: E. P. Dutton, 1966.

"Russian Ballet at Covent Garden." *The Times* (London), 23 July 1929, p. 12.

"The Russian Ballet: *Le Sacre du printemps.*" *The Times* (London), 28 June 1921, p. 8.

Le Sacre du printemps. Clippings Notebooks in the Theatre Museum, London.

"*Le Sacre du printemps.*" *L'Avant-scène: Ballet/danse* (August-October 1980).

"*Le Sacre du printemps.*" *The Guardian,* 19 April 1960, p. 7.

"*Le Sacre du printemps* at Drury Lane." *The Times* (London), 12 July 1913, p. 11.

"*Le Sacre du printemps.*" *L'Avant-scène-Ballet/danse* (August–October 1980).

"A Saison russe (i.e. Season's Rush) at the Hippodrome." *The Sketch* (30 July 1913), p. 111.

Schmitt, Florent. "Les Premiers: *Les Sacres du printemps* [sic] de M. I. Stravinsky au Théâtre des Champs-Elysées." *La France* 52 (4 June 1913): 2.

Schneider, Louis. "Au Théâtre des Champs-Elysées: *Le Sacre du printemps*—la mise-en-scène et des décors." *Comoedia* 7 (31 May 1913): 2.

——. "Le Théâtre des Champs-Elysées, La Saison Russe à Paris: *Boris Godounow, La Khovanchina,* les Ballets." *Le Théâtre* 349 (1 July 1913): 24.

Searle, Humphrey. *Ballet Music: An Introduction.* New York: Dover, 1973.

Sears, David. "Paul Taylor Reflects on His Work." *Dance News* 66 (April 1981): 1, 3.

Sergei Diaghilev and Russian Art: Articles, Open Letters, Interviews, Correspondence. Contemporaries (Write) on Diaghilev. 2 volumes. Compiled with author's introductory articles, and commentaries of I. S. Zilbershtein and V. A. Samkov. Moscow: Fine Arts, 1982.

Shattuck, Roger. *The Banquet Years: The Origins of the Avant-Garde in France, 1885 to World War I.* New York: Random House, 1968, revised ed., London: Cape, 1969.

Siegel, Marcia B. *At the Vanishing Point: A Critic Looks at Dance.* New York: Saturday Review Press, 1973.

——. *The Shapes of Change: Images of American Dance.* Boston: Houghton Mifflin, 1979.

——. *Watching the Dance Go By.* Boston: Houghton Mifflin, 1977.

Siohan, Robert. *Stravinsky.* Translated by Eric Walter White. New York: Grossman Publishers, 1970.

S.L.B. "Nijinsky and the Dancing Revolution." *The Sketch* (23 July 1913): 96.

S. M. "Voici revenir nos amis les russes." *Comoedia* 7 (6 May 1913): 1.

Sokolova, Lydia. *Dancing for Diaghilev.* Edited by Richard Buckle. London: John Murray, 1960.

Sorell, Walter. *The Dancer's Image: Points and Counterpoints.* New York and London: Columbia University Press, 1971.

——. *The Mary Wigman Book.* Middletown, Conn.: Wesleyan University Press, 1973.

——. "Maurice Béjart's Ballet of the Twentieth Century." *Dance News* 56 (May 1971): 5, 7.

——. "On Massine and Cocteau, Scandals and Audiences." *Dance Scope* 13 (1979): 12–17.

Souday, Paul. "Théâtre des Champs-Elysées: *Le Sacre de printemps.*" *L'Eclair* 26 (31 May 1913): 2.

Spaulding, Frances. *Roger Fry: Art and Life.* Berkeley: University of California Press, 1980.

Stengele, Roger. *Who's Béjart.* Edited by J. Verbeeck. Brussels: Théâtre royale de la monnaie, Opéra National (n.d.).

Stodelle, Ernestine. "Before Yesterday." *Dance Observer* 29 (January 1962): 5–7.

Stravinsky, Igor. *An Autobiography.* New York: W. W. Norton, 1962.

——. "Ce que j'ai voulu exprimer dans *Le Sacre du printemps.*" *Montjoie!* 1 (29 May 1913): 1.

——. *Poetics of Music.* Preface by George Seferis; translated by Arthur Knodel and Ingolf Dahl. Cambridge, Mass.: Harvard University Press, 1942.

Stravinsky, Igor, and Craft, Robert. *Conversations with Igor Stravinsky.* New York: Doubleday, 1959.

——. *Expositions and Developments.* Berkeley and Los Angeles: University of California Press, 1959; revised ed., 1981.

——. *Memories and Commentaries.* Berkeley and Los Angeles: University of California Press, 1981.

——. *The Rite of Spring Sketches 1911–1913.* Facsimile reproduction from the autographs. London: Boosey & Hawkes, 1969.

Stravinsky, Vera, and Craft, Robert. *Stravinsky in Pictures and Documents.* New York: Simon & Schuster, 1978.

Swift, Mary Grace. *The Art of the Dance in the U.S.S.R.* Notre Dame, Ind.: University of Notre Dame Press, 1968.

Taruskin, Richard. "From 'Firebird' to 'The Rite': Folk Elements in Stravinsky's Scores." *Ballet Review* 10 (Summer 1982): 72–87.

Taylor, Paul. *Private Domain: An Autobiography.* New York: Alfred A. Knopf, 1987.

"Théâtre des Champs-Elysées: *Le Sacre du printemps, Les Sylphides, Le Tricorne.*" Unsigned, clippings file on *Le Sacre du printemps,* Theatre Museum, London.

Thompson, Oscar. "Stage Schoenberg Opera and Stravinsky Ballet." *Musical America* 50 (25 April 1930): 5, 14.

Tobias, Tobi. "Excellent Women." *New York Magazine,* 19 March 1984, pp. 74–75.

———. "Taylor's Domain." *Dance Magazine* 54 (August 1980): 60–61.

Vallas, Leon. "*Le Sacre du printemps.*" *La Revue française de musique* 14 (June–July 1913): 601–3.

Van Vechten, Carl. *The Dance Writings of Carl Van Vechten.* Edited and with an introduction by Paul Padgette. New York: Dance Horizons, 1974.

———. *Music after the Great War.* New York: G. Schirmer, 1915.

Vaughan, David. "The Evolution of Ballet Rambert." *Dance Magazine* 54 (October 1982): 74–77.

Villiers, Anne. "A Berlin: Triomphe et scandale." *Danse et rythmes* 35 (October–November 1957): 14.

Vuillermoz, Emile. "La Nouvelle Version chorégraphique de *Sacre du Printemps* au Théâtre des Champs-Elysées." *La Revue musicale* 1 (February 1921): 161–64.

———. "La Saison russe au Théâtre des Champs-Elysées." *S.I.M. La Revue musicale* 9 (15 June 1913): 49–56.

Walker, Katherine Sorley. *De Basil's Ballets Russes.* New York: Atheneum, 1983.

Watkins, Mary. "Most Important Dance Event of Entire Year Takes Place This Week with the Philadelphia Orchestra." *New York Herald Tribune,* 20 April 1930, p. 8.

Welsh, Anne Marie. "The Life of Paul Taylor: Creativity amid Adversity." *The Washington Star,* 14 January 1980, pp. B1, 5.

White, Eric Walter. *Stravinsky: The Composer and His Works.* Berkeley and Los Angeles: University of California Press, 1966.

Whitworth, Geoffrey. *The Art of Nijinsky.* New York: McBride, Nast, 1914.

Wigman, Mary. Clippings File, Dance Collection. The Library and Museum of the Performing Arts at Lincoln Center, The New York Public Library.

———. *The Language of Dance.* Translated by Walter Sorell. Middletown, Conn.: Wesleyan University Press, 1966.

Wiley, Roland John. "Alexandre Benois' Commentaries on the First *Saison russe.*" *The Dancing Times* 70 (October 1980): 28–30.

———. "Benois' Commentaries on the First *Saison russe*-Part 4." *The Dancing Times* 71 (January 1981): 250–51.

———. "Benois' Commentaries on the First *Saison russe*-Part 7." *The Dancing Times* 71 (April 1981): 464–65.

Williams, Peter. *Ballet Rambert: 50 Years On.* Edited by Clement Crisp, Anya Sainsbury and Peter Williams. London: Scolar Press, 1976; revised and enlarged ed., 1981.

Interviews

Addison, Errol. Via telephone, London, January 1981.

Alston, Richard. New York, New York, October 1982; London, April 1983.

Andrien, Ruth. New York, New York, May 1983.

Béjart, Maurice. New York, New York, September 1983.

Lewitzky, Bella. Via Telephone, New York, New York, May 1983.

Mason, Monica. Houston, Texas, June 1978.

Mehlman, Lily. Via Telephone, New York, New York, January 1981.
Owen, Sally. London, April 1983.
Rambert, Marie. London, October 1978.
Schönberg, Bessie. Via Telephone, New York, New York, January 1981.
Sokolova, Lydia, London, April 1969.

Index

Italicized page numbers indicate references to illustrations.

Abramtsevo artists' colony, 8, 14
Acocella, Joan Ross, 14
Ailey, Alvin, 108
Alpine Symphony (R. Strauss), 76
Alston, Richard, 2, 125, 127, 128, 139, 140;
  work on *Le Sacre*, 128–29, 131, 133, 135,
  138, 139. *See also Le Sacre du printemps*
  (Alston, 1981)
American Ballet Theatre, 107
American Genesis (Taylor), 112
Anderson, Jack, 108
Andrien, Ruth, 113, 119, *114, 116, 120,*
  121
Annual of the Imperial Theaters, 10
Ansermet, Ernest, 68, 82
L'Après-midi d'un faune (Mallarmé), 25
L'Après-midi d'un faune (Nijinsky), 2, 21,
  22, 23, 24, 25, 30, 44, 113; choreography
  of, 25, 30, 54
Ashton, Frederick, 125, 126, 127
Astruc, Gabriel, 12, 24, 45, 46, 163n.42
Aureole (Taylor), 111
Autobiography (Stravinsky), 20, 26

Bakst, Léon, 9, 10, 22, 25, 29
Balakirev, Mili, 14
Balanchine, George, 108, 111, 127
Ballet, as a genre, 6, 7
Ballet Club, 126
Ballet Rambert, 126, 127, 128, 139
Les Ballets de l'Etoile, 92
Ballets Russes, 6, 8, 33–34, 40, 43, 62, 63,
  65, 75, 82; accomplishments of, 13–14,
  15, 20, 51; premieres by, 10, 13–14, 128;
  repertoire of, 15, 23, 24, 33–34, 40, 62;
  style of, 20
Bari, Tania, 94, *100*
Barnes, Clive, 104

Bauer, Flora, 84
Bauer, Marion, 84
Bausch, Pina, 109
Beaumont, Cyril, 14, 25
Béjart, Maurice, 2, 92, 101, 103, 104, 105,
  108; choreography of, 93–94; compared
  to predecessors, 94; and pop ballet, 89,
  104; style of, 92–93; work on *Le Sacre*,
  92, 93–95. *See also Le Sacre du printemps*
  (Béjart, 1959)
Bel Geddes, Norman, 76
Belville, Eugène, 25
Benois, Alexandre, 9, 10, 11, 12, 15, 21,
  22, 35, 36
Berger, Gaston, 92
Bhakti (Béjart), 93
Blanche, Jacques-Emile, 29, 43
Bland, Alexander, 139
Blaue Reiter, 16
Blue Schubert Fragments (Alston), 128
Bolm, Adolph, 13, 26
Bolshoi Ballet, 107, 127
Boris Godunov (Mussorgsky), 13
Borodin, Alexander, 13, 14, 15
La Boutique fantasque (Massine), 67
Bowne, William, 90
Boyarsky, Konstantin, 107
Braque, Georges, 51
Brown, Tricia, 127
Bruce, Christopher, 126
Brussel, Robert, 13, 16
Buckle, Richard, 21, 48
Busby, Gerald, 112
Butler, Ethel, 110

"The Call of the Sun" (Roerich), 27
Campbell, Joseph, 142, 144, 149
Capell, Richard, 61, 73

Le Carnaval (Fokine), 14
Carr, Nicolas, 128
Cecchetti, Enrico, 19, 125
CEMA (Council for the Encouragement of Music and the Arts), 126
Chaliapin, Feodor, 13, 15
Chappell, William, 125
Chesworth, John, 126
Childs, Lucinda, 127
Chopin, Frédéric, 33
Churchyard (Taylor), 112
Cimabue, 64
Clarke, Mary, 139
Cléopâtre (Fokine), 13, 14, 34
Cloven Kingdom (Taylor), 112
Clytemnestra (Graham), 110, 141
Cocteau, Jean, 45, 58, 61, 67
Coe, Robert, 110
A coeur perdu (Péladan), 14
Cohan, Robert, 127
Comoedia, 29, 44
Contes russes (Massine), 10, 65, 67
Coomaraswamy, Ananda, 142
Le Coq d'or (Rimsky-Korsakov), 35, 63
Coton, A. V., 12, 104
Craft, Robert, 20, 22, 40, 48
Crisp, Clement, 139
Croce, Arlene, 105, 109, 121, 123, 128, 147, 149
Cubism, 16, 29, 30, 51, 54, 58, 67, 81
Cunningham, Merce, 110, 127

Dada, 67
Daily Mail, 51, 61, 73
The Daily Telegraph, 61
Dalcroze, Emile Jaques, 26
Daniel, Oliver, 76, 79
Dante Alighieri, 142
Daphnis and Chloë (Fokine), 14, 24
"Daphnis and Chloë" (Longus), 11
Dark Elegies (Tudor), 126
Debay, Victor, 32
Debussy, Claude, 25, 29, 30, 33, 41, 76
Delarova, Eugenia, 76
De Mille, Agnes, 76, 78
Les Demoiselles d'Avignon (Picasso), 52
Diaghilev, Serge, 1, 9, 10, 11, 12, 19, 29, 44, 45, 75, 84; aesthetic of, 12, 15, 16; and Ballets Russes, 5, 8, 15, 34, 63; editor of *Mir iskusstva*, 8, 9, 10, 11; and Fokine, 21, 22, 23, 178n.3; and Massine, 64, 65; and Nijinsky, 24, 62; work on *L'Après-midi d'un faune*, 22; work on *Petrouchka*, 36; work on *Le Sacre*, 2, 17, 19, 20–21, 26, 32, 44, 65. *See also* individual productions of Le Sacre du printemps

Dial, 74
Didelot, Charles, 7
Dienis, Jean-Claude, 97, 99
Le Dieu bleu (Fokine), 14
Dolin, Sir Anton, 41
Dostoevski, Feodor, 14
Doublework (Alston), 128
Dougill, David, 139
Du côté de chez Swann (Proust), 58
Dudley, Jane, 127
Dukes, Ashley, 125
Duncan, Isadora, 12, 16

Egorova, Lubov, 92
Eliot, T. S., 74, 142
Elssler, Fanny, 6
Eng, Frank, 91
Episodes (Balanchine and Graham), 111
Eurythmics, 26
Evans, Edwin, 61, 81
"Exhibition of Russian Art," 12

Le Festin (Fokine), 13
The Field of Mustard (Alston), 128
Le Figaro, 60
La Fille du pharon (Petipa), 7
La Fille mal gardée (Ashton), 127
Filosofov, Dimitre, 9
The Firebird. See L'Oiseau de feu
Fletcher, John Gould, 61
Fokine, Mikhail, 11–12, 21, 45, 140; and Ballets Russes, 22, 23, 24, 34, 51, 63; choreography for *L'Oiseau de feu*, 35, 107; choreography for *Petrouchka*, 37; choreography of, 12, 14, 15
Folies-Bergère, 15
Folk dances, 38–39, 51–52, 57, 72, 93, 97, 139
Folk music, 38–39, 40, 64, 73
Formalism, 7
Four Epitaphs (Taylor), 110
Freud, Sigmund, 58
Fuller, Loïe, 15
Futurism, 16, 29

Le Gaulois, 13
Gautier, Théophile, 6, 12
Geva, Tamara, 79
Girard, Henri, 44, 46
Glinka, Mikhail, 35
Die glückliche Hand (Schoenberg), 77
Gogol, Nicolai, 6
Goldman, Debra, 6, 15

Golovin, Alexander, 9, 14
Goncharov, A. D., 107
Goncharova, Natalia, 64
Goodwin, Noel, 139
Gore, Walter, 125
Gould, Diana, 125
Graham, Martha, 2, 76, 78, 110, 111, 141,
    142, 144, 159; in *Le Sacre*, 79–80, 85, *86*,
    87; style of, 141–42, 147, 149. *See also Le
    Sacre du printemps* (Graham, 1984)
La Grande Revue, 33
Grey, Lord, 63
Grigoriev, Serge, 22, 23, 71, 75
Grigorovich, Yuri, 41
Gross, Valentine, 45, 52; drawings by, 52,
    53, *59*, 129, 138–39
Guardian, 104
Gunsburg, Baron de, 26
Guyon, Anne, 138

Hammond, Richard, 76, 78
Handel, George Frideric, 111
Harris, Dale, 147
Henry, Pierre, 92, 94
Hering, Doris, 108
Hernani, 2, 71
Hinkson, Mary, 127
Hodson, Millicent, 48
Horst, Louis, 80, 141
Horton, Lester, 89, 108
Hoving, Lucas, 109
Howard, Andrée, 125, 126
Howard, Robin, 127
Howland, Olin, 77
Hoyer, Doris, 92
Hughes, Robert, 51
Huisman, Maurice, 93
Humphrey, Doris, 76, 77, 111
Humphrey-Weidman troupe, 80
Husserl, Edmund, 58

Ivantzoff, Ivan, 77

Jackson, C., 111
Jackson, Shirley, 108
Jardin aux lilas (Tudor), 126
Jary, Jacques, 60
Jeux (Nijinsky), 2, 29, 30, *31*, 32, 43;
    choreography for, 30, 54
Johansson, Christian, 7
Johnson, A. E., 19
Jones, Robert Edmond, 77
Jooss, Kurt, 109
Jordan, Stephanie, 139
Journal of Orders, 7
Jowitt, Deborah, 93

Jung, Carl, 142
Juszkiewicz, Anton, 38

Kammersymphonie (Schoenberg), 76
Kandinsky, Vasily, 16
Karsavina, Tamara, 13, 29, *31*
Kasatkina, Natalia, 107
Kendall, Elizabeth, 112, 113
Kerensky, Oleg, 103
Khovanshchina (Mussorgsky), 13
King, Eleanor, 78, 79, 80, 82, 85
Kirstein, Lincoln, 111
Kisselgoff, Anna, 105, 109, 121
Kramer, A. Walter, 84
Kriegsman, Alan, 121
Kschessinska, Mathilda, 5
Kun, Zsuzsa, 108

Le Lac des cygnes, 75
Lady into Fox (Howard), 126
Lalo, Pierre, 30
Laloy, Louis, 25, 30, 33
Lanceray, Eugene, 9, 10
Langer, Susanne, 57
Larionov, Mikhail, 64–65, 66
Laurent, Jean, 92
Lawrence, D. H., 58
League of Composers, 76, 77, 81
Legat, Nicholas, 5
La Légende de Joseph (Fokine), 64
Lester Horton Dance Theatre, 89, 109
Levinson, André, 57, 58, 71, 74, 159
Lewitzky, Bella, 89, 90
Liadov, Anatol, 34
Lieven, Prince Peter, 37
Limón, José, 109
Liturgie (Massine), 64, 67
Lloyd, Maude, 125
Longus, 11
"The Lottery" (Jackson), 108

Macaulay, Alastair, 139
McDonagh, Don, 79
MacDonald, Brian, 108
MacMillan, Kenneth, 104, 105, 108, 138
Mallarmé, Stéphane, 25
Mamontov, Savva, 8
Mamoulian, Rouben, 77
Marinetti, Giacomo, 16
Marnold, Jean, 60
Martin, John, 78, 81, 84, 85
Maryinsky Ballet, 7, 11, 12, 13, 92
Mason, Monica, 105
Les Masques (Ashton), 126
Massine, Léonide, 2, 20, 40, 47, 76, 78, 79;
    aesthetic of, 66–67; and Ballets Russes,

64, 65; choreography for *Le Sacre*, 65, 66, 67–68, 71, 72, 73, 78, 85; choreography of, 65, 73; compared to Nijinsky, 71, 73; and Graham, 78–79; influences on, 81; in United States, 76–77. *See also Le Sacre du printemps* (Massine, 1920, 1930 and 1949)
Matisse, Henri, 110
Maus, Octave, 60
Mehlman, Lily, 78, 80, 81, 85
Mephisto Waltz (Ashton), 126
Mercury Theatre, 125
Metropolitan Opera, 76, 77, 82, 84, 87, 110
Midas (Fokine), 63
Mir iskusstva, 8, 9, 10, 11, 21, 34; group of, 12, 14, 16, 34
Modernism, 2, 16, 150
Monteux, Pierre, 25–26, 61; work on *Le Sacre*, 43, 46
Morrice, Norman, 126
Morton, Lawrence, 38
Moss, Howard, 147, 149
Mount Triglav (Rimsky-Korsakov), 13
Mumford, Peter, 138
Murray, John Middleton, 16
Musical America, 82, 84
Musical Leader, 84
Mussorgsky, Modest, 8, 13
My Life in Ballet (Massine), 79

Narcisse, 21
Neumeier, John, 105, 108
New York City Ballet, 111
New York Times, 46, 84
Night Journey (Graham), 110, 141
Nijinska, Bronislava, 21, 24, 26–27, 46, 55, 57, 128, 139; in *Jeux*, 29–30; in *Le Sacre*, 74
Nijinsky, Romola, 48
Nijinsky, Vaslav, 1, 13, 24, 26, *31*, 41, 62, 103, 125; aesthetic of, 61; choreography for *L'Après-midi d'un faune*, 25; choreography for *Jeux*, 29–30; choreography for *Le Sacre*, 26, 27, 28, 46–47, 50, 51–55, 57–58, 74, 149; choreography of, 2, 21, 24, 29, 45, 50, 54–55, 140; criticism of, 19, 30, 60; style of, 57, 149. *See also Le Sacre du printemps* (Nijinsky, 1913)
Noailles, Anna de, 13
Les Noces (Nijinska), 10, 41, 76, 128, 139
Nolan, Sidney, 104
Notebooks (Graham), 142
Nouvel, Walter, 9
Noverre, Jean-Georges, 5

Nugent, Ann, 139
Nuit obscure (Béjart), 93
The Nutcracker (Petipa), 7

The Observer, 40
October Revolution, 11
L'Oiseau de feu (Fokine), 10, 14, 16, 20, 107; compared to *Le Sacre*, 43; folk material in, 34, 35; reception of, 32, 33; scenario for, 34, 38
O'Keeffe, Georgia, 142
Oliver, W. E., 90, 91
Omphale (Gautier), 12
One Hundred Russian Folk Songs (Rimsky-Korsakov), 35, 38
Orphée (Béjart), 94
Orpheus (Boyarsky), 107
Owen, Sally, *130*, 135, *136*, *137*

Les Papillons (Fokine), 63
Parade (Massine), 67
Paris Opéra, 5, 13, 14
Parry, Jann, 139
Le Pavillon d'Armide (Fokine), 12, 13
Pavlova, Anna, 5, 13
Pawlowski, Gustave de, 60
Paxton, Steve, 127
Péladan, Joseph, 14
Perrot, Jules, 7
Peter Pan (Robbins), 111
Petipa, Marius, 7–8; choreography of, 7–8, 16, 35
Petrouchka (Fokine), 10, 14, 15, 21, 22, 107, 129; compared to *Le Sacre*, 43; folk material in, 34, 36, 37; reception of, 32, 33; scenario for, 36–37, 38; score for, 20, 37
Phenomenology (Husserl), 58
Philadelphia North American, 75
Picasso, Pablo, 51, 52, 67
Pierre, Dorothi Bock, 90
Piltz, Maria: in *Le Sacre*, *53*, 57, *59*, 74
Poème d'extase (Scriabin), 76
Polenova, Elena, 9
"Polovtsian Dances" (Fokine), 13, 14, 33, 45
Popova, Tatiana, 38
Preobrazhenska, Olga, 5
Primitive Mysteries (Graham), 141, 149, 159
Primitive Mythology (Campbell), 142
Primitivism, 14
Prince Igor (Borodin), 13
Profiles (Taylor), 113
Protas, Ron, 141, 142
Proust, Marcel, 58
Pulszky, Romola de. *See* Nijinsky, Romola

Queen, 73

Rachmaninoff, Sergei, 13
Radzinski, Jan, 113
Ramberg, Miriam. *See* Rambert, Marie
Rambert, Marie, 26, 46, 48, 57, 125, 126,
    133, 138, 140; and Ballet Rambert, 126,
    127; work on *Le Sacre*, 27–28, 128
Rauschenberg, Robert, 110
Ravel, Maurice, 3, 76
Rawlings, John, 115
Rech', 15
Redon, Odilon, 25
Reis, Claire, 76, 77, 78
Rhythm, 16
Ricketts, Charles, 61
Rilke, Rainer Maria, 142
Rimsky-Korsakov, Nicolai, 8, 13, 14, 35,
    38, 39, 63, 64
The Rite of Spring. See Le Sacre du printemps
"The Rite of Spring: Genesis of a
    Masterpiece" (Craft), 48
The Rite of Spring: Pictures of Pagan Russia.
    See Le Sacre du printemps (Alston, 1981)
Rivière, Jacques, 54, 55, 58, 60, 61, 111,
    139
Rivoire, Mary, 78
Robbins, Jerome, 111
Robertson, Bryan, 139, 140
Robertson, Rae, 68
Robinson, Jacqueline, 91
Rodin, Auguste, 25
Roerich, Nicholas, 1, 9, 14, 61, 76, 82; cri-
    ticism of, 19; and *Mir iskusstva*, 10;
    painting of, 27; and Stravinsky, 22;
    work on *Le Sacre*, 2, 16, 20, 22, 28–29,
    46, 55, 60, 69, 77, 133, 149. *See also Le
    Sacre du printemps* (Nijinsky, 1913)
Romanticism, 2, 5, 15
Romeo et Juliette (Béjart), 93
Rothafef, S. L., 76
Roxy Theater, 77
Royal Ballet, 107, 127, 128
Royal Swedish Ballet, 65, 87, 92
Runes (Taylor), 112, 113
Ruslan and Ludmila (Glinka), 35
The Russian Ballet (Johnson), 19
Russian folk art, 8–9, 10, 14–15, 16, 34, 38,
    60, 66
Russian Neonationalism, 8, 10

Le Sacre du printemps (Stravinsky), 20, 22,
    33, 37–41, 149, 150; adaptability of, 2,
    91, 108, 150; conception of, 17, 20, 22,
    23; folk material in, 34, 38, 39, 40; pro-
    ductions of, 2, 107, 108–9; reception of,

75, 76, 89; structure of, 26, 40; theme
in, 1, 91, 105, 108. *See also individual productions*
Le Sacre du printemps (Nijinsky, 1913), 14,
    17, 22, 47–50, *56*, 84, 90; choreography
    for, 40–41, 51–57, 57–58, 74, 149; docu-
    mentation of, 47–48, *53, 56, 59*, 174n.37,
    175n.61; premiere of, 2, 10, 19, 30, 33,
    45–47, 58, 60, 69; preparation of, 27–28,
    43–45; reception of, 19, 25, 52, 60, 69;
    scenario for, 2, 22–23, 37, 55; score for,
    26, 33, 38–41; significance of, 2, 3, 38,
    41; sources for, 51–52, 57
Le Sacre du printemps (Massine, 1920), 2,
    20, 40, 47, 62, 67, 69, *70*, 75, 135, 149;
    choreography for, 65, 67, 69, 71; com-
    pared to Nijinsky's *Le Sacre*, 71–72, 74;
    reception of, 71–72, 73
Le Sacre du printemps (Massine, 1930), 2,
    77, 79, 82, *83, 86*, 141; choreography
    for, 85, 87; reception of, 84; scenario
    for, 87
Le Sacre du printemps (Horton, 1937), 89,
    90, 91
Le Sacre du printemps (Massine, work film
    1949), 85, 157–60
Le Sacre du printemps (Wigman, 1957),
    91–92
Le Sacre du printemps (Béjart, 1959), 2, 89,
    93, 95, *96, 98, 100, 102*, 103; choreogra-
    phy for, 95–101; compared to Nijinsky's
    Le Sacre, 99; reception of, 89, 103, 105;
    scenario for, 93, 94
Le Sacre du printemps (MacMillan, 1962),
    104, 138
Le Sacre du printemps (Kasatkina and
    Vasilyov, 1965), 107, 108
Le Sacre du printemps (Bausch, 1975), 109
Le Sacre du printemps (The Rehearsal)
    (Taylor, 1980), 2, 109, 111, 113, *114*,
    115, *116, 117, 120, 122*; choreography
    for, 115, 118–19, 121; reception of, 109,
    121, 123; scenario for, 115
Le Sacre du printemps (Alston, 1981), 2,
    130, 132, 134, 136, 137, 138, 139;
    choreography for, 131, 133, 135, 138;
    preparations for, 129; reception of, 139
Le Sacre du printemps (Graham, 1984), 2,
    142, *143*, 144, *145, 146, 148*; choreogra-
    phy for, 144, 147; reception of, 147, 149
Le Sacre du printemps (Toth), 1
Sadler's Wells Theatre, 128, 138
Satie, Erik, 67
La Scala Ballet, 5, 65, 85, 87, 157
Schéhérazade (Fokine), 14, 33
Schmitt, Florent, 62

Schneider, Louis, 60
Schoenberg, Arnold, 76, 77, 82
Schönberg, Bessie, 76, 78, 79, 85
Scriabin, Alexander, 76
Scudorama (Taylor), 111, 112
Second Piano Concerto (Rachmaninoff), 13
Serait-ça la mort? (Béjart), 93
Sergeyev, Nicholas, 92
Serov, Alexander, 10
Sert, Misia, 13
Shankar, Uday, 141
Shapiro, Lillian, 78, *83*
Siegel, Marcia, 109, 111, 159
The Sketch, 61
The Sleeping Beauty (Petipa), 7
The Snow Maiden (Rimsky-Korsakov), 35, 64
Snow White (Taylor), 112
"Society for Self-Education," 9
Soft Verges (Alston), 128
Sokolova, Lydia, 47, 64; in *Le Sacre*, 68, 69, *70*, 71, 74, 135
Sokolow, Anna, 78, 111
Soleil de nuit (Massine), 64, 67
Somov, Konstantin, 9
Sons and Lovers (Lawrence), 58
Le Spectre de la rose (Fokine), 14, 45
Speyer, Louis, 44
Sports and Follies (Taylor), 112
Staats, Leo, 92
The Standard, 61
Stanislavsky, Konstantin, 8
Steiman, Maurice, 26, 43
Stokowski, Leopold, 75, 77; work on *Le Sacre*, 77, 78, 80, 82, 87
Strachey, Lytton, 61
Strauss, Richard, 63, 76
Stravinsky, Igor, 1, 3, 14, 22, 32, 46, 76, 128; aesthetic of, 34, 61; and Ballets Russes, 33, 34, 36; criticism of, 19; and Nijinsky, 40, 41, 66; in Russia, 107; and *Le Sacre*, 2, 20, 21, 23, 27, 28, 33, 40, 48, 55, 66, 67, 103, 149, 150; sources for, 34, 40. *See also Le Sacre du printemps* (Stravinsky)
Strumlauf, Helen, 78
Swan Lake. See Le Lac des cygnes
Swift, Mary Grace, 108
Les Sylphides (Fokine), 13, 14, 33, 45
Sylvia, 10
Symbolism, 10, 15, 51
Symphonie pour un homme seul (Béjart), 92, 93

Taglioni, Marie, 6
Talashkino artists' colony, 8, 9, 22, 39

Taras, John, 108
Taruskin, Richard, 37, 38, 39
Taylor, Paul, 2, 109, 110, 112, 123; choreography of, 119, 123; development of, 110–11; work on *Le Sacre*, 113, 115, 123. *See also Le Sacre du printemps* (Taylor, 1980)
Tchaikovsky, Peter Ilyich, 35
Tcherepnine, Nicholas, 12
Telegraph, 82
Teliakovsky, V. A., 10
Tenisheva, Princess Maria, 8, 9, 22, 39
Terry, Richard, 73
Tetley, Glen, 105, 108
Thamar (Fokine), 14, 23
Theatre Arts Monthly, 74
Théâtre des Champs-Elysées, 12, 43, 44, 62, 65, 67, 68, 69
Theatre Royal, 60
Théâtre Royal de la Monnaie, 89, 93, 103
Thompson, Oscar, 82
Time, 87
Times, 73, 75, 103
Tobias, Tobi, 147
Totem and Taboo (Freud), 58
Toth, Karol, 1
Touchard, Maurice, 60
Trisler, Joyce, 109
Tudor, Antony, 109, 126

Uber das Geistige in der Kunst (Kandinsky), 16
UnAmerican Activities (Alston), 127
Union Pacific (Massine), 81

Vallas, Leon, 60
Vasilyov, Vladimir, 107
Vasnetsov, Victor, 9
Vaughan, David, 126
Vechten, Carl Van, 46
Vershinina, Irina, 41
Vesna Sciaschennaia. See Le Sacre du printemps (Stravinsky): conception of
Villiers, Anne, 92
"Virgin" (Cimabue), 64
Volkonsky, Prince Serge, 10
Volkova, Vera, 92
Vorticism, 16, 58
Vrubel, Mikhail, 9
Vuillermoz, Emile, 71, 72, 75, 149

Walter, Eric, 108
Waring, James, 111
Wasserstrom, Sylvia, 78
Webern, Anton, 111
Weidman, Charles, 76, 77, 111
White, Eric Walter, 40

Wigman, Mary, 91, 108
Williams, Peter, 104
Wilson, Sallie, 111
Woizikovsky, Leon, 71
The World of Art. See Mir iskusstva

Yasgour, Rose, 78

Zemtsovsky, Izalii, 39